Teacher's Guide

American Government

Ethel Wood and Stephen C. Sansone

GReaT Source

EDUCATION GROUP

A Houghton Mifflin Company

AUTHORS | **Ethel Wood**

Princeton High School
Princeton, New Jersey

Ethel Wood has taught World History, U.S. Government, and Comparative Government for more than 16 years at Princeton High School. Previously she had taught in Texas at the high school, community college, and university levels. In addition, she is the author of "Teaching Guide: Comparative Government and Politics."

Stephen C. Sansone

Waukesha South High School
Waukesha, Wisconsin

Stephen C. Sansone has taught U.S. History, Government, and Honors Government for more than 20 years in the Waukesha School District and is currently at Waukesha South High School. He is also the author of the *Activity Book* and numerous articles, including most recently "Get Your Students Involved in Civics" for *Social Education* (1998–99).

CONSULTING AUTHOR | **Dr. Michael Hartoonian**

Professor of Education
University of Minnesota

Dr. Hartoonian has taught, lectured, and served as an education, business, and government consultant throughout the United States, Central America, Asia, and Europe. He has authored more than 50 articles and written and contributed to numerous books. He is also a past president of the National Council of Social Studies (1995–96).

Special thanks also to the following government teachers who consulted with us:

Michael Barry	David LaShomb
Tom Baumann	Karen Moore
Ann Connor	Paul Rykken
Karen Coston	Maria Schmidt
Jana Eaton	George Westergaard
Ellen Harmon	Mark Wise

A special thanks is owed to Michael Barry and George Westergaard for their help in writing the *Teacher's Guide*.

Printed in the United States of America

International Standard Book Number: 0-669-046798-7

1 2 3 4 5 6 7 8 9 — MZ — 08 07 06 05 04 03 02 01 00

Table of Contents

Unit III: Institutions of National Government

Unit IV: Civil Liberties and Civil Rights

OVERVIEW

What's different about this government book? Why not stick with the government book we've been using for years? What's wrong with the government book we have?

Questions such as these offer a formidable challenge. So why should government teachers look at a new program? What's so great about it?

The answer is: "Lots of things."

American Government puts students first.

1. The **writing** speaks to students. It's clear, concise, informal, and engaging. Standard topics are covered, but so are some unusual or amusing features. Chapters are clearly outlined and briefly summarized at the end.

2. The **artwork** offers touches of humor in place of staged photos of politicians.

3. The **Skills Handbook** outlines succinctly the key skills students need through their lifetime for understanding politics and government.

4. The **Almanac** offers up-to-date glimpses of various parts of government, from elections to the courts and the Constitution.

5. The **Activity Book** involves students in the process of government through hands-on, "let-me-solve-it" kinds of activities on everything from establishing voter eligibility to balancing the school budget.

6. The **Web site** offers study aids and resources for students, not just their teachers. Topic-by-topic, the Web site provides chapter outlines, study guides, Internet resources, and activities.

American Government considers what teachers need.

1. A **coursebook**—with brief, clear explanations—functions as a reference, as opposed to a bulky textbook that establishes the curriculum. A coursebook works better as one piece among many others—activities, Internet, and current articles and events—than a textbook does.

2. A coursebook for about **$20** seems far more practical for a semester course than a $50 textbook. Traditional texts are so expensive that they can only be purchased once every 7 to 10 years, leaving them out-of-date more than half the time they're in use.

3. A **cleaner, simpler approach** gives teachers what they want—clear explanations about the concepts of government—without all of the clutter of most textbooks. Gone are the section and chapter reviews, objectives, "getting involved" features, and pages and pages of uninformative photos.

4. A program that **substitutes resources for worksheets.** Aside from multiple-choice tests and a study guide, this program opts instead to give teachers bibliographies, Internet resources, and participatory activities.

5. The **Skills Handbook** offers a way to teach lifelong skills for understanding government in place of hit-or-miss lessons scattered throughout texts. Here, in one convenient place, are the resources to improve students' abilities to read maps, evaluate sources, give speeches, do research, and much more.

Still not convinced there's a better way? *American Government* may not be for every teacher. But we believe teachers who take charge of setting their own curriculum, who really care about having current information, who see the text as one element among many in their teaching repertoire, and who use the Internet— these teachers, we believe, will embrace *American Government*.

HOW TO USE *AMERICAN GOVERNMENT*

As *American Government* was being developed, teachers, along with three distinguished professors of government and two politicians, commented and reviewed the manuscript chapter by chapter. From their comments emerged the following suggestions about how to use this program.

1. Teaching the text

For many government teachers, the course consists of a march through several main topics that "have to be covered," such as the Constitution, the presidency, Congress, and the Supreme Court. To make this job somewhat easier, this *Teacher's Guide* has broken down the subject into 48 topics, or lectures.

These **48 topics** organize a curriculum of essential topics to cover. In a semester course, it is impossible to cover everything. The topics allow teachers to make considered choices about what to include and what to omit. Across the course of a semester, teachers can "cover" the subject by teaching two to three topics per week.

2. Integrating activities and lectures

To make a subject relevant and meaningful, nothing succeeds quite as well as involving students in good activities. By introducing activities from the *Activity Book* with lectures, teachers can strike a balance between theory and practice and give students the information they need as well as the practical experience they crave.

3. Using an eclectic approach

Government teachers have traditionally used articles on current events or political subjects of the moment as often as they have used information from a text. Many teachers we talked with had students on-line one week searching resources on the Internet and doing a simulation (for example, a jury trial) the next. After that, they might return to the text and then take a detour to look at some articles on a current event in the news. *American Government* works especially well in this teaching scenario, serving as a reference point for integrating all that teachers want to fold into their classrooms.

4. Adjusting to block scheduling

For most teachers, adjusting to block scheduling means giving up "lecture-style" classes in favor of ones that are more varied, mixing lectures, activities, discussions, and participation in each session. This program is designed for this scenario, and that's why the program includes

- *Activity Book* with dozens of activities
- Web site with loads of resources and a "research center"
- *Reader* to discuss issues raised by some of today's most distinguished politicians
- *Coursebook* with clear, brief explanations for easy reference
- *Teacher's Guide* with discussion questions and activities

COURSEBOOK

The coursebook breaks down the subject of government into six units:

I. Constitution and Foundations of Government

II. Political Behavior and Participation

III. Institutions of National Government

IV. Civil Liberties and Civil Rights

V. Public Policy and Comparative Government

VI. State and Local Government

Two additional units are:

VII. The Skills Handbook

VIII. The Almanac

To find a specific subject, use the Contents. It's the best way to find broad, general subjects such as "Voter Turnout." Use the Index for more specific subjects, such as "Independent Counsel Statute" or "Dennis Hastert."

To make navigation through the coursebook easier, each chapter begins with a preview. This helps the teacher look ahead to what's in the chapter. Each chapter concludes with a brief summary of one or two paragraphs, pulling together some of the main ideas that were discussed.

Preview

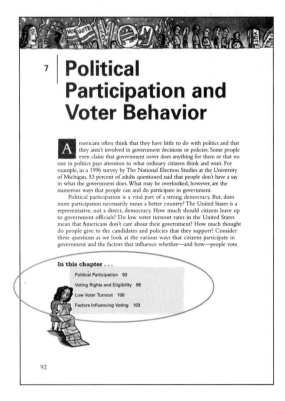

Summary

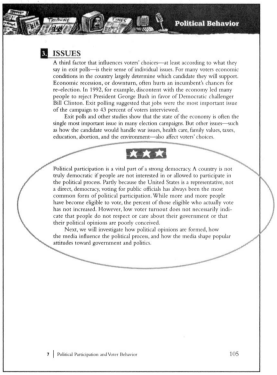

Throughout each chapter, several features are woven into the text to provide timely examples, historical perspective, or major points of comparison. At the bottom of pages, key vocabulary is defined. Definitions for the most essential (and tested) terms appear in red in the text and in a tinted box at the bottom of the page. Other vocabulary terms are boldfaced and set outside the tinted box in the footnote.

Vocabulary

- To help students learn the **vocabulary** of government, approximately 300 of the most important words have been defined and highlighted on the page. The essential terms are presented in color in the text and highlighted in color at the bottom of the page. Other helpful vocabulary words are defined in black and white.

Features

- A variety of unusual and pertinent features keeps students interested. The recurring **features** are

Headlines

Vs.

Quotes

E.G.

Then and Now

Timeline

Political Behavior

The Original Electorate

In 1789, only about 23 percent of the total population was eligible to vote. The Founders said little about the establishment of **suffrage** rights, leaving the question of voting requirements largely to the states. Article I of the Constitution states that members of the House of Representatives should be chosen by the "people of the several states." All states had property requirements at first, so that only white men who owned property could vote.

The End of Property Requirements

A very important part of President Andrew Jackson's (1829–1837) popularity was his appeal for "universal manhood suffrage," which meant that voting was reserved for all adult white men, regardless of property holdings. By 1852, all states had dropped property requirements for voting.

Voting and African Americans

After the Civil War (1861–1865), slaves were freed by the 13th Amendment, and voting rights were extended to African American men in 1870 by the 15th Amendment, although, as discussed in Chapter 16, the matter was not settled then. Because so many voting procedures were left up to the states, many former slave states chose to ignore the amendment. Such tactics as the **poll tax**, the **grandfather clause**, and **literacy tests** kept African Americans from voting for decades. Grandfather clauses were declared unconstitutional in 1915, but poll taxes went largely unchecked until 1964, and literacy tests were not banned until 1965.

Voting and Women

Starting in the late nineteenth century, states in the West were the first to extend voting rights to women. The 19th Amendment was not passed until 1920, when the right to vote was granted to all eligible women. Unlike African-American men, who had been kept from voting largely by intimidation and state and local laws, women almost immediately began to vote in large numbers.

def·i·ni·tions

suffrage—the right or privilege of voting.

poll tax—a fee, now unconstitutional, required of voters in many southern states; designed to discourage African-American voters.

grandfather clause—a now unconstitutional law that permitted persons to vote without meeting other requirements if they or one of their ancestors had been entitled to vote in 1866.

literacy test—an examination of reading and writing skills, now unconstitutional, that citizens had to pass before they were allowed to vote.

7 | Political Participation and Voter Behavior

97

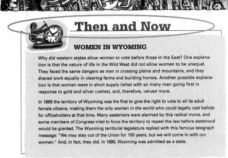

Then and Now

WOMEN IN WYOMING

Why did western states allow women to vote before those in the East? One explanation is that the nature of life in the Wild West did not allow women to be unequal. They faced the same dangers as men in crossing plains and mountains, and they shared work equally in clearing farms and building homes. Another possible explanation is that women were in short supply (what with so many men going first in response to gold and silver rushes), and, therefore, valued more.

In 1869 the territory of Wyoming was the first to give the right to vote to all its adult female citizens, making them the only women in the world who could legally cast ballots for officeholders at that time. Many easterners were alarmed by this radical move, and some members of Congress tried to force the territory to repeal the law before statehood would be granted. The Wyoming territorial legislature replied with this famous telegraph message: "We may stay out of the Union for 100 years, but we will come in with our women." And, in fact, they did. In 1890, Wyoming was admitted as a state.

Voting and 18 to 21-Year-Olds

A final major expansion of voting rights occured in 1971 when the 26th Amendment granted suffrage to 18 to 21-year-olds. Before that time, the general requirement was that individuals had to be at least 21 to vote. A few states—such as Georgia, Kentucky, Alaska, and Hawaii—had allowed people as young as age 18 to vote. The increased activism of young people, particularly on college campuses during the 1960s, almost certainly inspired this expansion of voting rights.

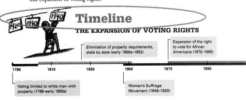

Timeline

THE EXPANSION OF VOTING RIGHTS

1790	1810	1830	1850	1870	1890

- Elimination of property requirements, state by state (early 1800s–1852)
- Expansion of the right to vote for African Americans (1870–1965)
- Voting limited to white men with property (1789–early 1800s)
- Women's Suffrage Movement (1848–1920)

98

ix

TEACHER'S GUIDE

The *Teacher's Guide* breaks down the subject of government into 48 topics, creating ready-made class periods for teachers. These "topics" are organized as "lectures," giving teachers the objectives, background, and bibliographies to discuss the subject in class. By covering 2 to 3 topics each week, teachers can easily make their way through the entire government curriculum in a semester.

Each topic is broken down into a four-page lesson plan.

I. Objectives, Background, and Resources

- Each **topic** is linked immediately to the appropriate **chapter.**
- A companion **activity** for each topic in the *Activity Book* is cited.
- **Objectives** define goals for each topic.
- **Vocabulary** highlights major terms for students to master. These terms will be tested.
- **Background** fills in the historical, cultural, and academic dimensions of each subject.
- **Further resources** give teachers ways to extend their knowledge of a subject.

II. Discussion Questions, Critical Thinking Questions, and Skills Development Activities

- **For Discussion** review questions help build students' comprehension of text material.
- **Critical Thinking** questions lead students to think in-depth about key ideas and issues.
- **Skills Development Activities** allow teachers to extend any topic in one of four ways:

  1 Writing
  2 Current Events
  3 Internet
  4 Special Sources

Objectives

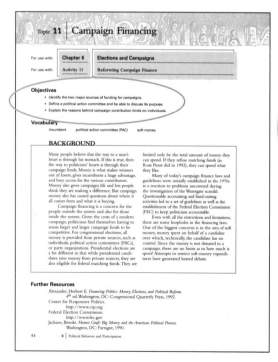

Discussion Questions

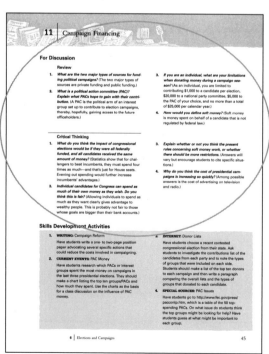

III. Study Guide and Vocabulary Quiz

A study guide is one of many tools included to help build student comprehension.

- Each topic includes a **study guide** to help students master basic concepts of each topic.
- The **outline** for each topic is included in the Web site: www.greatsource.com/amgov/.
- An **interactive practice quiz** is also included for each topic at the Web site.

The terms of government are one important way students come to know the subject. As a result, the vocabulary terms are specially called out in the text of the pupil's edition and defined at the bottom of each page.

- Each term is **highlighted in the text** and **defined at the bottom of the page** on which it appears.
- Each term is also defined again in the **glossary.**
- Each topic includes a **vocabulary quiz** (shown here) to help them master the terms.
- An additional interactive vocabulary quiz is included in the Web site: www.greatsource.com/amgov/.

IV. Multiple-choice Test and Essay Test

In addition, five skills lessons enable teachers to present key skills in an organized, succinct fashion.

A **multiple-choice test** serves as the primary assessment tool. It tests if students have mastered the main ideas of each topic.

An **essay test question** is also included to provide a written assessment possibility with every topic.

Study Guide and Vocabulary   ## Tests

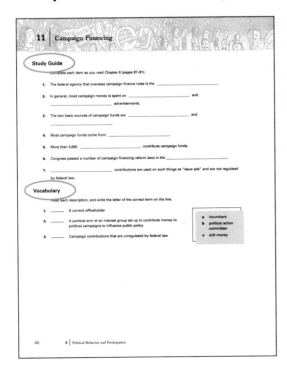

ACTIVITY BOOK

Because students learn through hands-on participation, *American Government* puts a great deal of emphasis on activities. In addition to the four Skills Development Activities for every topic in the *Teacher's Guide,* the *Activity Book* includes additional activities that connect meaningful projects with each topic.

The intent of the *Activity Book* is to make it easy for teachers to involve students in activities. Putting together worthwhile activities is time-consuming; and working through the logistics of what materials are needed and how long each stage ought to take is always something of an experiment.

That's why Stephen Sansone wrote the *Activity Book.* Committed to the idea of involving students, he has for years taught his students largely through participation in activities. Those activities—and many others—are included here.

Brief Activities (1–2 days)

Each topic has one Brief Activity. Activities begin with an **Overview** that describes the students' work. Immediately following is a **Time Frame,** giving teachers a step-by-step plan. Lists of **discussion questions,** a rubric for **assessment,** and further **resources** are also included.

Most of the Brief Activities then have **a worksheet** to coordinate a group's activity, whether it is collecting information, analyzing an issue, or making a speech.

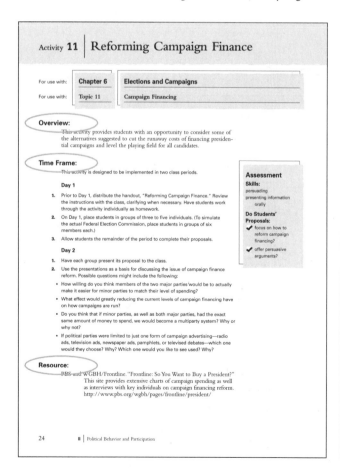

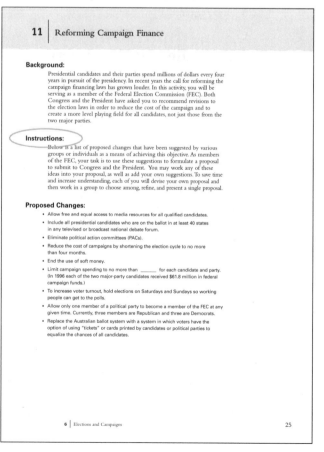

Extended Activities (3–40 days)

Each unit has four Extended Activities. The Extended Activities are long enough to involve students in simulations of the actual work of government, such as passing a bill or preparing a platform or budget. In addition to an **Overview**, a **Time Frame**, **discussion questions**, and a list of **Resources**, the Extended Activities also usually have accompanying information—party platforms, facts about court cases, background on both sides of an issue, and so forth—that students work through. A rubric to help teachers with **assessment** is also part of each Extended Activity.

The purpose of the Extended Activities is to give teachers a way to involve students in creative group projects or simulations and even, perhaps, to teach their entire course through activities, using the text as an informational resource when needed.

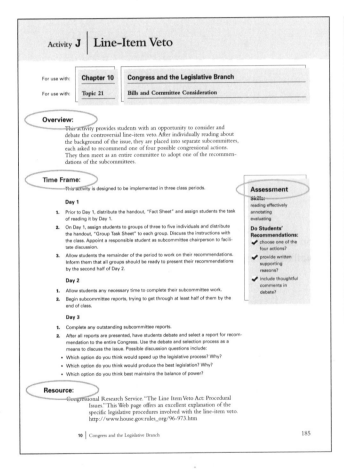

Activity **J** | Line-Item Veto

| For use with: | **Chapter 10** | **Congress and the Legislative Branch** |
| For use with: | **Topic 21** | **Bills and Committee Consideration** |

Overview:

This activity provides students with an opportunity to consider and debate the controversial line-item veto. After individually reading about the background of the issue, they are placed into separate subcommittees, each asked to recommend one of four possible congressional actions. They then meet as an entire committee to adopt one of the recommendations of the subcommittees.

Time Frame:

This activity is designed to be implemented in three class periods.

Day 1

1. Prior to Day 1, distribute the handout, "Fact Sheet" and assign students the task of reading it by Day 1.
2. On Day 1, assign students to groups of three to five individuals and distribute the handout, "Group Task Sheet" to each group. Discuss the instructions with the class. Appoint a responsible student as subcommittee chairperson to facilitate discussion.
3. Allow students the remainder of the period to work on their recommendations. Inform them that all groups should be ready to present their recommendations by the second half of Day 2.

Day 2

1. Allow students any necessary time to complete their subcommittee work.
2. Begin subcommittee reports, trying to get through at least half of them by the end of class.

Day 3

1. Complete any outstanding subcommittee reports.
2. After all reports are presented, have students debate and select a report for recommendation to the entire Congress. Use the debate and selection process as a means to discuss the issue. Possible discussion questions include:
   - Which option do you think would speed up the legislative process? Why?
   - Which option do you think would produce the best legislation? Why?
   - Which option do you think best maintains the balance of power?

Assessment

Skills:
reading effectively
annotating
evaluating

**Do Students'
Recommendations:**
✔ choose one of the four actions?
✔ provide written supporting reasons?
✔ include thoughtful comments in debate?

Resource:

Congressional Research Service. "The Line Item Veto Act: Procedural Issues." This Web page offers an excellent explanation of the specific legislative procedures involved with the line-item veto. http://www.house.gov.rules_org/96-973.htm

10 | Congress and the Legislative Branch   185

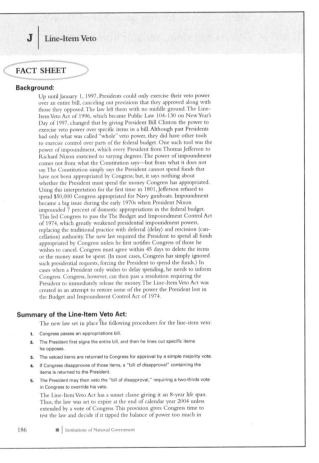

J | Line-Item Veto

FACT SHEET

Background:

Up until January 1, 1997, Presidents could only exercise their veto power over an entire bill, canceling out provisions that they approved along with those they opposed. The law left them with no middle ground. The Line-Item Veto Act of 1996, which became Public Law 104-130 on New Year's Day of 1997, changed that by giving President Bill Clinton the power to exercise veto power over specific items in a bill. Although past Presidents had only what was called "whole" veto power, they did have other tools to exercise control over parts of the federal budget. One such tool was the power of impoundment, which every President from Thomas Jefferson to Richard Nixon exercised to varying degrees. The power of impoundment comes not from what the Constitution says—but from what it does not say. The Constitution simply says the President cannot spend funds that have not been appropriated by Congress; but, it says nothing about whether the President must spend the money Congress has appropriated. Using this interpretation for the first time in 1801, Jefferson refused to spend $50,000 Congress appropriated for Navy gunboats. Impoundment became a big issue during the early 1970s when President Nixon impounded 7 percent of domestic appropriations in the federal budget. This led Congress to pass the The Budget and Impoundment Control Act of 1974, which greatly weakened presidential impoundment powers, replacing the traditional practice with deferral (delay) and rescission (cancellation) authority. The new law required the President to spend all funds appropriated by Congress unless he first notifies Congress of those he wishes to cancel. Congress must agree within 45 days to delete the items or the money must be spent. (In most cases, Congress has simply ignored such presidential requests, forcing the President to spend the funds.) In cases when a President only wishes to delay spending, he needs to inform Congress. Congress, however, can then pass a resolution requiring the President to immediately release the money. The Line-Item Veto Act was created in an attempt to restore some of the power the President lost in the Budget and Impoundment Control Act of 1974.

Summary of the Line-Item Veto Act:

The new law set in place the following procedures for the line-item veto:

1. Congress passes an appropriations bill.
2. The President first signs the entire bill, and then he lines out specific items he opposes.
3. The vetoed items are returned to Congress for approval by a simple majority vote.
4. If Congress disapproves of those items, a "bill of disapproval" containing the items is returned to the President.
5. The President may then veto the "bill of disapproval," requiring a two-thirds vote in Congress to override his veto.

The Line-Item Veto Act has a sunset clause giving it an 8-year life span. Thus, the law was set to expire at the end of calendar year 2004 unless extended by a vote of Congress. This provision gives Congress time to test the law and decide if it tipped the balance of power too much in

186   **III** | Institutions of National Government

PARTICIPATING IN GOVERNMENT READER

To get more students involved in government, Michael Dukakis and Paul Simon asked some of the most well-known and distinguished politicians of our day to contribute to a collection of essays for students. The purpose of the essays was to show students the different roads that led each of them into politics and the issues that motivated them.

The purpose of the reader is one part inspirational and an equal part discussion starter, creating the initial spark to generate conversations on a wide range of political subjects. Among the more than 25 distinguished contributors to the reader are:

- Kay Bailey Hutchinson, senator from Texas
- Willie Brown, mayor of San Francisco
- Mario Cuomo, former governor of New York
- Dianne Feinstein, senator from California
- Steve Goldsmith, mayor of Indianapolis
- Sandra Day O'Connor, Supreme Court justice
- Federico Peña, former cabinet member
- Alan Simpson, former senator from Wyoming
- Patricia Schroeder, former representative from Colorado
- Loretta Sanchez, representative from California

WEB SITE   WWW.GREATSOURCE.COM/AMGOV/

The Internet has become a worldwide library of information and a tool of inestimable communication. To take advantage of its possibilities, a companion Web site has been developed. Below is a **brief site map.**

American Government

  I.   **Program Overview**
- **A.** Table of Contents
- **B.** Introduction to the Program
- **C.** Meet the Authors
- **D.** Walk-through of the Book

  II. **Resource Center**
- **A.** Lesson Resources (for each topic)
    - **1.** Outlines
    - **2.** Vocabulary quiz
    - **3.** Practice quiz
    - **4.** Further resources
- **B.** Online Almanac
    - **1.** Links
    - **2.** Documents
    - **3.** Emerging Issues
    - **4.** Updates and Corrections

FREQUENTLY ASKED QUESTIONS

1. **How is this book different from other government texts?**

   This text was written by practicing high school government teachers, not by professors. But the greatest difference between this book and others comes in its commitment to be student-centered. The writing is directed at students; the art will appeal to students; the Skills Handbook and Almanac are tools designed for students. Other books for high school government students do not put students first but rather are assembled to appeal to "adoption" committees. We think students will recognize a difference.

2. **Why is vocabulary emphasized so much? Why are some words highlighted in red and others are not?**

   Part of knowing a subject is knowing the "lingo." To understand government, students first need to know the terms used to describe it and discuss it. When government authors throw around so many different terms, how can anyone know which ones are the most important? That's a good question, which is why we highlighted the key terms in red in the text. Lesser terms are presented, but not highlighted. These secondary terms are still important but represent a second tier of mastery. By spotlighting key terms, students know instantly which ones they absolutely must master.

3. **How does the Skills Handbook work with the chapters on government content?**

   Teachers report spending between 15 to 30 percent of their class time teaching skills, such as evaluating sources, preparing a speech, or writing a position paper. To help students with these assignments, the authors decided to create one succinct yet comprehensive resource to which students can turn. Instead of treating "skills" as instruction sprinkled across a text in bite-sized bits, the authors developed one resource that students can turn to for all kinds of assignments, whether it is understanding a graph or political cartoon, preparing an impromptu talk for the class, or doing research.

4. **Why is there an Almanac? Why not put all of the information in it in the chapters?**

   An almanac is a timely record of what's happening, usually one that is updated annually. Government teachers often expressed their frustration with "out-of-date" texts. Time and again they explained how they used current newspaper articles to update subjects for their classes. The Almanac offers a way to update *American Government* on a regular basis in more than a cosmetic fashion. In addition, the Web site (www.greatsource.com/amgov/) expands upon the Almanac in the back of the book. It also has still more recent updates and corrections.

5. **Why is the *Teacher's Guide* broken down into 48 "topics"?**

   In the government curriculum, some subjects—such as the presidency or Supreme Court—are longer and more weighty than others. As a result, those chapters run longer. To break down the curriculum into relatively "equal" segments, such as class periods, the content was broken into equal units called "topics." Each topic can be presented in approximately one class period. Big subjects, such as Congress, have more topics associated with them than smaller subjects, such as Comparative Government. On the whole, topics were created as a convenience. They list the 48 main class periods or major ideas on government.

SKILLS DEVELOPMENT ACTIVITIES

TEACHING GOVERNMENT

By Ethel Wood

"Mrs. Wood, I can't do my presentation today because I have an appointment for my senior class picture. . . ."

"Mrs. Wood, my printer went haywire last night, but can you read my paper from this disk?"

"Mrs. Wood, that test wasn't fair . . . it was too hard, and anyway, I was absent two days for field trips!"

These all too familiar teenage laments are captured by the logo on my favorite coffee mug, a gift from a student: "The little joys of teaching are without number." Teaching teenagers challenges the most patient among us because their demands—though few in number individually—accumulate, each day, every day of the school year. Add the fire drills, endless attendance procedures, faculty meetings, and classroom management problems, and most teachers wonder how they ever find time to teach. But then, buried in the trivia of the day, a student will ask, "Who really runs foreign policy in this country anyway?" And another student will say, "The President," and another will add, "No, Congress," and another, "No, big interest groups control everything." Suddenly the class is off and running on a great discussion about political power in the United States.

Helping students to make links between their lives and the world around them is what good teaching is all about, and our biggest challenge in the classroom lies in finding ways to maximize positive learning experiences within environments that don't always encourage them. The last thing a teacher needs is a textbook that appears to be somewhere in space, flashing colorful pictures of people in out-of-date clothing or using words and phrases to which students can't relate. My own real-life teaching experiences have guided my every step in writing *American Government*. In my approach to each topic, these questions have been in the front of my mind: How do I explain this important concept in my own classroom? What questions do students typically ask? What examples will clarify the difficulties many will have? Which issues related to this topic can be discussed? I hope that the text will help bring about more of those special moments in class—times when students and subject matter click.

A textbook is an essential component of my classroom. I count on the text to provide my students with basic knowledge of American government and politics. If the text isn't interesting, students are less likely to read it, and the infrastructure of the class is seriously damaged. On the other hand, it is my responsibility to bring the subject to life through class activities, discussions, and extra resources, such as original documents, Internet materials, videos, and up-to-date magazine and newspaper articles. Students also must learn important skills, such as reading maps, cartoons, and graphs, writing essays and research papers, and studying effectively for exams. Typically, I spend quite a bit of class time helping students improve these skills.

Most of us can be better teachers if we have time-saving yet creative support for our efforts. By the very nature of our jobs, we sometimes feel isolated in the classroom, overwhelmed by our responsibility, and yet never doing as well as we would like. The best support comes from our colleagues—those that are struggling with similar issues of curriculum, organization, school and national environments, and student concerns.

GET STUDENTS INVOLVED IN CIVICS

by Stephen C. Sansone

On April 25, 1983, *U.S. News & World Report* featured a one-page editorial by Marvin Stone entitled, "Civics Gap: Alarming Challenge." The article summarized what was wrong with civics education in this country. Stone stated, "Nearly all states require some instruction in government for high school graduation. How, then, is it possible for so many students to know so little and hold such wrong ideas? Much of the blame is placed by experts on dull teaching methods and on teachers' excessive reliance on textbooks that fail to relate theory to the actual workings of government."

Apparently, very little has changed in civics education in the years since Stone wrote this article. In early September 1998, the National Constitution Center released the results of a nationwide phone survey of 600 teens between the ages of 13 and 17. Cassandra Burrell of the Associated Press reported on the findings: "[O]nly 2% can name the chief justice of the United States; . . . 21% know there are 100 members of the Senate; . . . 25% know the Constitution was written in Philadelphia; . . . less than 33% can name . . . the speaker of the House."

These concerns, expressed some 15 years apart, beg the question: How do we educate students to join the ranks of the informed citizenry? It is clear, as Stone stated, that we must reduce our over-reliance on textbooks as the main vehicle for teaching civics. One way to achieve this is by implementing a participatory component into curriculum units. In science class we refer to this as a lab, in English class we publish, and in driver's education we call it getting "behind the wheel." It is the "behind the wheel" stuff—more specifically, participatory activities—of citizenship that civics education is lacking. Students of civics spend too much time memorizing the specific parts of the car and too little time learning how to drive it.

I believe that textbooks or other informational components are a necessary part of every unit. However, many unit designs leave the inclusion of participatory activities to happenstance. What I am suggesting is that teachers routinely incorporate a participatory component into their classes.

Perhaps the best rationale for inserting this element into unit designs lies in an ancient Chinese proverb, which simply states: "Tell me, I forget. Show me, I remember. Involve me, I understand." Traditional unit designs, which lack the participatory element, address only the first two statements of the proverb. They simply "tell" and "show" students. Unit designs that include the participatory component "involve" students, thus increasing their understanding. Incorporating the participatory component into the unit design ensures that students get the "behind the wheel" training of civics education. The major roadblock to routinely inserting this component into the curriculum is that many educators think that the term participatory component translates into either a rather sophisticated, or overly generic, "boxed" simulation. The idea of using such simulations in every unit is unnatural, and these components tend to be relegated to "sidebar" status.

Using this book as a vehicle to reshape unit designs to include the participatory component should go a long way toward getting students "behind the wheel" of citizenship. It addresses the issue Stone raised in 1983 of "dull teaching methods," without having to throw out the textbooks. When the primary function of a civics course is providing information to students, we reduce the concept of citizenship to a study. Citizenship is an act. It involves action.

HOLDING THE OFFICE OF CITIZEN

by Michael Hartoonian

I know of no safe depository of the ultimate powers of the society but with the people themselves; and if we think them not enlightened enough to exercise their control with a wholesome discretion, the remedy is not to take power from them, but to inform their discretion through instruction . . . Education.

—Thomas Jefferson, 1820

In 1789 the Framers of the Constitution wrote with two thoughts in mind: This document must not only control uncontrollable government, but it must also control a people without the discipline or virtue to govern themselves. In 1820 Thomas Jefferson added to this thinking with his own thoughts about creating an educated populace that could govern itself. If done correctly, it would be through education that individuals would assume the all-important office of citizen. In fact, the people should and would create public schools with this first purpose in mind—to develop enlightened citizens who could ensure the survival and health of the Republic.

It was known, if only dimly, that if the process for federalism were to continue, and if citizens were to govern themselves in the new states, they would have to be educated. Even as late as 1862, when President Lincoln signed the Morrill Act establishing a land grant of 30,000 acres to every state for higher education, the first priority or mission of these schools was civic competence. A look at the charters that established these universities tells us that their main purpose was the development of citizens who could govern themselves.

We have always understood this simple fact: Send our citizens to school, not to become better off, but to become better, period. And, if each of us becomes better—a better scholar, a better citizen, a better person—we each have a better opportunity to become better off. Most importantly, we will understand that our personal well-being is always tied to the well-being of our fellow citizens. We will come to know that there can be no private wealth without common wealth.

Our first responsibility as teachers is to the health and sustainability of the Republic. Education must always be defined within the context of a particular society, and, because our society is constructed on the precept of the enlightened citizen, scholarship takes on an intentional public purpose. Citizens understand the principles of rule of law, legal limits to freedom, and majority rule with minority rights. They are knowledgeable about their cultural heritage, understanding how contemporary institutions and conditions came to be, and they possess the attitudes of civility, fair play, cooperation, and a demand for quality in the character and work of themselves and others. This, again, is a public purpose, meaning that citizens understand that their responsibility is to the ideals of the nation. As a citizen, one has the responsibility to know these things; one must work hard to learn this knowledge, because it is a high honor to hold the office of citizen, the highest office in the land. Without a conscious effort to teach and learn these attitudes, this knowledge, and the ability to participate in the public life of the nation, a free republic will not long endure.

You hold, perhaps, the most important office in the world . . . the office of citizen of the United States of America. The materials, activities, and knowledge presented here will enhance your abilities to perform the responsibilities of that office. This program is designed to improve the intellectual, ethical, and participatory fitness of citizens.

Constitution and Foundations of Government

For use with:	**Chapter 1**	**Principles of Government**
For use with:	Activity 1	Services Governments Provide

Objectives

- List and demonstrate an understanding of the origins and purposes of governments.
- Define and describe the four characteristics of a nation-state.
- Analyze the main purposes of governments and apply those to definitions and purposes of governments.

Vocabulary

government   nation-state   sovereignty   politics

BACKGROUND

How did the idea of government develop? Was it a natural evolution from the family unit? Aristotle described man as a "political animal" and thought it was the only natural way for people to live. His experience was of the city-states in ancient Greece, small self-governing communities that were often at war with one another. Others, such as the Chinese scholars Lao-tzu and Confucius, developed theories about ways that people should live together. These theories were among those that became the core of people's beliefs about how societies should function.

In later centuries the concept of the nation-state emerged as a primary method for justifying governing bodies. Nation-states were a way for communities with similar ethnic bonds and territories to band together to create communities with governments.

The usual definition for *government* is an institution that enforces public policies. But what does that mean? Government organizes a community around common goals and common cultures. It provides a way for people to live together peacefully and prosper. It organizes life

in nation-states—defined as entities with territory, population, sovereignty, and government.

Over the years, the purposes of governments have been fairly consistent. They have offered protection. Nation-states have also provided some justification for their existence by using the idea of a common culture to protect and develop their own interests as well as to develop common policies for resolving disputes (e.g., lawsuits or arbitration) and for creating a peaceable society (e.g., curfew, or traffic laws).

Today, it may seem difficult to imagine a time when an army could invade a community, slaughter the men, and enslave the women and children. But that practice was quite common. In fact, such actions still occur, even with international enforcement against such practices.

In this lesson, students will have the opportunity to examine theories of government, such as the Evolution Theory, the Force Theory, the Divine Right Theory, and the Social Contract Theory, as they begin to study the purposes and origins of governments.

Further Resources

Diamond, Jared. *Guns, Germs, and Steel.* New York: Knopf, 1997.

Fishkin, James S. *The Voice of the People.* New Haven: Yale University Press, 1996.

Tinder, Glenn. *Political Thinking—The Perennial Questions.* 4th ed. Boston: Little, Brown, 1986.

For Discussion

Review

1. *What four characteristics define a nation-state?* (The characteristics of nation-states are territory, population, sovereignty, and government.)

2. *What are the purposes of government?* (The purposes of government are protection, maintenance of public order, resolution of social conflicts, and responsibility for a stable economy.)

3. *From where did governments come originally?* (Government may have evolved from the traditional family structure, from the conquest and domination of one group over another, from rulers claiming divine right to govern, or from the effort to establish order in a chaotic world through a social contract.)

4. *What are two characteristics of a nation-state?* (One characteristic of a nation-state is that it chooses its own form of government, and another characteristic is that it has a government to help create a stable and peaceful way of life for its people.)

Critical Thinking

1. *Why do you think all countries have governments?* (A government is an integral aspect of being a country and providing sovereignty, and it benefits the people who live in the country.)

2. *What do you think is the most plausible explanation for how governments originated?* (Encourage students to offer reasons to explain their choices.)

3. *Why do you think governments were appealing to citizens of Greek city-states, to ancient peoples of China, and to early Native Americans?* (In those cultures, people were often at war with one another, so governments offered them protection.)

4. *Why do you think places such as Bosnia and Kosovo wish to become countries?* (By becoming a country, a territory gains sovereignty—the ability to choose its own form of government—and the right to establish its own culture in the form of a nation-state.)

5. *What, in your own words, is a good definition for government?* (Encourage students to be specific and to explain government's benefits. For example, a government is a way for people to organize a way to live together and resolve their disputes and make a better life for themselves.)

Skills Development Activities

1. **WRITING:** Contract with Government

   Ask students to imagine dealing with the government. Each party supplies something the other needs. Ask students to list three things that the government would give them. Then have them list things they would give to the government.

2. **CURRENT EVENTS:** Sovereignty

   Have students conduct research about a contemporary territory that is trying to achieve sovereignty, such as Guam, Puerto Rico, or Samoa. Ask them to find articles from the last five years and have them identify two or three major issues in the effort to achieve sovereignty. They should then prepare a short oral overview for the class in which they explain what they learned and what they think the chances are for the territory's sovereignty.

3. **INTERNET:** Political Philosophers

   Direct the students to research Web sites devoted to political philosophers such as Aristotle or John Locke. Have them use a search engine to search for sites with the philosophers' names and then locate a site devoted to their works. Students should report their findings in a 60-second oral review of the sites.

4. **SPECIAL SOURCES:** Theories of Government

   Have students find a copy of Thomas Paine's *Common Sense* or the Confucian *Analects* in the library. Ask them to read the introduction or part of a chapter and paraphrase it in their own words.

Study Guide

Name: _____

Complete each item as you read Chapter 1 (pages 2–7).

1. What is government? _____

_____

2. What are commonly called *countries* are actually _____.

3. The four characteristics of nation-states are _____,

_____, _____, and

_____.

4. Governments share the same basic purposes of protection, maintenance of _____,

resolution of _____, the responsibility for a _____,

and the provision of _____.

5. The four main theories of the origin of governments are the _____ Theory, the

_____ Theory, the _____ Theory, and

the _____ Theory.

Vocabulary

Read each description, and write the letter of the correct term on the line.

1. _____ Institutions by which a country is ruled and its public policy created and administered.

2. _____ A political unit with a defined territory and government

3. _____ A nation-state's right to rule itself

4. _____ Methods of managing government

a	government
b	politics
c	sovereignty
d	nation-state

Multiple-Choice Test

Name: _____

Find the best answer for each item. Then completely fill in the circle for that answer.

1. A _____ is an institution that rules a nation-state.
   - **a.** country
   - **b.** sovereign
   - **c.** social contract
   - **d.** government

2. A nation-state has
   - **a.** territory
   - **b.** people
   - **c.** government
   - **d.** all of the above

3. What does *sovereignty* mean?
   - **a.** attempts to influence government
   - **b.** a nation-state's right to rule itself
   - **c.** a government based on a social contract
   - **d.** the institution through which a state makes policy

4. Which is NOT a basic purpose of government?
   - **a.** to expand its territory
   - **b.** to maintain public order
   - **c.** to resolve social conflicts
   - **d.** to provide public services

5. Sovereignty is most closely related to which basic purpose of government?
   - **a.** protection
   - **b.** public service
   - **c.** resolving conflicts
   - **d.** maintaining the economy

6. Which theory of the origins of government sees government as a result of warfare and conquest?
   - **a.** the Evolution Theory
   - **b.** the Force Theory
   - **c.** the Divine Right Theory
   - **d.** the Social Contract Theory

7. Which theory of the origins of government sees government rulers as representatives of God?
   - **a.** the Evolution Theory
   - **b.** the Force Theory
   - **c.** the Divine Right Theory
   - **d.** the Social Contract Theory

8. Which theory of the origins of government was supported by John Locke?
   - **a.** the Evolution Theory
   - **b.** the Force Theory
   - **c.** the Divine Right Theory
   - **d.** the Social Contract Theory

9. Which theory of the origins of government sees government as an extension of the family?
   - **a.** the Evolution Theory
   - **b.** the Force Theory
   - **c.** the Divine Right Theory
   - **d.** the Social Contract Theory

10. Native-American governments provide evidence for which theory?
    - **a.** the Evolution Theory
    - **b.** the Force Theory
    - **c.** the Divine Right Theory
    - **d.** the Social Contract Theory

	a	b	c	d
1	a	b	c	d
2	a	b	c	d
3	a	b	c	d
4	a	b	c	d
5	a	b	c	d
6	a	b	c	d
7	a	b	c	d
8	a	b	c	d
9	a	b	c	d
10	a	b	c	d

Essay Question

Which theory of the origins of government do you find least believable? Explain your answer.

For use with: | **Chapter 1** | **Principles of Government**

For use with: | **Activity 2** | **Living in a Direct Democracy**

Objectives

- Define and identify different theories of elites' political power.
- List and explain three major ways political power is distributed.
- Explain the key similarities and differences among the major forms of government.

Vocabulary

unitary government	federal government	parliamentary government
presidential government	confederation	democracy

BACKGROUND

Democracy and *power* often seem as though they are terms in conflict. The uses of power appear to be associated with decision-making that is arbitrary and often dictatorial, and so it can be. But power can also be wielded by large groups of people in a wide variety of ways. *The American Heritage Dictionary* defines power as "the ability or official capacity to exercise control. . . . A person, group or nation having control over others."

The ways power is distributed and used are usually determined in part by the culture of each nation-state. In the United States, a parliamentary system evolved into a federal system, created by a group of men in the 1780s. They held *de facto* (actual) power that became *de jure* (legal) power as they placed the power in a constitutional framework. The Founders created a form of representative democracy that worked for the culture they represented. Other forms of government, whether dictatorial or representative, have developed in other countries and have worked as well or at least lasted as long.

One of the major questions concerning power in government is whether or not the power used is perceived as legitimate by those governed. Legitimacy exists only when those governed believe that the forms of government are legitimate and those who wield the power have gained it in a legitimate way. Otherwise, while the system of government may be maintained by force for a while, eventually the government will fall and a new, more legitimate system will arise. The collapse of the former Soviet Union provides an illustration of such a situation.

Many people believe that forms of government work only if the people governed perceive that those who hold *de jure* and even temporary *de facto* power are the legitimate decision makers for the country.

Further Resources

Almond, Gabriel A., and G. Bingham Powell. *Comparative Politics Today: A World View.* 6th ed. New York: HarperCollins, 1996.

Gilliam, Richard, ed. *Power in Postwar America.* Boston: Little, Brown, 1971.

Lasswell, Harold D. *Politics: Who Gets What, When, and How.* New York: McGraw-Hill, 1938.

For Discussion

Review

1. **What is an elite and what are some theories that can be used to define elites?** (An elite is a group who possesses special privileges and powers. Some theories used to define elites are Marxist, as well as theories of a "power elite," bureaucrats, and pluralists.)

2. **How can forms of government be distributed geographically?** (Government forms can be distributed through unitary or federalist systems or some form of confederation.)

3. **What are the major differences between parliamentary and presidential governments?** (Parliamentary forms combine the executive and legislative branches of government. Presidential forms separate the executive and legislative branches into two distinct branches that function independently.)

4. **What are the three major forms of government participation as defined by Aristotle?** (They are autocracy, oligarchy, and democracy.)

Critical Thinking

1. **Why do you think that some people become members of an elite and others do not?** (Have the students identify the elite in their own community, in the United States, and in another country before they answer.)

2. **What are some potential advantages of an autocracy or an oligarchy over a democracy?** (Encourage students to consider speed of decision-making and short-term efficiency as they prepare their answers.)

3. **What are some potential advantages of a democracy over an autocracy?** (Encourage students to consider participation and legitimacy as they share their answers.)

4. **What are some of the factors that you believe motivate people to participate in their government?** (Answers will vary, but students should cite specifics.)

5. **What do you believe is the best form of government for most people in most countries?** (Have students explain their answers using examples.)

Skills Development Activities

1. **WRITING:** Political Participation

   Have students write a short essay in the form of a letter to the editor or a political speech explaining why they believe it is or is not important to participate in one's government.

2. **CURRENT EVENTS:** Power and Politics

   Ask students to locate in one or more news sources examples of people trying to wield power by either participating or attempting to participate in the operation of their government.

3. **INTERNET:** Elites

   Have students search for Web sites explaining contemporary political ideologies and the kinds of elites potentially created by such ideologies. They should report their findings to the class in the form of a short review of the sites and their contents.

4. **SPECIAL SOURCES:** Political Philosophy

   Have students locate abstracts of two political philosophy statements, such as the *Communist Manifesto* and *Mein Kampf,* and ask them to be prepared to present a short critique of each to the class.

Study Guide

Name: _____

Complete each item as you read Chapter 1 (pages 7–15).

1. What four main groups of elites have political scientists identified? _____

   _____

2. The distribution of political power can be analyzed in terms of its _____ location, its distribution between _____ and _____ branches, and by the _____ of people who participate.

3. Governments that concentrate power in one geographic location are said to have a

   _____ system of government.

4. Virtually all modern governments have a(n) _____ branch responsible for making laws and a(n) _____ branch responsible for executing laws.

5. According to Aristotle, the three major categories of government, according to the number of elites, are

   _____, _____, and

   _____.

6. The type of democracy that exists in the United States is a _____.

Vocabulary

Read each description, and write the letter of the correct term on the line.

1. _____ Form of government in a single unit that holds all the power

2. _____ Form of government in which power is divided between a central government and regional governments

3. _____ Form of government in which the leaders are chosen by and responsible to the legislature

4. _____ Form of government in which legislative and executive power are separate

5. _____ Political system marked by a weak central government and powerful states

6. _____ System of government in which the people exercise power

a	confederation
b	democracy
c	federal government
d	parliamentary government
e	presidential government
f	unitary government

Multiple-Choice Test

Name: _____

Find the best answer for each item. Then completely fill in the circle for that answer.

1. Elites exist in

   a. governments   **c.** the military

   b. business   **d.** all of the above

2. Who wrote that a "power elite" exists in the United States?

   a. Karl Marx   **c.** C. Wright Mills

   b. Max Weber   **d.** Aristotle

3. Who argues that there is not a single, super-powerful group of elites?

   a. the bureaucrats   **c.** Aristotle

   b. the pluralists   **d.** Max Weber

4. A strong central government shares power with weaker state governments under a

   a. confederation   **c.** autocracy

   b. federal government   **d.** unitary government

5. Confederations tend to be

   a. short-lived   **c.** headed by a strong central government

   b. long-lasting   **d.** parliamentary

6. The two basic forms of dividing power among branches of government are

   a. federal and unitary   **c.** monarchy and dictatorship

   b. parliamentary and presidential   **d.** direct and representative

7. A prime minister is the chief executive of

   a. a presidential government   **c.** a unitary government

   b. a federal government   **d.** a parliamentary government

8. The United States has

   a. a theocracy   **c.** an aristocracy

   b. a federal government   **d.** none of the above

9. An oligarchy, an aristocracy, and a theocracy are all examples of

   a. rule by one   **c.** rule by many

   b. rule by a few   **d.** rule by all

10. Aristotle categorized governments according to

   a. geographic locations   **c.** the number of people who rule

   b. division of powers into branches   **d.** the age of the rulers

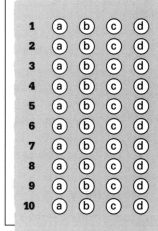

Essay Question

Identify the four main theories that political scientists use to describe elites. Then identify the one that you think best describes elites in the United States. Explain the reasons for your choice.

| For use with: | **Chapter 2** | **Beginnings of American Government** |
| For use with: | **Activity 3** | **Updating the Declaration** |

Objectives

- Demonstrate an understanding of how early colonial governments were structured.
- Explain the major ideas in the Declaration of Independence and the series of events that led to its creation.
- Analyze the meanings of ideas such as limited government, representative government, liberty, and equality and explain how they apply to the origins of U.S. government.

Vocabulary

limited government	representative government
bicameral	unicameral

BACKGROUND

The writers of the U.S. Constitution were men of the Enlightenment. Many read widely and had very clear ideas about the relationship between humans and their government. They had little faith in the virtues of men and so attempted to create a government based on laws and on institutions subject to such laws. With the recent impeachment of a U.S. President, we can still see the thinking of the Framers as they attempted to create ways that laws and institutions, not men, would govern human affairs.

Some still find it strange that English colonies could revolt against possibly the most democratic society in the world in the eighteenth century. However, it is not so strange when we consider that these colonies had gained a measure of freedom—often through neglect by England—from general arbitrary rule. Without the representation of the colonists that might have made English rules seem less arbitrary, the developing political ideology of many of the colonists was offended. And so a revolution occurred.

It was to be a revolution, starting with the Declaration of Independence, that would establish a foundation for new ways of looking at humanity in ways that declared the virtues of freedom, equality, and limited government. While economics certainly played a part in this revolution, it was also a revolution of perceptions and ideals, some unrealized for a century and more. We still try to understand, to follow, and to develop that enlightened thinking.

Further Resources

Becker, Carl L. *The Declaration of Independence: A Study in the History of Political Ideas.* New York: Random House, 1942.

Peltason, J.W. *Understanding the Constitution.* New York: Holt, Rinehart and Winston, 1994.

Wills, Garry. *Inventing America: Jefferson's Declaration of Independence.* New York: Doubleday, 1978.

For Discussion

Review

1. *What does the term* limited government *mean?* (*Limited government* refers to a system in which governmental powers are restricted and by which individuals' rights are protected.)

2. *Define* representative government. (The governed have the right to choose those who represent them. Elected officials are accountable to the people who elected them.)

3. *How do documents such as the Magna Carta, the Petition of Right, and the Declaration of Independence reflect and expand the idea of limited government?* (These documents show the development of models of decision-making that impose limitations on those who would make it arbitrary.)

4. *How can John Locke's influence be seen in the Declaration of Independence?* (Students should mention natural rights and the consent of the governed.)

Critical Thinking

1. *Why do you think that the American revolutionaries felt it necessary to write and publish a Declaration of Independence?* (Students may conclude that others needed to know the rationale for this revolution, and Jefferson and the others provided it.)

2. *How effective do you think boycotts are?* (Students' answers will vary. Urge them to consider any boycotts they may have heard of.)

3. *If it is true, as stated, that the eighteenth-century English government was one of the most democratic in the world at that time, why do you think that the colonists felt it necessary to revolt?* (Students may choose several answers here, including economic, political, and even ethical reasons.)

4. *Do you believe that there is such a thing as natural rights and that such rights actually exist?* (Students may advance many different answers for this question, but most will probably state that such rights exist.)

Skills Development Activities

1. **WRITING:** Social Contract

   Have students develop a written social contract for your classroom or interpret the one that they believe already exists. Ask them to explain the responsibilities, obligations, and rights that concern all those covered by this contract.

2. **CURRENT EVENTS:** Public Opinion

   Have students use a contemporary news source to locate a table, graph, or chart illustrating how people currently feel about the way they are governed. Ask them to be prepared to explain whether they are surprised by what they found.

3. **INTERNET:** Thomas Jefferson

   Using a search engine, have students locate one or more Web sites about the life and political views of Thomas Jefferson. Ask them to make a short list of several facts they learned from their research.

4. **SPECIAL SOURCES:** Equality

   Students should locate a political cartoon that they feel makes a comment about whether all people really are "created equal." Invite students to share their cartoons with classmates.

Study Guide

Name: _____

Complete each item as you read Chapter 2 (pages 16–23).

1. Two important English political traditions established by the late 1600s were _____ and _____.

2. Three historical English political documents are the _____, the _____, and the _____.

3. The document that created and governed each English colony in America was called its _____.

4. The three types of English colonies in America were _____, _____, and _____.

5. Who was the primary author of the Declaration of Independence? _____

6. Two fundamental ideas of John Locke that influenced the Declaration of Independence were _____ and _____.

Vocabulary

Read each description, and write the letter of the correct term on the line.

1. System in which government's powers are restricted and individuals' rights are protected

2. System in which policies are made by elected officials

3. Having two legislative chambers or houses

4. Having one legislative chamber or house

a	bicameral
b	limited government
c	representative government
d	unicameral

Multiple-Choice Test

Name: _____

Find the best answer for each item. Then completely fill in the circle for that answer.

1. Which was NOT a political tradition in England by the 1600s?
   a. representative government
   b. presidential government
   c. written limits on the monarch's power
   d. limited government

2. Which was the first attempt to limit the power of the English monarchy?
   a. the English Bill of Rights
   b. the Declaration of Independence
   c. the Magna Carta
   d. the Petition of Right

3. The most common type of English colony in America was
   a. the royal colony
   b. the proprietary colony
   c. the charter colony
   d. none of the above

4. Royal colonies had
   a. no legislatures
   b. unicameral legislatures
   c. bicameral legislatures
   d. no governors

5. How many English colonies were established in America?
   a. 12
   b. 13
   c. 14
   d. 15

6. The First Continental Congress did all of the following EXCEPT
   a. call for a boycott of British goods
   b. call for a Second Continental Congress
   c. resolve to declare independence from England
   d. resolve to send a Declaration of Rights to England

7. Who is the author of the Declaration of Independence?
   a. George Washington
   b. Benjamin Franklin
   c. John Adams
   d. Thomas Jefferson

8. John Locke wrote
   a. the Magna Carta
   b. the English Bill of Rights
   c. the Declaration of Rights
   d. the Second Treatise of Government

9. According to Locke, what "natural rights" do all people have?
   a. the right to life
   b. the right to own property
   c. the right to liberty
   d. all of the above

10. The Declaration of Independence is based most closely on
    a. the Petition of Right
    b. the English Bill of Rights
    c. the Declaration of Rights
    d. the Second Treatise of Government

	a	b	c	d
1	ⓐ	ⓑ	ⓒ	ⓓ
2	ⓐ	ⓑ	ⓒ	ⓓ
3	ⓐ	ⓑ	ⓒ	ⓓ
4	ⓐ	ⓑ	ⓒ	ⓓ
5	ⓐ	ⓑ	ⓒ	ⓓ
6	ⓐ	ⓑ	ⓒ	ⓓ
7	ⓐ	ⓑ	ⓒ	ⓓ
8	ⓐ	ⓑ	ⓒ	ⓓ
9	ⓐ	ⓑ	ⓒ	ⓓ
10	ⓐ	ⓑ	ⓒ	ⓓ

Essay Question

The American Colonies fought a war to secure their independence from England. Explain how two of John Locke's ideas justified that action.

For use with:	**Chapter 2**	**Beginnings of American Government**
For use with:	**Activity 4**	**Arguing Against the Articles**

Objectives

- Explain the accomplishments and key figures of the Second Continental Congress.
- Interpret and explain the major compromises leading to the completion of the Constitution.
- Compare and contrast the weaknesses of the Articles of Confederation with the strength of the Constitution.

Vocabulary

constitution	Articles of Confederation	republic
ratification	Federalists	Anti-Federalists

BACKGROUND

One way to look at the evolution of the U.S. Constitution from the Articles of Confederation is to consider it as a search for order. The Articles of Confederation clearly placed the new United States (or Confederated States) in danger. In a continent possessing such vast resources, many peoples and nations certainly would attempt to gain those resources for themselves, especially if getting them was relatively easy.

In their search for order, the Founders also wished to develop and maintain a republican style of government. In such a government, representation would help to maintain liberty without permitting the kind of license they feared democracy might bring. They had little trust in the ability of individual humans to consider any interest but a personal, selfish one.

So they wrote a constitution, not trusting an unwritten constitution such as the one followed by the English. They wanted written guidelines, similar to the way the early colonial charters were written down—social contracts on paper—establishing rules of law that could not be changed by the immediate whim of an autocrat or even a legislature.

They also had to deal with the human rights outlined in their Declaration of Independence. To do so, they compromised and left future generations to work out the rough edges of the compromises they created. These authors and statesmen added a Bill of Rights to their document as a final compromise toward gaining ratification.

So far, although Americans still struggle with its interpretation in areas such as limits to free speech and privacy, the Constitution ratified in 1789 has worked.

Further Resources

Lipset, Seymour Martin. *The First New Nation.* New York: Basic Books, 1963.

Morris, Richard B. *The Forging of the Union, 1781–1789.* New York: Harper and Row, 1987.

Rossiter, Clinton. *1787: The Great Convention.* New York: Macmillan, 1966.

For Discussion

Review

1. *What were some of the weaknesses of the Articles of Confederation?* (Some weaknesses include no power to tax, no national judicial system, and the inability to regulate trade or establish a common currency.)

2. *What did the authors of the U.S. Constitution mean when they said that they favored a republican form of government?* (They meant that they wanted a government based on representation because, while they believed in consent of the governed, they failed to trust the people to govern directly.)

3. *What two major compromises were made during the Constitutional Convention that allowed completion of the Constitution?* (The two compromises are the Connecticut Compromise, which created a bicameral legislature, and the Three-Fifths Compromise, which allowed states to count slaves for representation.)

4. *Why did the Anti-Federalists initially oppose ratification of the Constitution?* (They believed that it made the national government too powerful, and it contained no bill of rights.)

Critical Thinking

1. *Why do you think that the authors of the Constitution believed that the majority of people could not be trusted to govern directly?* (Students may say that the Founders believed that the people behaved as a mob and that most people were selfish. Encourage students to think creatively about this question.)

2. *What is your definition of liberty? Would your definition be similar to that of the authors of the Constitution?* (Encourage students to think analytically and creatively here.)

3. *Reread Jefferson's words to Abigail Adams on page 26. Why does he like rebellion?* (Student answers will vary.)

4. *Why do you think many of the essays in* The Federalist *were written anonymously?* (Encourage students to think about why authors today choose to use pseudonyms.)

Skills Development Activities

1. **WRITING:** The Iroquois Confederation

   Have students work in groups to research the Iroquois Confederation. Ask them to prepare one-page summaries of their findings.

2. **CURRENT EVENTS:** Order in the World

   Ask students to locate and summarize one or more contemporary news sources showing the perceived need for established order somewhere in the world. They might choose Russia, Iraq, or Rwanda as examples. Ask that they explain whether or not they agree or disagree with the sources they located.

3. **INTERNET:** Liberty

   Have students use a search engine to locate one or more Web sites dealing with the concept of liberty (or freedom) and summarize their findings.

4. **SPECIAL SOURCES:** *The Federalist*

   Have students locate a copy of *The Federalist* and read all of one of the essays excerpted in the Almanac on pages 515–516. Ask them to list the two or three main points that are made.

Study Guide

Name: _____

Complete each item as you read Chapter 2 (pages 24–31).

1. What was the name of the first constitution of the United States? _____

2. The Articles of Confederation did not give the national government the power to regulate

   _____, to establish _____ to raise money, or the

   power to make the 13 _____ obey its laws.

3. Two men who resisted the establishment of a strong government were _____ and

   _____.

4. Four men who favored a strong government in the United States were _____,

   _____, _____, and _____.

5. What was the Connecticut (or Great) Compromise of the Constitutional Convention? _____

   _____

6. What was the Three-Fifths Compromise? _____

   _____

7. In the debate over the ratification of the Constitution, its supporters were called the

   _____ and their opponents were called the _____.

8. The essays of *The Federalist* were written by _____

   _____ and _____.

Vocabulary

Read each description, and write the letter of the correct term on the line.

1. _____ A written plan of government

2. _____ The first constitution of the United States

3. _____ Term for a democracy in which citizens hold the power and exercise it through elected officials

4. _____ Formal approval of a constitution or constitutional amendment

5. _____ Supporters of the strong national government outlined in the U.S. Constitution

6. _____ Those who opposed the adoption of the U.S. Constitution

a	Anti-Federalists
b	Articles of Confederation
c	constitution
d	Federalists
e	ratification
f	republic

Multiple-Choice Test

Name: _____

Find the best answer for each item. Then completely fill in the circle for that answer.

1. The first constitution of the United States was called
   a. the New Jersey Plan
   b. the Iroquois Confederation
   c. the Articles of Confederation
   d. the Virginia Plan

2. Which statement about the Articles of Confederation is FALSE?
   a. It gave the national government the power to establish a national currency.
   b. It was ratified by the 13 states.
   c. It was influenced by the Iroquois Confederation.
   d. It provided for a weak national government.

3. Who was a delegate to the Constitutional Convention?
   a. Thomas Jefferson
   b. James Madison
   c. Alexander Hamilton
   d. Daniel Shays

4. Who is known as the "Father of the Constitution"?
   a. George Washington
   b. Benjamin Franklin
   c. Alexander Hamilton
   d. James Madison

5. At the Constitutional Convention, large states supported
   a. the establishment of a bicameral legislature
   b. representation in a legislature based on population
   c. veto power in the executive branch
   d. all of the above

6. The Great Compromise resulted in all of the following EXCEPT
   a. a bicameral Congress
   b. equal state representation in the upper house
   c. representation by population in the lower house
   d. the creation of a presidency

7. To go into effect, the Constitution had to be ratified by
   a. a national election
   b. at least nine states
   c. the delegates to the Constitutional Convention
   d. the governors of the states

8. The Anti-Federalists opposed the Constitution because
   a. it wasn't ratified
   b. it failed to protect individual rights
   c. it had been written too quickly
   d. it abolished slavery

9. Who was NOT an author of the essays of *The Federalist*?
   a. John Jay
   b. "Publius"
   c. Alexander Hamilton
   d. George Washington

10. When was the Constitution ratified?
    a. 1776
    b. 1787
    c. 1789
    d. 1799

Answer grid:

	a	b	c	d
1	a	b	c	d
2	a	b	c	d
3	a	b	c	d
4	a	b	c	d
5	a	b	c	d
6	a	b	c	d
7	a	b	c	d
8	a	b	c	d
9	a	b	c	d
10	a	b	c	d

Essay Question

Explain the significance of Madison's quotation from *The Federalist* No. 51 on page 31. Do you agree or disagree with his view of human nature?

For use with:	**Chapter 3**	**The Constitution**
For use with:	**Activity 5**	**Rank-Ordering the Bill of Rights**

Objectives

- Explain the basic principles and structure of the Constitution.
- Explain at least two ways each branch of government may check the other two.
- Detail the main steps in the amendment process.

Vocabulary

popular sovereignty	separation of powers	federalism
amendment	checks and balances	Bill of Rights

BACKGROUND

The U.S. Constitution is more than 200 years old and, except when it is being challenged, you rarely hear about it. It has been amended only 27 times, and two of those cancel each other out. The genius of the Constitution is in the detail, or more precisely, the lack of detail. To get an idea of how simple it is, all you need to do is look at any state constitution and compare the two. The difference is in the level of detail that defines the roles and powers of the different participants at the state level. The national relationships have developed as part of usage and custom. The state relationships are defined by strict constitutional guidelines.

The guiding principles set forth in the Constitution—popular sovereignty, limited government, separation of powers, checks and balances, and federalism—have been defined and redefined as each new generation has put its own unique stamp on the framework of the Constitution. Think of the Constitution as the framework and walls of a house. At first the walls are plain white with little distinction. Each generation that "moves into the house" has changed the appearance of the walls to suit its situation; some painted, some wallpapered, some paneled, and some may have even cut out a window. Regardless of what has happened to the wall's surface, though, the framework has stayed much the same.

The changes made to the Constitution over the years have come by many different methods. The passing of laws by Congress has been the most obvious method of change. Executive actions, judicial interpretations, the amendment process (formal and informal), and changing customs have all helped the Constitution to evolve.

It is interesting to note that in the 1999 impeachment trial of President Bill Clinton, each side argued that the Constitution was on its side! Is it possible they were both right? Only history will tell.

Further Resources

Congressional Research Service, Library of Congress. "Analysis and Interpretation: Annotations of Cases Decided by the Supreme Court of the United States."
http://www.access.gpo.gov/congress/senate/constitution/toc.html

Hamilton, Alexander, James Madison, and John Jay. *The Federalist Papers.* Cambridge, MA: Harvard University Press, 1961.

Peltason, J. W. *Understanding the Constitution.* 13th ed. New York: Holt, Rinehart & Winston, 1994.

For Discussion

Review

1. *What are at least two ways the different branches of government can check each other?* (Suggest that students refer to the chart on page 36.)

2. *What are the steps in the amendment process and who is involved?* (See the chart on page 40 for explanation of the four paths a proposed amendment may take.)

3. *What are the different methods of keeping the U.S. Constitution current and up to date?* (Answers should include as many of the following as you deem necessary—the amendment process, legislative actions, executive actions, judicial interpretations, or changing customs.)

4. *How many articles are in the Constitution?* (There are seven.)

Critical Thinking

1. *The Constitution is old but not perfect. Create a new amendment and explain why you think the new amendment is necessary.* (Answers will vary. Make sure students have demonstrated the need for the change in their responses.)

2. *Why was the Bill of Rights so important to many people during the ratification debates?* (Many individual rights are not clearly spelled out in the Constitution, and there was fear the new government might become oppressive.)

3. *Is the formal amendment process too difficult?* (Student answers may vary. Some mention of the large majorities needed both in Congress and the states is appropriate when discussing difficulty. Students may also mention it is supposed to be hard to make a permanent change, and minor matters can be handled informally.)

Skills Development Activities

1. **WRITING:** Presidential Terms

    Have students write a brief position paper in which they argue for or against allowing a President to serve for more than two terms.

2. **CURRENT EVENTS:** Bill Clinton's Impeachment

    The defenders of both President Bill Clinton and President Andrew Johnson claimed removal might upset the balance of power between the President and Congress. In a one-page essay, have students identify three specific areas or situations in which that relationship might have been altered if President Clinton had been removed. Have students think about both long- and short-term situations.

3. **INTERNET:** The Constitution

    Many of us take for granted that the Constitution was going to be ratified, though it was hardly automatic. Have students research Web sites discussing the arguments for and against the Constitution and have them make a chart that includes at least five positions from each side. In a paragraph at the bottom of the chart, ask students to evaluate which side proved more accurate.

4. **SPECIAL SOURCES:** The Preamble

    Ask students to read the Preamble to the Constitution on page 497. Ask them to paraphrase it in modern, informal language. Have the class discuss the various versions.

Study Guide

Name: _____

Complete each item as you read Chapter 3.

1. The Constitution rests on the five basic principles of _____,

_____, _____, _____,

and _____.

2. The idea that government must be based on the will of the people is called _____.

3. _____ guarantees that government does not hold all of the power.

4. The powers of the government are separated among three branches: the _____

branch, the _____ branch, and the _____ branch.

5. Article I is about _____, Article II is about _____, and

Article III is about _____.

6. The division of power between the central government and the states is called

_____.

7. The three parts of the Constitution are the _____,

the_____, and the _____.

8. There are _____ amendments to the Constitution; the first ten are called the

_____ _____ _____.

9. Amendments to the Constitution can be proposed in _____ ways and ratified in

_____ ways.

Vocabulary

Read each description, and write the letter of the correct term on the line.

1. _____ Idea that people are the most important source of governmental power

2. _____ Division of governmental power among different branches of government

3. _____ System designed to prevent a single branch of government from becoming too powerful

4. _____ The sharing of power between the national and state governments

5. _____ A change or addition to the Constitution

6. _____ The first ten amendments to the Constitution

a	amendment
b	Bill of Rights
c	checks and balances
d	federalism
e	popular sovereignty
f	separation of powers

Multiple-Choice Test

Name: _____

Find the best answer for each item. Then completely fill in the circle for that answer.

1. Which of the following is NOT a basic principle of the Constitution?
   - **a.** federalism
   - **b.** checks and balances
   - **c.** limited government
   - **d.** equality

2. To keep one branch of government from becoming too powerful, the Framers of the Constitution created a system of
   - **a.** federalism
   - **b.** checks and balances
   - **c.** popular sovereignty
   - **d.** amendments

3. The last constitutional convention was held in
   - **a.** 1776
   - **b.** 1892
   - **c.** 1992
   - **d.** 1787

4. The legislative branch checks and balances the power of
   - **a.** the executive branch
   - **b.** the judicial branch
   - **c.** both a and b
   - **d.** neither a nor b

5. How many articles are there in the U.S. Constitution?
   - **a.** 1
   - **b.** 6
   - **c.** 7
   - **d.** 10

6. Which part of the Constitution identifies the goals of the American government?
   - **a.** the Preamble
   - **b.** the articles
   - **c.** the Bill of Rights
   - **d.** the amendments

7. The Bill of Rights consists of
   - **a.** the Preamble and the Articles only
   - **b.** all of the Articles
   - **c.** the first ten amendments only
   - **d.** all of the amendments

8. There have been _____ amendments to the Constitution.
   - **a.** 26
   - **b.** 32
   - **c.** 10
   - **d.** 27

9. One way amendments to the Constitution can be proposed is by
   - **a.** specially called state conventions
   - **b.** a 3/4 vote of the state legislatures
   - **c.** a 2/3 vote of each house of Congress
   - **d.** executive action

10. Informal changes to the Constitution have
    - **a.** never occurred
    - **b.** been made through executive actions
    - **c.** been made through the amendment process
    - **d.** been made through the Preamble

	a	b	c	d
1	ⓐ	ⓑ	ⓒ	ⓓ
2	ⓐ	ⓑ	ⓒ	ⓓ
3	ⓐ	ⓑ	ⓒ	ⓓ
4	ⓐ	ⓑ	ⓒ	ⓓ
5	ⓐ	ⓑ	ⓒ	ⓓ
6	ⓐ	ⓑ	ⓒ	ⓓ
7	ⓐ	ⓑ	ⓒ	ⓓ
8	ⓐ	ⓑ	ⓒ	ⓓ
9	ⓐ	ⓑ	ⓒ	ⓓ
10	ⓐ	ⓑ	ⓒ	ⓓ

Essay Question

List the six goals of American government that are identified in the Constitution. Which goal do you think is most important? Explain the reason for your choice.

For use with:	**Chapter 4**	**Federalism**
For use with:	Activity 6	**National and State Powers Collage**

Objectives

- Define and explain the six powers of government.
- Trace key developments in the establishment of national supremacy.
- Identify and give examples of the three different responsibility relationships between federal and state governments.

Vocabulary

delegated powers	implied powers	inherent powers
reserved powers	concurrent powers	prohibited powers
Elastic Clause		

BACKGROUND

Federalism and the debates surrounding it are ever changing. As long as there has been a Constitution, the nature of federalism has been debated. The early Americans saw a system in which the states were the predominant centers of power. With the Civil War and the rise of industrialism, the national government became increasingly involved in managing the country, though it did so rather reluctantly. The New Deal under Franklin Roosevelt pushed the pendulum farther than most ever anticipated by firmly placing the national government in the role of chief problem solver. This level of national involvement continued with LBJ's Great Society. Today the debate has taken a turn in the opposite direction. A key issue facing the government today is how we can give power back to the states. Only time will tell if momentum in that direction will be maintained.

The Constitution spells out certain powers for certain groups within our system. As the responsibilities of government have grown, so have the powers, but there are no nice, neat guidelines. The Elastic Clause has made it easier for our modern-day Congress to claim many of these new responsibilities and the power that goes with them. The question seems to be this: Is this really what we want as a nation? It is difficult to imagine our system ever going back to a point where the states are more important than the federal government, but it's possible. (One example of a potential change: Now, abortion is a federally guaranteed right, but if the Supreme Court overturns that right, it will be up to the individual states to decide if abortion rights will be protected within their borders.)

Grodzins's "marble cake" government is a useful analogy for understanding the relationship between national and state powers and responsibilities. And welfare is a great case study for demonstrating the "marble cake."

Further Resources

Grodzins, Martin. "The Federal System." *American Government: Readings and Cases,* ed. Peter Woll. 11th ed. New York: HarperCollins, 1993.

The Urban Institute. "Assessing the New Federalism Project." http://newfederalism.urban.org/html/reports.htm

Walker, David B. *The Rebirth of Federalism.* Chatham, MA: Chatham House, 1994.

For Discussion

Review

1. **What are three powers the Constitution gives to the national government?** (They are delegated, implied, and inherent powers.)

2. **What part of the Constitution is the source of the implied powers?** (It is the Elastic Clause.)

3. **What are the three types of responsibilities that state and federal governments have toward each other?** (Answers could include: the federal government guarantees a republican form of government, the states are responsible for elections, and both must give "full faith and credit" to acts and actions of the other.)

Critical Thinking

1. **Why do you think the powers of the national government have increased in the last 100 years?** (The responsibilities of government have increased as demands made upon the government have increased.)

2. **Many people think the government is too involved in our lives. If you could take away one power the government has, what would it be?** (Answers may vary, but students should explain what they see as possible consequences of the power being gone.)

3. **Do you believe it's fair for a state university to charge a lower tuition rate to citizens of its state than to citizens of other states?** (Students will have different opinions, but they should try to be specific in their answers.)

4. **Should a school board be allowed to require drug screenings of high school athletes? Why or why not?** (As students explain their views, review the concept of reserved powers.)

Skills Development Activities

1. **WRITING:** Federal Programs

   Have students research a federal program that is shared by both state and national governments. It is their job to make a recommendation to Congress, explaining the role of the different levels of government and whether or not there should be an adjustment in how the program is administered.

2. **CURRENT EVENTS:** Education

   Education is always up for discussion. Have students speculate what would happen if the national government, not the states, ran education in the United States. Make sure students note both concerns and benefits. Have students create a chart to explain their findings. Place students in groups if you think they can work together.

3. **INTERNET:** Native-American Casinos

   Have students research Native-American casinos. Both state and national governments have claimed jurisdiction. Ask students to pick a side—the tribes, the states, or the national government—and argue their positions in a one- to two-page presentation.

4. **SPECIAL SOURCES:** Federalism

   Have students find a political cartoon that illustrates a conflict between states and the national government. Suggest as an alternative that students create their own "federalism" cartoon based on a controversial issue in their state.

Study Guide

Name: _____

Complete each item as you read Chapter 4 (pages 44–49).

1. The national government has three basic types of powers: _____ ,

   _____ , and _____ .

2. The implied powers of the national government are inferred from the _____ .

3. The powers of the states are guaranteed by the _____ Amendment to the Constitution.

4. The powers of the states are called _____ .

5. Powers held by both the national and state governments are called _____ .

6. Three responsibilities of the national government to the states are to ensure that each state has a

   _____ form of government, to protect states against

   _____ , and to _____ new states to the union.

7. Two responsibilities of the states to the federal government are to provide a _____

   and to conduct _____ .

Vocabulary

Read each description, and write the letter of the correct term on the line.

1. _____ Powers expressly given to the national government by the Constitution

2. _____ Powers of the national government based on the Elastic Clause

3. _____ Part of the Constitution that lets the national government make all laws that are "necessary and proper"

4. _____ Powers, usually in foreign affairs, that grow out of the very existence of the national government

5. _____ Powers given only to the states

6. _____ Powers held by both the national and state governments

7. _____ Powers forbidden to both the national and state governments

a	concurrent powers
b	delegated powers
c	Elastic Clause
d	implied powers
e	inherent powers
f	prohibited powers
g	reserved powers

Multiple-Choice Test

Name: _____

Find the best answer for each item. Then completely fill in the circle for that answer.

1. Which of the following is NOT a delegated power?

   a. to coin money

   b. to declare war

   c. to ratify constitutional amendments

   d. to raise and maintain armed forces

2. Implied powers are based on

   a. delegated powers

   b. the Elastic Clause

   c. extradition

   d. the Full Faith and Credit Clause

3. An example of a reserved power is the power to

   a. grant patents and copyrights

   b. coin money

   c. declare war

   d. conduct elections

4. An example of a concurrent power is the power to

   a. coin money

   b. ratify constitutional amendments

   c. collect taxes

   d. establish local governments

5. Reserved powers are guaranteed by

   a. the Full Faith and Credit Clause

   b. the Elastic Clause

   c. the 10th Amendment

   d. all of the above

6. The national government can acquire new territory. This is an example of

   a. a prohibited power

   b. an inherent power

   c. a delegated power

   d. a reserved power

7. The U.S. Constitution requires the national government to

   a. make sure each state has a republican form of government

   b. protect states against domestic insurrection

   c. not interfere with the abilities of states to perform their responsibilities

   d. all of the above

8. Conducting elections is a power and responsibility of

   a. the national government

   b. the state governments

   c. both the national and state governments

   d. neither the national nor state governments

9. What does the Full Faith and Credit Clause require?

   a. that the national government fulfills its responsibilities to the states

   b. that the states fulfill their responsibilities to the national government

   c. that the states fulfill their responsibilities to each other

   d. that states determine their own polling places

10. The legal process of returning an alleged criminal to the state where the crime was committed is called

    a. ratification

    b. cooperative federalism

    c. concurrence

    d. extradition

1	ⓐ	ⓑ	ⓒ	ⓓ
2	ⓐ	ⓑ	ⓒ	ⓓ
3	ⓐ	ⓑ	ⓒ	ⓓ
4	ⓐ	ⓑ	ⓒ	ⓓ
5	ⓐ	ⓑ	ⓒ	ⓓ
6	ⓐ	ⓑ	ⓒ	ⓓ
7	ⓐ	ⓑ	ⓒ	ⓓ
8	ⓐ	ⓑ	ⓒ	ⓓ
9	ⓐ	ⓑ	ⓒ	ⓓ
10	ⓐ	ⓑ	ⓒ	ⓓ

Essay Question

Explain why you think the Elastic Clause is called that.

| For use with: | **Chapter 4** | **Federalism** |
| For use with: | **Activity 7** | **How Much Federal Government?** |

Objectives

- Explain the significance of the ruling in *McCulloch v. Maryland*.
- List at least five rights that have been incorporated by various court decisions.
- Define and provide examples of the different types of grants.
- Differentiate between block grants and categorical grants.

Vocabulary

grants-in-aid   categorical grants   block grants

revenue sharing   mandate

BACKGROUND

The nature of federalism and the relationship between the states and the national government have evolved over time. *McCulloch v. Maryland* clearly made the national government supreme when there was a conflict between state and national law, but states remained extremely powerful throughout the 1800s. As society asked governments to do more, the national government took on a larger portion of those new responsibilities. The national government was in a better position to do this than the states because it had passed the new national income tax and had significant tariff revenue. It was also in a position to look at issues from a national perspective, which was not practical for the states.

Today federalism is demonstrated through two vastly different vehicles—incorporation and the grants-in-aid system. Incorporation has forced all of the states to adopt national standards in many legal applications, such as Miranda warnings, providing public defenders, and applying civil rights. The grants-in-aid program has provided a way for the national government to share the wealth, so to speak, with state and local governments. This has been accomplished through categorical grants, block grants, and, for a while, revenue sharing. The grants provide a political advantage to incumbents because it helps with their re-election. The practice of credit claiming, ironically enough, is why revenue sharing disappeared—no one could directly take credit for the money returning to the states and municipalities, so it never gathered much support from Congress and its members.

The final topic in this section is mandates. Mandates have become a great tool for Congress but are loathed by state and local governments. Mandates require state and/or local governments to carry out some activity, and often no money is provided. These mandates or conditions for aid are commonly called *strings*. Congress gets the credit while states get the bills!

Further Resources

Kenyon, Daphne A., and John Kincaid, eds. *Competition Among State and Local Governments.* Washington, DC: The Urban Institute Press, 1991.

Michigan State University Libraries, ed. Jon Harrison. "Grants and Related Resources: Federal Funding Tools and Information Sources." http://www.lib.msu.edu/harris23/grants/federal.htm

7 | The Changing Nature of Federalism

For Discussion

Review

1. *What was the significance of the ruling in McCulloch v. Maryland?* (The Supreme Court ruled that the National Bank was constitutional under the Elastic Clause and that when state law and national law conflict, national law is supreme.)

2. *What is the purpose of incorporation?* (The main purpose is to apply common standards to certain laws all across the country.)

3. *What are the different types of grants that are used now or have been used in the last 30 years?* (Block grants, categorical grants, and revenue sharing are the types of grants used.)

4. *Why do state and local governments prefer block grants to categorical grants?* (Categorical grants have specific purposes and often restrict the user's choice of how the funds are used; block grants are given with less restriction on how they are used.)

Critical Thinking

1. *Why do you think it was important for the country that McCulloch v. Maryland was decided the way it was?* (The national government had to be supreme or it would allow the states to do whatever they wanted—this is really why the Civil War was fought. Which was more important, states' rights or national supremacy?)

2. *What, in your own words, is the importance of the incorporation of the 14th Amendment to the Civil Rights movement?* (The incorporation of the 14th Amendment brought national enforcement of civil rights to states that otherwise would never have moved to desegregate.)

3. *Put yourself in a politician's shoes. Explain why you prefer categorical grants to block grants and block grants to revenue sharing.* (From a political point of view, the more specific the grant, the easier it is to take credit for it at election time.)

4. *Do you think a state should ever have the right to secede from the Union?* (Help sudents refer to John Calhoun's thinking as they formulate their own answers.)

Skills Development Activities

1. **WRITING:** Grant Proposal

   Grants are given not only to governments but to institutions and individuals as well. Have students write a proposal for a categorical grant from the federal government for their school. They must explain their purpose, what they intend to do, and what the end product will be. Students may work alone or in pairs. Have the students present their proposals; then let the class vote on the best proposal.

2. **CURRENT EVENTS:** The 55-mph Speed Limit

   To prompt all the states to lower the speed limit to 55, the national government threatened to withhold transportation funds. Have students make a list of things they think the federal government might use to pressure states to go along with a federal policy. The list should be at least five items long.

3. **INTERNET:** The Commerce Clause

   Have students research one of the Supreme Court cases described on page 53. Have them summarize the key issues in a short oral report.

4. **SPECIAL SOURCES:** Local Government

   Have students contact a local government agency (such as the school board). They should find out where that government (or agency) gets the money it spends to keep itself going. Once they obtain this information, have them make a pie chart or bar graph based on the data. Invite them to share their findings with classmates.

Study Guide

Name: _____

Complete each item as you read Chapter 4 (pages 50–57).

1. Alexander Hamilton supported a very strong national government, while _____ opposed it.

2. In the case _____, the Supreme Court held that the federal government had broad power under the Elastic Clause.

3. In the years before the Civil War, southern states declared they had the right to declare any federal law banning slavery as "_____ and _____."

4. The Supreme Court expanded the power of the national government under the Commerce Clause in the 1824 case of _____.

5. Through a process called _____, the Bill of Rights has been applied to the states over the years.

6. The _____ Amendment reads that "No state shall . . . deprive any person of life, liberty, or property without due process of law. . . ."

7. Grants of money given by the federal government to the states are called _____.

8. The three types of federal grants are_____, _____, and _____.

9. A rule issued by the federal government to the states is called a _____.

Vocabulary

Read each description, and write the letter of the correct term on the line.

1. _____ Grants of money given by the federal government to the states

2. _____ A type of grant-in-aid given for a particular purpose

3. _____ A type of grant-in-aid given for general purposes

4. _____ Process by which part of federal tax money is distributed to state and local governments

5. _____ A rule issued by the federal government to the states

a	block grants
b	categorical grants
c	grants-in-aid
d	mandate
e	revenue sharing

Multiple-Choice Test

Name: _____

Find the best answer for each item. Then completely fill in the circle for
that answer.

1. When was *McCulloch v. Maryland* decided?

   a. 1791

   b. 1819

   c. 1912

   d. 1864

2. *McCulloch v. Maryland* resulted in

   a. a weaker national government

   b. the creation of federalism

   c. a stronger national government

   d. a constitutional amendment

3. In the years before the Civil War, southern states argued that

   a. the national government did not have the authority to ban slavery

   b. the states had the right to leave the Union

   c. the states had the right to declare a federal law "null and void"

   d. all of the above

4. The Commerce Clause gives

   a. the federal government the power to regulate interstate commerce

   b. the states the power to regulate internal commerce

   c. the states the power to regulate interstate commerce

   d. the federal government the power to regulate international commerce

5. John Calhoun was

   a. a states' rights supporter

   b. a nationalist position supporter

   c. a Supreme Court justice

   d. an attorney in *Barron v. Baltimore*

6. The Civil Rights Act of 1964 was authorized under

   a. the 14th Amendment

   b. grants-in-aid

   c. *Barron v. Baltimore*

   d. the Commerce Clause

7. Originally, the Bill of Rights protected individuals against abuses by

   a. the federal government

   b. some state governments

   c. all state governments

   d. all state governments and the federal government

8. Which Supreme Court case led to the application of the Bill of Rights to the states?

   a. *Gibbons v. Ogden*

   b. *Katzenbach v. McClung*

   c. *Barron v. Baltimore*

   d. *Gitlow v. New York*

9. The federal government grants money to a state to build a new school. This is an example of

   a. revenue sharing

   b. a categorical grant

   c. a block grant

   d. a mandate

10. The federal government orders a state to decrease its air pollution. This is an example of

    a. a grant-in-aid

    b. a categorical grant

    c. a block grant

    d. a mandate

	a	b	c	d
1	ⓐ	ⓑ	ⓒ	ⓓ
2	ⓐ	ⓑ	ⓒ	ⓓ
3	ⓐ	ⓑ	ⓒ	ⓓ
4	ⓐ	ⓑ	ⓒ	ⓓ
5	ⓐ	ⓑ	ⓒ	ⓓ
6	ⓐ	ⓑ	ⓒ	ⓓ
7	ⓐ	ⓑ	ⓒ	ⓓ
8	ⓐ	ⓑ	ⓒ	ⓓ
9	ⓐ	ⓑ	ⓒ	ⓓ
10	ⓐ	ⓑ	ⓒ	ⓓ

Essay Question

The federal government has the power to order a state to do something without
providing the necessary funds. Do you think this is a fair policy? Why or why not?

Political Behavior and Participation

For use with:	**Chapter 5**	**Political Parties**
For use with:	**Activity 8**	**Educating the Public**

Objectives

- Identify the four roles of political parties.
- Name three differences between a one-party and a two-party system.
- Explain proportional representation with an example.

Vocabulary

political party	proportional representation	patronage
independent	grassroots	

BACKGROUND

Political parties are organizations with which the public in the United States believes it is very familiar. Parties are in the news all the time. The party labels are constantly referred to at election time. In reality, however, the public is much less informed about what parties really do, how they are organized, and for what they stand.

Our political parties exist in a two-party (dominant) system. It doesn't really occur to most Americans that there are other types of systems. In most people's minds, one-party systems are the same as no-party systems, because the party has no competition and the government and the party are one and the same. What is often overlooked in these systems is that the party is usually the most important group in the decision-making process. The government serves to carry out decisions made by the party. Multiparty systems are easier to understand because they make sense. They are more reflective of a diverse population, and proportional representation allows that diversity to have a voice. The hidden problem is that the government is often made up of a coalition of parties, and this situation can lead to instability.

Political parties today have taken on many roles that help maintain their own existence as well as keep the government running smoothly. Parties are responsible for recruiting candidates and providing "labels" for easier identification at election time. Parties also perform a watchdog function, with the minority party keeping the majority party honest. While performing the watchdog role, parties try to keep the public informed as to their stances on issues and why the public should support each. Finally, parties help organize the government by bringing structure and organization.

The final issue facing parties today is their declining influence. Students may be surprised to learn that more and more voters are claiming to be independent, rather than Democrat or Republican.

Further Resources

Broder, David. *The Party's Over.* New York: Harper & Row, 1971.
Maisel, L. Sandy, ed. *The Parties Respond.* 2nd ed. Boulder, CO: Westview Press, 1994.
Democratic National Committee.
　　　　http://democrats.org
Republican National Committee.
　　　　http://rnc.org

For Discussion

Review

1. *What is the definition of a political party?* (It's defined as a group of people organized to influence government through winning elections and setting public policy.)

2. *What are the four roles of political parties?* (The four functions of parties are recruiting and labeling, acting as a watchdog, providing information, and organizing the government.)

3. *What are three differences between one-party and two-party systems?* (Some differences are competitive elections, alternative policy choices, and having a minority party to perform watchdog functions.)

4. *How are representatives chosen in a proportional representation system?* (Voters vote for a party, as opposed to a candidate, and the makeup of the legislative branch matches the proportion of the vote that each party receives.)

Critical Thinking

1. *Why do many political scientists consider multiparty systems the most representative of all the systems?* (In multiparty systems a wide variety of interests are represented in the party choices. Voters feel they can more easily find a party that represents their viewpoints as opposed to having to compromise.)

2. *How successful are political parties in your area in getting out information?* (Answers will vary.)

3. *Why do you think more people consider themselves independents instead of Democrat or Republican?* (Answers may include some mention of favoring issues that are supported by different parties.)

4. *Are any minor parties active in your community or state?* (Answers will vary.)

Skills Development Activities

1. **WRITING:** Party Platforms

   Have students meet in groups of two or three. Each group is to form and name their own political party and write a mini-platform. Each group should create a platform of the six issues they consider most important and clearly state the issues and their positions on them. Post the platforms for all students to read, and then have the class vote on which they like the best.

2. **CURRENT EVENTS:** Mexico

   Have students reread the passage on Mexico on page 62. Then have them research recent developments concerning the PRI and elections.

3. **INTERNET:** Multiparty Systems

   Have students look up various countries and their party systems on the Internet. Students should create a list of at least five nation-states that have multiparty systems.

4. **SPECIAL SOURCES:** Party Organization

   Have students create a chart that shows the relationship between the national, state, and local party organizations. The box(es) at each level should include a brief description of what the party organization at that level does. Post the charts around the room for all to see and discuss.

Study Guide

Name: _____

Complete each item as you read Chapter 5 (pages 60–66).

1. There are three types of party systems: _____,

    _____, and _____.

2. The United States has had a _____-party system for most of its history.

3. Political parties simplify elections by choosing candidates that carry a party

    "_____."

4. Political parties who are not in power serve as _____, keeping an eye on the party

    in power.

5. Political parties provide _____ to citizens and voters about important issues.

6. Congress and state legislatures are organized according to _____, giving parties a

    key role in running the government.

7. Voters who do not consistently vote for one party are called _____.

8. Political parties are _____ organizations, which means their power comes from

    the bottom up.

Vocabulary

Read each description, and write the letter of the correct term on the line.

1. _____ A group of people organized to influence government through
    winning elections

2. _____ A system in which candidates are elected in proportion to the
    percentage of the vote their party receives

3. _____ Term for a voter who is not aligned with a political party

4. _____ Term for an organization based on local, unprofessional support

5. _____ Practice of rewarding political supporters with government jobs

a	grassroots
b	independent
c	patronage
d	political party
e	proportional representation

Mulitple-Choice Test

Name: _____

Find the best answer for each item. Then completely fill in the circle for that answer.

1. Which statement about political parties is FALSE?

   a. Political parties exist in almost every country.

   b. Political parties are set up only by government officials.

   c. Political parties work to have their candidates elected to office.

   d. Political parties seek to influence public policy.

2. A political party in effect is the government under a

   a. one-party system

   b. two-party system

   c. multiparty system

   d. democracy

3. Coalitions are most likely found in countries with

   a. one-party systems

   b. a lot of patronage

   c. multiparty systems

   d. few independents

4. Which best describes the party system in the United States?

   a. a one-party system

   b. a two-party system

   c. a multiparty system

   d. an independent system

5. What are the main political parties in the United States?

   a. Locals and Nationals

   b. Republicans and Independents

   c. Independents and Democrats

   d. Democrats and Republicans

6. Which of the following is an important role political parties play?

   a. recruiting candidates

   b. serving as watchdogs

   c. getting out information

   d. all of the above

7. In the United States, people can become a member of a political party by

   a. simply choosing to do so

   b. registering with the government

   c. paying a fee to the party

   d. any of the above

8. In the United States, what is an "independent"?

   a. any voter

   b. any voter not consistently aligned with a particular party

   c. any party leader

   d. any voter who refuses to vote

9. In the United States, the organization of political parties is best described as

   a. top-down

   b. corporate

   c. grassroots

   d. governmental

10. Political parties use a system of _____ to reward their supporters.

    a. patronage

    b. grassroots

    c. proportional representation

    d. coalition

	a	b	c	d
1	ⓐ	ⓑ	ⓒ	ⓓ
2	ⓐ	ⓑ	ⓒ	ⓓ
3	ⓐ	ⓑ	ⓒ	ⓓ
4	ⓐ	ⓑ	ⓒ	ⓓ
5	ⓐ	ⓑ	ⓒ	ⓓ
6	ⓐ	ⓑ	ⓒ	ⓓ
7	ⓐ	ⓑ	ⓒ	ⓓ
8	ⓐ	ⓑ	ⓒ	ⓓ
9	ⓐ	ⓑ	ⓒ	ⓓ
10	ⓐ	ⓑ	ⓒ	ⓓ

Essay Question

Multiparty systems are far more common than two-party systems. What advantages might multiparty systems have over two-party systems that account for this fact?

For use with: **Chapter 5** **Political Parties**

For use with: **Activity 9** **Surfing Party Platforms**

Objectives

- Demonstrate an understanding of the four historical factors at the core of America's two-party system.
- Identify and describe the four types of minor parties.
- Explain the two primary roles that minor parties serve in relation to the two major parties.

Vocabulary

winner-take-all   single-member district   split ticket

BACKGROUND

Political parties have been part of the U.S. system since the very beginning. The earliest parties formed around two distinguished individuals with opposite points of view. The two groups established a pattern of two-party dominance that has carried through to modern day. Most Americans do not realize that there are alternatives. Our two-party system is so ingrained that its continuance is a given.

There are reasons for the acceptance of our present system. Since we have been a homogeneous society ideologically, Americans have been fairly satisfied with only two options. There are also a number of legal reasons why we have two dominant parties. One of the most important reasons is the winner-take-all electoral system. A third party often finds it difficult to overcome both major parties, and you don't get anything for finishing second. Another issue is the "wasted vote" psychology. A vote for a third party is often portrayed as a wasted vote. This only makes minor party success that much less likely.

The historic party eras each have different characteristics, but the most relevant is the current era—the era of divided government. The voters, intentionally or not, have been reluctant to give only one party the "keys" to the nation. How long this will continue is difficult to predict.

There are four distinct types of minor parties—splinter parties, economic protest parties, ideological parties, and single-issue parties—each with a different purpose for existing. In some instances these minor parties force the "big two" to pay attention through their impact on an election result, but those cases are rare. Unfortunately for these minor parties, this situation is not likely to change in the near future.

Further Resources

The Libertarian Party.
         http://www.lp.org/lp.html
Rosenstone, Steven J., Roy L. Behr, and Edward H. Lazarus.
         Third Parties in America: Citizen Response to Major Party Failure.
         New York: Prometheus Books, 1995.
Sundquist, James L. *Dynamics of the Party System.* Rev. ed. Washington,
         DC: Brookings Institute, 1983.

For Discussion

Review

1. *What are the four historic factors behind the U.S. two-party system?* (The four historic influences on the U.S. two-party system are tradition, the shared principles and beliefs of the people, the winner-take-all system, and single-member districts.)

2. *What are the three most recent party eras?* (The three most recent party eras are the Republican era, the second Democratic era, and the era of divided government.)

3. *What are the four types of minor parties that exist in America?* (The four types are economic protest, splinter, single-issue, and ideological.)

4. *What are the most important impacts of minor parties historically in the United States?* (Minor parties have influenced the outcome of elections at times, and they have forced the major parties to pay more attention to some important issues.)

Critical Thinking

1. *Why has it been so difficult for H. Ross Perot, with all of his money, to obtain electoral votes in recent presidential elections?* (Answers should include some mention of two-party tradition, winner-take-all system, and wasted vote psychology.)

2. *Why do you think today's voters seem to prefer divided government?* (Some mention of a balancing of power between the two major parties should be included in the answer.)

3. *Why do you think that of all types of minor parties, splinter parties have the best chance of getting electoral votes?* (Splinter parties will usually take part of the party faithful with them when they leave the original party. This tends to guarantee them a constituency that will vote for them.)

Skills Development Activities

1. **WRITING:** Consensus

   Have students work in groups to list at least five political beliefs and values that they believe nearly everyone in their class shares.

2. **CURRENT EVENTS:** Issues

   Major political parties are always trying to get by controversial issues without really taking a position. Have students create a list of five issues that they think either did not get enough attention in the last election or are likely to be missed in upcoming elections. An example might be term limits for elected senators and representatives.

3. **INTERNET:** Minor Parties

   Have students find home pages of no less than three and no more than five minor political parties. Have them print out those home pages and then pick one of those parties and write a brief one-paragraph summary of the major positions of that party. See how many different minor parties the class can find.

4. **SPECIAL SOURCES:** Exit Polls

   Have students examine the 1996 presidential election exit poll results on page 521. Ask them to present some of the information about Perot's supporters in the form of a pie chart or bar graph.

Study Guide

Name: _____

Complete each item as you read Chapter 5 (pages 67–75).

1. List four reasons why the two-party system has endured in the United States: _____;
_____; _____; _____.

2. What is the "winner-take-all" system? _____

_____

3. The first political party in the United States was the _____ party.

4. The Federalist party was opposed by the Anti-Federalists, later called the _____.

5. The Democratic party was founded by _____ in 1828.

6. The _____ party was led by Henry Clay and Daniel Webster.

7. The _____ party emerged as an antislavery party in the 1850s.

8. The 1932 election of Franklin Roosevelt marked the beginning of the _____,
1932–1968.

9. From 1932 to 1968, the _____ party was more powerful than the
_____ party.

10. The four main types of minor parties are _____,
_____, _____, and
_____.

Vocabulary

Read each description, and write the letter of the correct term on the line.

1. _____ System in which the winner receives the largest number of votes

2. _____ System in which one person represents an entire voting district

3. _____ A vote for candidates of different parties in the same election

a	single-member district
b	split ticket
c	winner-take-all

Multiple-Choice Test

Name: _____

Find the best answer for each item. Then completely fill in the circle for that answer.

1. When did political parties arise in the United States?
- **a.** during the debate over ratification of the Constitution
- **b.** during the debate over slavery
- **c.** during the debate over the Great Depression
- **d.** during the debate over the Vietnam War

2. All of the following are reasons that the two-party system exists in the United States EXCEPT
- **a.** broad ideological consensus
- **b.** historical tradition
- **c.** a winner-take-all system
- **d.** a legal requirement

3. The first political party in the United States was the _____ party.
- **a.** Federalist
- **b.** Anti-Federalist
- **c.** Whig
- **d.** Democratic–Republican

4. From 1828 to 1860, the chief rival of the Democratic party was the _____ party.
- **a.** Whig
- **b.** Anti-Federalist
- **c.** Republican
- **d.** Democratic-Republican

5. Which party arose in the 1850s to oppose slavery?
- **a.** the Federalist party
- **b.** the Whig party
- **c.** the Democratic party
- **d.** the Republican party

6. Which party dominated the period from 1860 to 1932?
- **a.** the Whig party
- **b.** the Democratic–Republican party
- **c.** the Democratic party
- **d.** the Republican party

7. Which party dominated the period from 1932 to 1968?
- **a.** the Reform party
- **b.** the American Independent party
- **c.** the Democratic party
- **d.** the Republican party

8. Which of the following is NOT a type of minor party?
- **a.** economic protest
- **b.** single-issue
- **c.** split ticket
- **d.** ideological

9. The _____ system gives minor parties very little chance of winning elections.
- **a.** split ticket
- **b.** democratic
- **c.** single-issue
- **d.** winner-take-all

10. Which statement about minor parties is true?
- **a.** Minor parties have never won the presidency.
- **b.** Minor parties have influenced presidential elections.
- **c.** Minor parties have existed for many years.
- **d.** all of the above

1	ⓐ	ⓑ	ⓒ	ⓓ
2	ⓐ	ⓑ	ⓒ	ⓓ
3	ⓐ	ⓑ	ⓒ	ⓓ
4	ⓐ	ⓑ	ⓒ	ⓓ
5	ⓐ	ⓑ	ⓒ	ⓓ
6	ⓐ	ⓑ	ⓒ	ⓓ
7	ⓐ	ⓑ	ⓒ	ⓓ
8	ⓐ	ⓑ	ⓒ	ⓓ
9	ⓐ	ⓑ	ⓒ	ⓓ
10	ⓐ	ⓑ	ⓒ	ⓓ

Essay Question

Do you think minor parties will have significant influence on elections in the future? Include references to several past minor parties and their influence in your answer.

For use with:	**Chapter 6**	**Elections and Campaigns**
For use with:	**Activity 10**	**Self-Announcement**

Objectives

- Identify the main types of primaries and explain how they work.
- List the four types of elections or processes states use to choose candidates for general elections.
- Describe the four distinct phases in presidential campaigns.

Vocabulary

nomination	open primary	caucus
direct primary	general election	closed primary

BACKGROUND

Free, open, and competitive elections separate democratic systems from all other types of systems. Elections are not unique to the United States, but we do have a certain set of guidelines that establish procedures we must follow. Some examples include: voters must register before they can vote; we vote on the first Tuesday after the first Monday in November of even-numbered years; and we go through a long campaign and conventions before the general election.

Primary elections were started by progressives in the early 1900s as a reform intended to end the corruption of political machines. Different types of primaries have developed over the years, including open primaries, closed primaries, blanket primaries, and runoff primaries. The purpose of these preliminary elections (and caucuses) is to allow party members in the electorate to pick their party's candidate for the general election. The winners of each of the parties' primaries then compete against one another for the right to occupy the contested position.

The highest-profile election is the race for the presidency. Running for President is a full-time job for those that choose the undertaking. Bob Dole opted to resign his Senate seat rather than try to be both a senator and a candidate in 1996. Running for President involves a number of phases. The first stage involves deciding to run. Often at this stage, if people do decide to run, they put together staffs and organizations so they can begin the campaign as soon as they announce their candidacy. This stage may begin up to two years before the actual election.

Next is competing for delegates in the presidential primaries that lead up to the official nominating convention and the election itself. Congressional elections occur at the same time, but given the limited constituency, they are not nearly as involved or as expensive. The last phase involves the expensive and tiring campaigning before the national election.

Further Resources

Holbrook, Thomas M. *Do Campaigns Matter?* Thousand Oaks, CA: Sage Publications, 1996.

Jacobson, Gary C. *The Politics of Congressional Elections.* 3rd ed. New York: HarperCollins, 1992.

Wayne, Stephen J. *The Road to the White House.* 6th ed. New York: St. Martin's Press, 1997.

For Discussion

Review

1. *What is a direct primary?* (A direct primary is an election in which the voters of a party get to choose the party's candidate for the general election.)

2. *What state's caucus is an early indicator of a presidential candidate's popularity?* (The state is Iowa.)

3. *What are the two distinct phases of a presidential campaign?* (The first phase is the campaign before the nomination, and the second is the effort between the nomination and the general election.)

4. *What is "Super Tuesday"?* (It is a day in early March when several southern states hold their primaries.)

Critical Thinking

1. *What impact do you think holding an election on a weekend day might have?* (Answers may vary, but some mention of it being easier to vote because people generally do not work on weekends should be included.)

2. *Why do you think some states choose closed primaries as opposed to open primaries?* (In open primaries it is possible for members of the opposite party to vote in your primary and choose a weaker candidate for the general election.)

3. *What has been the impact on political parties of the primary system?* (When parties lost control of the nominating process, they also lost their leverage to "encourage" their party members to follow a party line when voting in Congress. This has allowed candidates to vote as they wish and made party discipline almost nonexistent.)

4. *Are you surprised by Walter Mondale's statement on page 81 about campaigning?* (Student opinions will vary.)

Skills Development Activities

1. **WRITING:** Election Reform

    Most people in America believe the presidential election process is too long and complicated. Have students pretend they have been assigned to a special commission to reform elections. They are given the task of making recommendations for simplifying the process. Students should write one to two pages on what their reforms are and how they would improve the election process. They can work individually or in pairs.

2. **CURRENT EVENTS:** Elected Officials

    Have students find out who all of their elected officials are—President, Vice President, national senators and representative, governor, state senator, state representative, and local mayor or executive. When is the next chance to elect each? Students should make a chart to show their results.

3. **INTERNET:** Candidate Registration

    Have students research registration requirements for all 50 states (give each student a number of states) and have them make a chart to compare the results. A discussion on the impact of the differences in registration should follow.

4. **SPECIAL SOURCES:** Keynote Addresses

    Ask students to find out who gave the keynote addresses at the last five Republican and Democratic conventions. Suggest that they read part of one of the actual speeches or a newspaper review of one of them. Have students report on their findings in several paragraphs.

Study Guide

Name: _____

Complete each item as you read Chapter 6 (pages 76–87).

1. Most election law is _____ law, but the Constitution gives

   _____ much power to regulate presidential elections.

2. The basic types of elections in the United States are the _____ election, the

   _____ , and the _____ election.

3. The two basic kinds of direct primaries are the _____ and the

   _____ .

4. A vote in which a member of one party votes in the other party's primary is a _____ .

5. Identify the two main phases of most national campaigns.

   _____

   _____

6. In what state has the first primary of each presidential campaign traditionally been held?

   _____

7. One who receives unexpected support for the nomination at a political convention is a

   _____ .

Vocabulary

Read each description, and write the letter of the correct term on the line.

1. _____ Selection and naming of a candidate for office

2. _____ Nominating election that chooses a party's candidate

3. _____ Election that chooses which candidate wins an office

4. _____ Primary in which voting is limited to registered party members

5. _____ Primary in which voting is open to all voters

6. _____ Private meeting of party leaders held to select candidates

a	caucus
b	closed primary
c	direct primary
d	general election
e	nomination
f	open primary

Multiple-Choice Test

Name: _____

Find the best answer for each item. Then completely fill in the circle for that answer.

1. Most election law is _____ law.
   a. local
   b. state
   c. national
   d. constitutional

2. What is the most common type of primary in the United States?
   a. blanket
   b. open
   c. caucus
   d. closed

3. Which accurately describes an Australian ballot?
   a. secret
   b. sent through the mail
   c. illegal
   d. all of the above

4. Which comes LAST?
   a. a general election
   b. a direct primary
   c. a caucus
   d. a closed primary

5. Direct primaries were first used
   a. in the early nineteenth century
   b. by Anti-Federalists
   c. by Federalists
   d. in the late nineteenth and early twentieth centuries

6. In a closed primary, only _____ can participate.
   a. registered candidates
   b. registered voters
   c. registered officeholders
   d. registered party members

7. Which results in party candidates being elected to office?
   a. a direct primary
   b. a runoff primary
   c. a general election
   d. a caucus

8. In a campaign, which comes first?
   a. the campaign before the party nomination
   b. the campaign after the general election
   c. the campaign between the nomination and the general election
   d. the general election

9. The first presidential primary is traditionally held in
   a. New York
   b. New Jersey
   c. New Mexico
   d. New Hampshire

10. The formal written statement of the principles and beliefs of a political party is called
    a. a keynote address
    b. a platform
    c. a roll call
    d. none of the above

	a	b	c	d
1	a	b	c	d
2	a	b	c	d
3	a	b	c	d
4	a	b	c	d
5	a	b	c	d
6	a	b	c	d
7	a	b	c	d
8	a	b	c	d
9	a	b	c	d
10	a	b	c	d

Essay Question

Would it be better if every state selected candidates in the same way? Why or why not?

For use with:	**Chapter 6**	**Elections and Campaigns**
For use with:	**Activity 11**	**Reforming Campaign Finance**

Objectives

- Identify the two major sources of funding for campaigns.
- Define a political action committee and be able to discuss its purpose.
- Explain the reasons behind campaign contribution limits on individuals.

Vocabulary

incumbent   political action committee (PAC)   soft money

BACKGROUND

Many people believe that the way to a man's heart is through his stomach. If this is true, then the way to politicians' hearts is through their campaign funds. Money is what makes winners out of losers, gives incumbents a huge advantage, and buys access for the various contributors. Money also gives campaigns life and lets people think they are making a difference. But campaign money also has caused questions about where it all comes from and what it is buying.

Campaign financing is a concern for the people outside the system and also for those inside the system. Given the costs of a modern campaign, politicians find themselves having to amass larger and larger campaign funds to be competitive. For congressional elections, all money is provided from private sources, such as individuals, political action committees (PACs), or party organizations. Presidential elections are a bit different in that while presidential candidates raise money from private sources, they are also eligible for federal matching funds. They are limited only by the total amount of money they can spend. If they refuse matching funds (as Ross Perot did in 1992), they can spend what they like.

Many of today's campaign finance laws and guidelines were initially established in the 1970s as a reaction to problems uncovered during the investigation of the Watergate scandal. Questionable accounting and fund-raising activities led to a set of guidelines as well as the establishment of the Federal Election Commission (FEC) to keep politicians accountable.

Even with all the restrictions and limitations, there are some loopholes in the financing laws. One of the biggest concerns is in the area of soft money, money spent on behalf of a candidate over which, technically, the candidate has no control. Since the money is not donated to a campaign, there are no limits as to how much is spent! Attempts to restrict soft-money expenditures have generated heated debate.

Further Resources

Alexander, Herbert E. *Financing Politics: Money, Elections, and Political Reform.*
      4th ed. Washington, DC: Congressional Quarterly Press, 1992.
Center for Responsive Politics.
      http://www.crp.org
Federal Election Commission.
      http://www.fec.gov
Jackson, Brooks. *Honest Graft: Big Money and the American Political Process.*
      Washington, DC: Farragut, 1990.

For Discussion

Review

1. *What are the two major types of sources for funding political campaigns?* (The two major types of sources are private funding and public funding.)

2. *What is a political action committee (PAC)? Explain what PACs hope to gain with their contribution.* (A PAC is the political arm of an interest group set up to contribute to election campaigns, thereby, hopefully, gaining access to the future officeholders.)

3. *If you are an individual, what are your limitations when donating money during a campaign season?* (As an individual, you are limited to contributing $1,000 to a candidate per election, $20,000 to a national party committee, $5,000 to the PAC of your choice, and no more than a total of $25,000 per calendar year.)

4. *How would you define soft money?* (Soft money is money spent on behalf of a candidate that is not regulated by federal law.)

Critical Thinking

1. *What do you think the impact of congressional elections would be if they were all federally funded, and all candidates received the same amount of money?* (Statistics show that for challengers to beat incumbents, they must spend four times as much—and that's just for House seats. Evening out spending would further increase incumbents' advantages.)

2. *Individual candidates for Congress can spend as much of their own money as they wish. Do you think this is fair?* (Allowing individuals to spend as much as they want clearly gives advantage to wealthy people. This is probably not fair to those whose goals are bigger than their bank accounts.)

3. *Explain whether or not you think the present rules concerning soft money work, or whether there should be more restrictions.* (Answers will vary but encourage students to cite specific situations.)

4. *Why do you think the cost of presidential campaigns is increasing so quickly?* (Among possible answers is the cost of advertising on television and radio.)

Skills Development Activities

1. **WRITING:** Campaign Reform

   Have students write a one- to two-page position paper advocating several specific actions that could reduce the costs involved in campaigning.

2. **CURRENT EVENTS:** PAC Money

   Have students research which PACs or interest groups spent the most money on campaigns in the last three presidential elections. They should make a chart listing the top ten groups/PACs and how much they spent. Use the charts as the basis for a class discussion on the influence of PAC money.

3. **INTERNET:** Donor Lists

   Have students choose a recent contested congressional election from their state. Ask students to investigate the contributions list of the candidates from each party and to note the types of groups that were included on each side. Students should make a list of the top ten donors to each campaign and then write a paragraph comparing the overall lists and the types of groups that donated to each candidate.

4. **SPECIAL SOURCES:** PAC Issues

   Have students go to http://www.fec.gov/press/paccontp.htm, which is a table of the 50 top-spending PACs. On what issue do students think the top groups might be looking for help? Have students guess at what might be important to each group.

Study Guide

Name: _____

Complete each item as you read Chapter 6 (pages 87–91).

1. The federal agency that oversees campaign finance rules is the _____.

2. In general, most campaign money is spent on _____ and _____ advertisements.

3. The two basic sources of campaign funds are _____ and _____.

4. Most campaign funds come from _____.

5. More than 4,000 _____ contribute campaign funds.

6. Congress passed a number of campaign financing reform laws in the _____.

7. _____ contributions are used on such things as "issue ads" and are not regulated by federal law.

Vocabulary

Read each description, and write the letter of the correct term on the line.

1. _____ A current officeholder

2. _____ A political arm of an interest group set up to contribute money to political campaigns to influence public policy

3. _____ Campaign contributions that are unregulated by federal law

a	incumbent
b	political action committee
c	soft money

Multiple-Choice Test

Name: _____

Find the best answer for each item. Then completely fill in the circle for that answer.

1. Most campaign money is spent on
   a. paying campaign workers
   b. radio and television ads
   c. flyers and signs
   d. government registration fees

2. A presidential candidate can use campaign funds
   a. from his or her own personal sources
   b. from the federal government
   c. from personal and organizational contributions
   d. from all of the above

3. Who regulates campaign financing?
   a. the Federal Election Commission
   b. the national political parties
   c. the Justice Department
   d. the states

4. Most campaign funds come from
   a. the federal government
   b. PACs
   c. the Federal Election Commission
   d. individual donors

5. Which best describes a PAC?
   a. an interest group
   b. a branch of state government
   c. a political party committee
   d. a financial arm of an interest group

6. About how many PACs are there?
   a. 10
   b. 50
   c. 600
   d. 4,000

7. In a presidential campaign, the federal government provides
   a. matching funds
   b. PAC money
   c. free advertisements
   d. all of the above

8. Which is an example of soft money?
   a. $250 donated to a presidential candidate by a construction worker
   b. $10,000 spent by a political party on issue ads
   c. $62 million given to a presidential candidate by the federal government
   d. all of the above

9. Vice President Gore was investigated for
   a. starting a PAC
   b. contributing too much to President Clinton's campaign
   c. misusing the power of his office to ask for donations
   d. all of the above

10. In recent years overall campaign costs and spending have been
    a. increasing
    b. decreasing
    c. remaining about the same
    d. It is impossible to tell.

	a	b	c	d
1	ⓐ	ⓑ	ⓒ	ⓓ
2	ⓐ	ⓑ	ⓒ	ⓓ
3	ⓐ	ⓑ	ⓒ	ⓓ
4	ⓐ	ⓑ	ⓒ	ⓓ
5	ⓐ	ⓑ	ⓒ	ⓓ
6	ⓐ	ⓑ	ⓒ	ⓓ
7	ⓐ	ⓑ	ⓒ	ⓓ
8	ⓐ	ⓑ	ⓒ	ⓓ
9	ⓐ	ⓑ	ⓒ	ⓓ
10	ⓐ	ⓑ	ⓒ	ⓓ

Essay Question

In the United States, citizens are free to spend their money on anything they choose. Why, then, are there laws limiting how much a person can donate to a campaign? Do you think these laws are proper? Explain your position.

Topic **12** | Political Participation

Objectives

- Identify various types of political participation.
- Explain the impact of education on voting.
- List which age groups have the highest political participation percentage.

Vocabulary

electorate   political socialization   activist

BACKGROUND

The backbone of any democratic system is the participation of the citizens. Without participation, democracy does not work. Without participation, a small minority can come to have influence that is out of proportion to its numbers.

Political participation is what separates democracies from dictatorships and other authoritarian systems. In the United States participation takes many different forms, including voting, reading articles in newspapers and magazines, and trying to influence other people's vote. The people who go beyond just voting and are involved more extensively are considered activists. Activists make a more significant contribution to the system by working for a campaign, running for local office, or volunteering to fill a local government post. Incidentally, activists tend to be more extreme philosophically, meaning Republican activists tend to be more conservative while Democratic activists tend to be more liberal.

Since most people's level of involvement is not as significant as that of the activists, many of the analyses of political participation examine lower levels of activity. Most of the studies look at the characteristics of those who participate. The studies have found that certain factors are important in encouraging participation. The three most common factors are education level, age, and race or ethnic background.

The impact of education is significant—the higher the level of education, the greater the likelihood an individual will be politically active. Age as a factor is similar to education; the older you are (up until age 75), the stronger the chances you will be politically active. The last factor, racial and ethnic background, needs careful study. Based on flat percentages, minority groups participate at lower levels than whites, but when controlled for economic factors, participation is similar for all groups.

Further Resources

Conway, M. Margaret. *Political Participation in the United States.* 2nd ed. Washington, DC: Congressional Quarterly Press, 1990.

Flanigan, William H., and Nancy H. Zingale. *Political Behavior of the American Electorate.* 8th ed. Washington, DC: Congressional Quarterly Press, 1994.

The National Election Studies, Center for Political Study, University of Michigan. http://www.umich.edu/~nes/

For Discussion

Review

1. *What are reported as the two most common forms of political participation?* (The two most common forms of participation reported are watching the campaign on television and voting in elections.)

2. *What impact does a person's level of education have on his or her political participation?* (Statistics show the more education a person has, the greater the chances he or she will be politically active.)

3. *Who are political activists?* (Activists are people who are involved in political activities, such as national campaigns or local protests.)

4. *What age group has the highest percentage voter turnout level?* (The group with the highest percentage turnout is those 65 to 74 years old.)

Critical Thinking

1. *This section points out that not many people are political activists. Why do you think so few people are willing to be involved at the activist level?* (Answers will probably include some mention of lack of time or fear of not knowing enough to make an impact or to do the job adequately.)

2. *Why do you think the level of participation goes up as people get older?* (Students may note that as people get older, they become more aware of the world around them and how government decisions can impact them.)

3. *Under what circumstances do you think you would most likely become politically active?* (Answers will vary, but students may mention an issue that would directly impact them.)

4. *What people do you know who are politically active?* (Student responses will vary. Encourage them to consider family, friends, neighbors, and members of the community and to think about the reasons these people participate politically.)

Skills Development Activities

1. **WRITING:** Political Activism

   Have students write a one- to two-page essay that supports one of the following opinions: "Participating in our political system is important because . . . ," or "It really doesn't matter if participation in our political system is low because. . . ." Have students read their essays to the class and conduct a follow-up discussion.

2. **CURRENT EVENTS:** Poll

   Have students create a poll to get information like that in the chart on political participation on page 93. (They may need some help from you.) Have them interview between 15 and 30 adults and then make charts to reflect their findings. They should evaluate their findings and compare them to the text results.

3. **INTERNET:** Demographic Factors

   Have students go on-line and research voting turnout for two other demographic factors, such as religion and gender. They should report their findings in graph or chart form.

4. **SPECIAL SOURCES:** Participation Chart

   Have students create a chart to reflect some of the statistical information presented on pages 92–95 from The National Election Studies or the U.S. Bureau of the Census. Remind them to give their charts a title and to provide all necessary information, so that others can understand the data.

Study Guide

Name: _____

Complete each item as you read Chapter 7 (pages 92–95).

1. In a democracy, the most common form of political participation is _____.

2. In the 1996 election, about _____ percent of eligible voters actually voted.

3. _____ is the branch of political science dealing with citizens and their activities.

4. People who exercise their right of political participation frequently and in a variety of ways are called

   _____.

5. _____ is the single biggest factor in determining an individual's level of political

   participation.

6. Political participation of older people is _____ than that of younger people.

7. If race alone is considered, African Americans, Hispanics, and other ethnic groups have a lower rate of political

   participation than _____ people.

8. People of different races have similar political participation rates if their income and

   _____ levels are similar.

Vocabulary

Read each description, and write the letter of the correct term on the line.

1. _____ People who are qualified to vote in an election

2. _____ Person who has a high degree of political participation

3. _____ Process by which people develop attitudes toward government

a	activist
b	electorate
c	political socialization

Multiple-Choice Test

Name: _____

Find the best answer for each item. Then completely fill in the circle for that answer.

1. Which is an example of political participation?

   a. casting a vote

   b. volunteering for a campaign

   c. writing to a member of Congress

   d. all of the above

2. What is the most common form of political participation in the United States?

   a. volunteering

   b. voting

   c. running for office

   d. raising campaign funds

3. Who is a member of the electorate?

   a. any American citizen

   b. any American over 18

   c. any American who is eligible to vote

   d. any American who votes

4. In a recent presidential election, about _____ of eligible voters voted.

   a. one-fourth

   b. one-half

   c. three-fifths

   d. three-fourths

5. Which BEST describes a delegate to a national party convention?

   a. a member of the electorate

   b. a PAC member

   c. an eligible voter

   d. an activist

6. _____ is the study of citizens and their activities.

   a. The electorate

   b. Civics

   c. Political participation

   d. Government

7. As a rule, the more education a person has, the _____ his or her level of political participation will be.

   a. lower

   b. higher

   c. more difficult to determine

   d. less expensive

8. In general, who is most likely to cast a vote?

   a. a person over 35 years old

   b. a person under 35 years old

   c. both a and b are just as likely

   d. It is impossible to tell.

9. If race alone is considered, which group has the HIGHEST level of political participation?

   a. Asian and Pacific Islanders

   b. African Americans

   c. Hispanics

   d. whites

10. Political socialization is the process by which people

    a. discuss their voting habits

    b. volunteer in a campaign

    c. develop their political identity

    d. become activists

	a	b	c	d
1	ⓐ	ⓑ	ⓒ	ⓓ
2	ⓐ	ⓑ	ⓒ	ⓓ
3	ⓐ	ⓑ	ⓒ	ⓓ
4	ⓐ	ⓑ	ⓒ	ⓓ
5	ⓐ	ⓑ	ⓒ	ⓓ
6	ⓐ	ⓑ	ⓒ	ⓓ
7	ⓐ	ⓑ	ⓒ	ⓓ
8	ⓐ	ⓑ	ⓒ	ⓓ
9	ⓐ	ⓑ	ⓒ	ⓓ
10	ⓐ	ⓑ	ⓒ	ⓓ

Essay Question

Identify and explain three social and economic characteristics that influence who participates politically and who does not.

For use with:	**Chapter 7**	**Political Participation and Voter Behavior**
For use with:	**Activity 13**	**Increasing Voter Turnout**

Objectives

- List the major requirements for voting.
- Describe the additional groups that have been given the right to vote since the Constitution was written.
- Identify several factors that may lead to low voter turnout.
- List three factors that influence the choices voters make.

Vocabulary

citizen   suffrage   political efficacy   absentee ballot

BACKGROUND

One of the great mysteries to many political scientists is why in the United States, a country so proud to be democratic, is the voting turnout so low. When compared to other democratic nations, our voting numbers indicate that we are near the bottom of these statistics. There are many factors that seem to explain our low turnout, though no one cause seems to be responsible for this poor showing.

The tradition of voting in America goes back to a time before the writing of the Constitution. Once we became independent, the Founders continued this system, allowing white male property owners who were 21 or older to vote. Over the years the qualifications for voting have changed and the electorate has expanded. The first significant change was the gradual removal of the property ownership requirement for voting. After the Civil War, African Americans were added to the list of voters by the 15th Amendment. Women were given the right to vote initially on a state-by-state basis, and then finally the passage of the 19th Amendment included all women as voters. The final group added to the list of eligible voters was 18- to 20-year-olds. Many of the protesters during the Vietnam War asked why, if members of this age group were old enough to be drafted by this country, they weren't they old enough to vote? Apparently Congress and the states agreed and ratified the 26th Amendment. It is ironic that this very vocal group that demanded the right to vote has the lowest turnout of any age group!

Given that all these people are now qualified voters, why is turnout so low? There seem to be numerous possible answers. Political efficacy (the feeling that your vote can make a difference), registration requirements, and other minor factors all combine to lessen turnout. Since it seems that there are a number of reasons, no one solution is likely to increase voter turnout.

For those who do vote, there are three key factors that most influence voter choice: candidate appeal, party identification, and issues.

Further Resources

Lupia, Arthur, and Matthew D. McCubbins. *The Democratic Dilemma.* New York: Cambridge University Press, 1998.

Nelson, Michael, ed. *The Elections of 1996.* Washington, DC: Congressional Quarterly Press, 1997.

Teixeria, Ruy. *The Disappearing American Voter.* Washington, DC: Brookings Institute, 1992.

For Discussion

Review

1. *What are the main voting requirements that need to be met in all states?* (To be eligible to vote, you have to be a U.S. citizen, at least 18 years old, a resident at your current address for a certain amount of time [it varies by state], and registered.)

2. *Which groups of citizens have become voters since the writing of the Constitution?* (Since the late 1700s, white males without property, African-American men, all women, and finally, those between the ages of 18 and 20 have been added as voters.)

3. *What are several factors that may contribute to low voter turnout in the United States?* (Five factors that contribute to low voter turnout are low political efficacy, the registration requirement, weekday voting, weak efforts by parties to turn out voters, and general satisfaction with the status quo.)

4. *What are the key factors that significantly influence the choices of those who do vote?* (Voters are most influenced by candidate appeal, party identification, and issues.)

Critical Thinking

1. *Do you think it is important to require registration before being allowed to vote?* (Requiring registration before voting is one way to try and guarantee a fair election. It helps identify a valid list of eligible voters and discourages vote fraud.)

2. *Many people believe low voter turnout is not something to be worried about and is actually a good sign. Do you agree? Explain.* (Those who agree should say that non-voters may be satisfied with the way things are or that non-voters are the least informed and wouldn't make a rational vote choice anyway.)

3. *You either are 18 or soon will be 18 and eligible to vote. What factors will most influence you when you go to cast your ballot for the very first time? Explain.* (Answers will vary.)

4. *What government officials or politicians would you say have high candidate appeal?* (Encourage students to explain their judgments as specifically as they can.)

Skills Development Activities

1. **WRITING:** Voter Turnout

   Some people have argued that the weakness of modern political parties is primarily to blame for the low voter turnout. Have students write a one-page essay that discusses whether it is the party's responsibility to motivate voters, or whether it is up to the individual to take it upon himself or herself to be an active citizen?

2. **CURRENT EVENTS:** Motor-Voter Bill

   Have students find two or three articles in newspapers or magazines that discuss the 1995 National Voter Registration Act (NVRA)—whether it was a good idea, its long-term effects, and so on. Ask them to summarize their findings in several paragraphs.

3. **INTERNET:** Voter Trends

   Have students visit The National Election Study Web site at the University of Michigan and find some voter studies or statistics that interest them. Ask students to print out the results they find, and then in a paragraph or two have them analyze any developing trends or surprising data.

4. **SPECIAL SOURCES:** Women's Suffrage

   One of the most hotly debated additions to the Constitution was the 19th Amendment. Have students use original sources to research some arguments made at the time of its passage. Ask them to find five positions for each side of the issue and report them in a table or poster.

Study Guide

Name: _____

Complete each item as you read Chapter 7 (pages 95–105).

1. A person who has rights and responsibilities as a member of a country is called a _____.

2. The right to vote is called _____.

3. Originally, only adult white males who owned _____ were eligible to vote.

4. The _____ Amendment extended suffrage to African-American men in 1870.

5. Among tactics designed to keep African Americans from voting were the poll _____,

    the _____, and _____ tests.

6. In 1920 the _____ Amendment extended suffrage to women.

7. In 1971 the _____ Amendment extended suffrage to people aged 18 to 21.

8. To vote, a person must be a _____ of the United States and have

    _____ to vote.

9. A lack of political _____ is one reason for low voter turnout.

10. The National Voter Registration Act, or "Motor-Voter" bill, allows people to register to vote when they apply

    for a _____.

11. Three factors that might explain why few people vote are _____,

    _____, and _____.

12. Three factors that influence voting are _____,

    _____, and _____.

Vocabulary

Read each description, and write the letter of the correct term on the line.

1. _____ A member of a nation who has certain rights and responsibilities

2. _____ The right to vote

3. _____ The feeling that one's vote has an effect

4. _____ The means by which a person can vote without going to the
    polling place

a	absentee ballot
b	citizen
c	political efficacy
d	suffrage

Multiple-Choice Test

Name: _____

Find the best answer for each item. Then completely fill in the circle for that answer.

1. In the 1700s and early 1800s, only people who owned

   _____ were eligible to vote.

   a. slaves
   b. property
   c. registration cards
   d. citizenship cards

2. What does *suffrage* mean?

   a. membership in a country
   b. registration
   c. a feeling that one's vote matters
   d. the right to vote

3. Which constitutional amendment extended suffrage to African-American men?

   a. the 1st
   b. the 15th
   c. the 19th
   d. the 26th

4. Which constitutional amendment extended suffrage to women?

   a. the 1st
   b. the 15th
   c. the 19th
   d. the 26th

5. The 26th Amendment lowered the voting age from 21 to 18 in

   a. 1946
   b. 1953
   c. 1965
   d. 1971

6. All of the following are voting requirements EXCEPT

   a. residency
   b. registration
   c. citizenship
   d. income

7. In the United States, the rate of voter turnout is best described as

   a. low
   b. increasing steadily
   c. high
   d. decreasing steadily

8. Political efficacy refers to the

   a. amount of influence people feel they have
   b. relative efficiency of a political party
   c. number of people who vote
   d. difficulties of voter registration

9. Turnout rates for primary elections are

   a. about half those for general elections
   b. about twice those for general elections
   c. about five times those for general elections
   d. none of the above

10. The most important single predictor of whom people will vote for is

    a. age
    b. registration
    c. party identification
    d. issues

1	ⓐ	ⓑ	ⓒ	ⓓ
2	ⓐ	ⓑ	ⓒ	ⓓ
3	ⓐ	ⓑ	ⓒ	ⓓ
4	ⓐ	ⓑ	ⓒ	ⓓ
5	ⓐ	ⓑ	ⓒ	ⓓ
6	ⓐ	ⓑ	ⓒ	ⓓ
7	ⓐ	ⓑ	ⓒ	ⓓ
8	ⓐ	ⓑ	ⓒ	ⓓ
9	ⓐ	ⓑ	ⓒ	ⓓ
10	ⓐ	ⓑ	ⓒ	ⓓ

Essay Question

Trace the expansion of voting rights in the United States, identifying when and how the pool of eligible voters has grown.

For use with:	**Chapter 8**	**Public Opinion and Mass Media**
For use with:	Activity 14	Testing Your Political Identity

Objectives

- Identify and define terms describing various political ideologies.
- Compare and contrast the concepts of liberalism and conservatism in regard to the place of each on a political spectrum.
- Analyze the reasons why many Americans choose a moderate position on a political spectrum.
- Understand perceptions of the ideologies of the two major parties.

Vocabulary

ideology   liberal   conservative   moderate,

BACKGROUND

American approaches to ideology arise out of U.S. political culture. The tenets of that culture are set forth in the Declaration of Independence—the right to life, government by consent of the governed, liberty, property, and the pursuit of happiness. The pursuit of happiness is often interpreted as some combination of the right to hold property and the access to success.

Children learn about the culture at very early ages, even though they probably know very little about the Declaration of Independence. They learn about the culture and about different ideological positions from such agents of socialization as the family, schools, peers, the media, religion, and, later on, political parties and the workplace. However, it's important to be cautious about using broad labels (such as liberal or conservative) to describe ideological positions.

As recent public opinion polls and election results tell us, most Americans are moderate in their beliefs. Those candidates with ideas from the far right or the far left attract few supporters. The spectrum of ideological beliefs, whether Democrat or Republican, tends toward pragmatism and moderation. Protecting our rights and having the right and the opportunity to live a good, meaningful life are things that most of us want.

In the United States, liberalism and conservatism exist in the moderate range. Most Democrats want what most Republicans want. Each party and those who identify with each party generally approach solutions to the nation's problems somewhat differently, but they are still within the confines of the political culture. Most of us support the system and the system's constraints. We may not always support those who govern us, but we believe in the system.

Further Resources

Almond, Gabriel A., and Sidney Verba, eds. *The Civic Culture Revisited: An Analytic Study.* Newbury Park, CA: Sage Publications, 1989.

Devin, Donald J. *The Political Culture of the United States.* Boston: Little, Brown, 1972.

Flanigan, William H., and Nancy H. Zingale. *Political Behavior of the American Electorate.* 8th ed. Washington, DC: Congressional Quarterly Press, 1994.

For Discussion

Review

1. *What do the terms* ideology, liberal, conservative, *and* moderate *mean?* (Encourage students to develop their definitions from the text material.)

2. *What are some of the major differences between the political points of liberals and conservatives?* (Students should see that liberals are more likely to favor government intervention for problem solving and conservatives generally favor less government intervention.)

3. *In what decade did Franklin Roosevelt begin the New Deal programs?* (They were developed in the 1930s.)

4. *Where do the Republican and Democratic parties fit on a political spectrum?* (Republicans generally locate a bit to the right of moderate, and Democrats generally fall a bit to the left.)

Critical Thinking

1. *Why do you think that most people believe that Republicans are more conservative than Democrats?* (Students may respond that Republicans wish to preserve the status quo and that they favor less change.)

2. *Why do you think that few Americans identify themselves as radicals or reactionaries on a spectrum of political ideologies?* (Some students may respond that Americans are pragmatic and that such radical positions just aren't intelligent.)

3. *Why do you think that most Americans hold a moderate political ideology?* (Encourage students to identify a number of specific reasons.)

4. *Where on the political spectrum would you place the members of Congress from your state?* (Encourage students to research and/or cite specific views before trying to make broad generalizations.)

Skills Development Activities

1. **WRITING:** Presidential Policies

   Have students research the policies and programs of two Presidents. Have them classify the President as liberal, conservative, or moderate in several policy areas.

2. **CURRENT EVENTS:** Television and Politics

   Ask students to view and perhaps videotape examples from one or two television news analysis programs, such as *Meet the Press*. Have them identify one or more ideological points of view on the program as liberal or conservative and present their findings to the class.

3. **INTERNET:** Ideologies

   Have students search the Internet for Web sites dealing with several different political ideologies. They may need to use terms such as *Democrat, Republican,* or even *communist* or *fascist* to find these sites. They should list the sites and make the list available to the class.

4. **SPECIAL SOURCES:** Liberals and Conservatives

   Have students locate and read several editorials and op ed articles in your local newspaper. Ask them to identify the opinions expressed in terms of each author's ideological position on the political spectrum.

Study Guide

Name: _____

Complete each item as you read Chapter 8 (pages 106–110).

1. The three main terms for describing political ideologies in the United States are

   _____, _____, and

   _____.

2. A person who believes in using governmental powers to protect individual rights and achieve social progress is

   often called a _____.

3. A person who supports the status quo and wants sharp limits on government is often called a

   _____.

4. A person with political attitudes that fall between liberal and conservative ideologies is often called a

   _____.

5. Racial equality, social progress, and individual rights are generally associated with

   _____ political ideology.

6. The belief that human needs should be taken care of by families and charities as opposed to the government is

   generally associated with _____ political ideology.

Vocabulary

Read each description, and write the letter of the correct term on the line.

1. _____ A body of ideas or beliefs

2. _____ A person whose beliefs lie on the left of the political spectrum

3. _____ A person whose beliefs lie on the right of the political spectrum

4. _____ A person whose beliefs lie in the center of the political spectrum

a	conservative
b	ideology
c	liberal
d	moderate

Multiple-Choice Test

Name: _____

Find the best answer for each item. Then completely fill in the circle for that answer.

1. All of the following are major political ideologies in the United States today EXCEPT

    a. liberal
    b. conservative
    c. party
    d. moderate

2. Who is the farthest to the right on the political spectrum?

    a. a moderate
    b. a reactionary
    c. a liberal
    d. a radical

3. Who is the farthest to the left on the political spectrum?

    a. a moderate
    b. a reactionary
    c. a conservative
    d. a radical

4. Which group is most closely associated with using the powers of government to promote social progress?

    a. moderates
    b. liberals
    c. conservatives
    d. reactionaries

5. Which group is most closely associated with decreasing government power and spending?

    a. moderates
    b. liberals
    c. conservatives
    d. radicals

6. Originally, liberalism was associated with

    a. monarchies
    b. maintaining the status quo
    c. protecting individual rights
    d. all of the above

7. Liberals generally _____ the New Deal programs of the Great Depression.

    a. supported
    b. opposed
    c. ignored
    d. benefitted from

8. Conservatives generally _____ the New Deal programs of the Great Depression.

    a. supported
    b. opposed
    c. ignored
    d. benefitted from

9. Which statement is true?

    a. American political parties are primarily electoral.
    b. American political parties are primarily ideological.
    c. American political parties are primarily reactionary.
    d. American political parties are primarily radical.

10. In general, the Republican party is considered _____ and the Democratic party is considered _____

    a. moderate, reactionary
    b. liberal, conservative
    c. conservative, liberal
    d. radical, reactionary

1	a	b	c	d
2	a	b	c	d
3	a	b	c	d
4	a	b	c	d
5	a	b	c	d
6	a	b	c	d
7	a	b	c	d
8	a	b	c	d
9	a	b	c	d
10	a	b	c	d

Essay Question

Is it possible to be both a liberal and conservative at the same time? Explain your answer.

| For use with: | **Chapter 8** | **Public Opinion and Mass Media** |
| For use with: | **Activity 15** | **Surveying the Community** |

Objectives

- Identify and explain major influences on political attitudes.
- Assess public opinion polls as to their effectiveness and accuracy.
- Analyze the results of public opinion polls in terms of the way they reflect public opinion.

Vocabulary

public opinion   straw poll   sample

BACKGROUND

Politicians, political scientists, and businesspeople constantly concern themselves with public opinion. Public opinion determines how people will vote, why they will vote, and even what they will buy. Polling organizations spend a great deal of time and money trying to determine what the public thinks about a given topic, issue, or product at a given time.

Public opinion consists of the attitudes people hold toward given issues at a particular time. However, these attitudes are based on the combined ideologies of those holding the opinions and the political culture that generated the ideologies. Remember that people learn about the political culture through agents of socialization, and they form their ideological beliefs from the culture. Of course, demographics also play a part in forming public opinion, because demographics play a part in socialization. One's ethnicity, geographic location, gender, and age, as well as the economic and social climate of the time, influence an individual's opinions.

Public opinion pollsters need to take all of these characteristics of opinion into account when they conduct their polls. They need to construct their questions in a way that will provide the most accurate information possible for those who have contracted them to conduct the poll, for public opinion polling is big business.

No politician or marketer would continue to employ a polling firm that made the kind of error that occurred in 1936 when the *Literary Digest* predicted that Republican Alf Landon would win over Franklin Roosevelt, who won that election by a landslide.

The critics of polling maintain that such activity subverts the electoral process. Perhaps it does. However, others believe that such polls assist in making policy that reflects what the people really want at a given time. One thing is clear: politicians or marketers who ignore the results of polls do so at their own risk.

Further Resources

Lipset, Seymour Martin. *Political Man: The Social Basis of Politics.* Garden City, NJ: Doubleday, 1959.

McClain, Paula D., and Joseph Stewart, Jr. *Can We All Get Along?* Boulder, CO: Westview Press, 1998.

Yahoo! "Surveys and Public Opinion Polls." http://dir.yahoo.com/Government/U_S__Government/Politics/Forums.Surveys_and_Polls/

For Discussion

Review

1. *Why do we study public opinion and public opinion polls?* (Both have a profound influence on forming policy agenda and public policy.)

2. *What are some of the influences that help form public opinion?* (Students should list the factors on pages 111 to 114.)

3. *What are the major differences between straw polls and scientific polls?* (Students should say samples, accuracy, and usefulness.)

4. *What are some of the uses of public opinion polls?* (They can be used to guide politicians and help Americans determine what other Americans believe at a given time.)

Critical Thinking

1. *Which of the major influences on public opinion do you believe is the most important? Why do you feel as you do?* (Encourage open discussion here. Students will express a variety of opinions. Family is generally considered the most influential.)

2. *Why do you think that politicians pay so much attention to the results of public opinion polls?* (They wish to be elected and they wish to know how a given position on a policy position will resonate with the electorate.)

3. *Have you ever been part of a poll? If so, explain your experiences.* (Encourage students to share specific details of their experiences.)

4. *What, if any, influence do you think your gender has on your views on certain political issues?* (Help students avoid broad generalizations as they share their ideas.)

Skills Development Activities

1. **WRITING:** Political Activities

   Have students interview a person of another generation and ask about his or her political beliefs. For example, the student might ask about this person's position on a current issue and then ask how he or she learned to think that way.

2. **CURRENT EVENTS:** Political Issue

   Ask students to identify one current political issue and then locate at least two differing opinions about the issue in a news magazine such as *Time* or *Newsweek*. Have them summarize their findings in a report to the class.

3. **INTERNET:** Public Opinion

   Students should locate a Web site showing a public opinion poll dealing with a political issue. They might find http://www.ABCNews.com such a site. They should critique the questions used in the poll and summarize their critiques in one or more paragraphs.

4. **SPECIAL SOURCES:** Scientific Polling

   Brainstorm together a list of five controversial issues in your school or community. Ask students to work in small groups to devise a survey and identify a representative sample they could poll to assess public opinion on the issue. Have groups share their work with the class. If time permits, have the class actually administer the survey.

Study Guide

Name: _____

Complete each item as you read Chapter 8 (pages 111–116).

1. The collective views of individuals about government and politics are called _____.

2. Six factors that influence an individual's political opinions are _____, _____, _____, _____, _____, and _____.

3. Which major political party are women more likely to support? _____

4. Two kinds of issues deeply influenced by a person's religion are _____ issues and _____ issues.

5. Are college-educated people more likely to be liberal or conservative? _____

6. Public opinion is measured through _____.

7. Another name for an informal poll is a _____ poll.

8. A small number of people polled to determine the opinions of a larger population is called a _____.

Vocabulary

Read each description, and write the letter of the correct term on the line.

1. _____ Attitudes expressed by many individuals about government and politics

2. _____ An unofficial vote or poll

3. _____ A small group that represents a larger population in a poll

a	public opinion
b	sample
c	straw poll

Multiple-Choice Test

Name: _____

Find the best answer for each item. Then completely fill in the circle for that answer.

1. Which of the following is likely to influence a person's political attitude?

   a. family
   b. gender
   c. education
   d. all of the above

2. Women tended to support what party through the 1950s?

   a. the Republican party
   b. the Democratic party
   c. both the Republican and Democratic parties equally
   d. neither party

3. Religion is likely to shape an individual's attitude about

   a. social issues
   b. economic issues
   c. both a and b
   d. neither a nor b

4. Political opinions of college-educated people tend to be

   a. conservative
   b. liberal
   c. impossible to identify
   d. none of the above

5. Statistics indicate that African Americans tend to be more _____ than whites.

   a. liberal
   b. conservative
   c. moderate
   d. reactionary

6. Polls indicate that Latinos tend to

   a. vote Democratic
   b. vote Republican
   c. vote equally for both parties
   d. not vote for either party

7. Which region is most closely associated with liberal political views?

   a. the West
   b. the South
   c. the Northeast
   d. the Midwest

8. An informal poll is also called a _____ poll.

   a. survey
   b. straw
   c. sample
   d. biased

9. The part of a population that is questioned to determine the public opinion of an entire population is called

   a. the straw poll
   b. the scientific poll
   c. the sample
   d. the pollster

10. Which statement about public opinion polls is true?

    a. A sample that is not representative of the population can affect the results of a poll.
    b. Biased questions can affect the results of a poll.
    c. No poll can claim 100 percent accuracy.
    d. all of the above

	a	b	c	d
1	a	b	c	d
2	a	b	c	d
3	a	b	c	d
4	a	b	c	d
5	a	b	c	d
6	a	b	c	d
7	a	b	c	d
8	a	b	c	d
9	a	b	c	d
10	a	b	c	d

Essay Question

A person's political attitude is shaped by many factors. Identify a factor that helps shape your political attitude. How does it do so?

For use with:	**Chapter 8**	**Public Opinion and Mass Media**
For use with:	**Activity 16**	**Working with the Media**

Objectives

- Explain the five types of mass media and trace their development.
- Identify the ways government regulates the media.
- Analyze the impact of the mass media on the policy agenda in the U.S. government.

Vocabulary

mass media   prior restraint   shield law   libel

BACKGROUND

In the decades following the founding of the Republic, editing and publishing a newspaper could be dangerous. The press was very partisan, and often editors would engage in the most defamatory libel against each other. While the courts were sometimes used to settle the disputes that arose, editors would challenge each other to duels, sometimes ending in the death of one or both of the duelists.

As the press strove to become more objective, such violent disputes became rare. However, with the advent of the "penny press" and "yellow journalism," news stories sometimes were either promoted and or created by the press as ways to sell more newspapers. During the early 1970s (and the Watergate episode), investigative journalism gained credence. A new era of journalism arose that allowed reporters to search for the "truth behind the truth" in news stories.

And even before television and the Internet, the news media became a truly mass medium. Many cities had several newspapers, national news magazines gained in popularity,

and with the invention of radio, reports could be, or seemed to be, instantaneous. The media became big business, and with the rise of television, the essence of "being there" existed in every person's living room.

To say that the press and now the mass media in all its various incarnations have had a profound influence on life in the United States would be a gross understatement. With all their shortcomings and faults, the media have had a strong, if not vital, influence in educating and keeping people informed about the affairs of the day. As people become better educated and more sophisticated in understanding how the media work, the media must expand their offerings to meet that expanded education and sophistication.

As new sources of news and other kinds of specialized information become available to us, we will be better able to choose not only what we wish to learn, but when, where, and how. And we can also ask why in many different ways.

Further Resources

Barber, James D. *The Pulse of Politics: Electing Presidents in the Media Age.* Englewood Cliffs, NJ: Prentice-Hall, 1992.

Graber, Doris A. *Mass Media and American Politics.* 5th ed. Washington, DC: Congressional Quarterly Press, 1997.

Linsky, Martin. *Impact: How the Press Affects Federal Policymaking.* New York: Norton, 1986.

16 | Politics and Mass Media

For Discussion

Review

1. *What are the major kinds of mass media? Why are they called the mass media?* (Students should at least know the media mentioned in the textbook. They are mass media because they reach almost all segments of the population.)

2. *What protections does the print media have against government interference?* (They have at least the 1st Amendment, shield laws, and protections against prior restraint and libel.)

3. *In what ways does the government regulate the broadcast media?* (Regulations, such as the equal time doctrine, are imposed by the FCC.)

4. *What political influence do the mass media have?* (Students should explain how they can influence campaigns and elections and set the public agenda.)

Critical Thinking

1. *Why do you think television appears to have such great influence in shaping public opinion?* (Television appears to have great influence because of its immediacy, its pervasive presence, and its easy access.)

2. *Do you believe, as some do, that protections against prior restraint and support for shield laws from government interference provide too much freedom for the media? Why or why not?* (Encourage students to support their answers with evidence, using perhaps Supreme Court decisions and other data from various sources.)

3. *Do you think that the government power to restrict the airwaves through the FCC is too much power to place in the hands of the government?* (Some students will answer yes because government interference can be dangerous, and others will say no since the media is a profit-making institution.)

4. *Do you think that the media encouraged the promotion of style over substance in marketing political candidates in political campaigns? Why or why not?* (Encourage students to develop their answers using data from their text and from their knowledge of recent political campaigns.)

Skills Development Activities

1. **WRITING:** News

   Have students write a short news article reporting on a real (or fictional) political event, such as a city council meeting, a student council meeting, or a political rally. Is the article strictly factual or have some of the writer's own biases entered into it? Each student should have one or more other students read and critique the article.

2. **CURRENT EVENTS:** Agenda Setting

   Ask students to select a news article or a television news report about one or more recent political events. They should try to detect any attempts in the article or news report to affect the political agenda in some way. Encourage them to share their findings with the class.

3. **INTERNET:** Political Influence

   Locate one or more Web sites dealing with a political figure (such as the President, a candidate in the news, or a U.S. senator). Students should try to decide whether or not the information on the Web site attempts to influence public opinion. They should compare information with several classmates to see if they have the same interpretations.

4. **SPECIAL SOURCES:** Negative Advertising

   Ask students to read the paragraph about negative advertising on page 527. Then have them locate at least one newspaper or magazine article from 1964 that reported on the daisy commercial and/or included a poll concerning the public's reaction to it. Ask students to report on their findings orally or in writing.

Study Guide

Name: _____

Complete each item as you read Chapter 8 (pages 116–123).

1. Means of communication that reach large audiences are called the _____.

2. There are three main types of mass media: the _____ media, the _____ media, and the _____.

3. The print media consist of _____ and _____.

4. The broadcast media consist of _____ and _____.

5. Which constitutional amendment protects the freedom of the mass media? _____

6. The broadcast media is regulated by the _____.

7. The requirement that equal radio or television airtime must be available to opposing candidates is called the _____.

8. The mass media have a powerful influence on the _____ opinions of U.S. citizens.

9. Reporters can help set the government's _____ by focusing on certain issues.

Vocabulary

Read each description, and write the letter of the correct term on the line.

1. _____ Radio, television, newspapers, magazines, the Internet

2. _____ Governmental censorship of a work before it is published or broadcast

3. _____ Protects journalists from revealing confidential sources

4. _____ Publication of falsehoods that damage someone's reputation

a	libel
b	mass media
c	prior restraint
d	shield law

Multiple-Choice Test

Name: _____

Find the best answer for each item. Then completely fill in the circle for that answer.

1. Which is NOT part of the mass media?
   - **a.** newspapers
   - **b.** the Internet
   - **c.** radio stations
   - **d.** none of the above

2. Which is the newest part of the mass media?
   - **a.** radio stations
   - **b.** television stations
   - **c.** the Internet
   - **d.** magazines

3. The freedom of the media in the United States is guaranteed by
   - **a.** the FCC
   - **b.** the Equal Time Doctrine
   - **c.** the 1st Amendment
   - **d.** libel laws

4. Journalists are protected by
   - **a.** shield laws
   - **b.** prior restraint
   - **c.** libel laws
   - **d.** all of the above

5. Today, prior restraint is
   - **a.** never practiced by the government
   - **b.** rarely practiced by the government
   - **c.** frequently practiced by the government
   - **d.** always practiced by the government

6. The _____ regulates the broadcast media.
   - **a.** 1st Amendment
   - **b.** network president
   - **c.** FCC
   - **d.** shield law

7. Americans learn most about political candidates through
   - **a.** word of mouth
   - **b.** speeches
   - **c.** posters and billboards
   - **d.** mass media

8. Which statement about political candidates and the mass media is true?
   - **a.** Candidates tend to ignore the mass media.
   - **b.** Candidates center their campaigns on media events.
   - **c.** Candidates appear in the mass media, but don't expect it to affect their success.
   - **d.** Candidates know the mass media will focus on their messages about policy.

9. By focusing on certain issues, the mass media influence the government's
   - **a.** agenda
   - **b.** policy
   - **c.** decisions
   - **d.** all of the above

10. The mass media reflect—and also _____ —public opinion.
    - **a.** influence
    - **b.** report on
    - **c.** create
    - **d.** all of the above

1	ⓐ	ⓑ	ⓒ	ⓓ
2	ⓐ	ⓑ	ⓒ	ⓓ
3	ⓐ	ⓑ	ⓒ	ⓓ
4	ⓐ	ⓑ	ⓒ	ⓓ
5	ⓐ	ⓑ	ⓒ	ⓓ
6	ⓐ	ⓑ	ⓒ	ⓓ
7	ⓐ	ⓑ	ⓒ	ⓓ
8	ⓐ	ⓑ	ⓒ	ⓓ
9	ⓐ	ⓑ	ⓒ	ⓓ
10	ⓐ	ⓑ	ⓒ	ⓓ

Essay Question

Should there be stricter regulations to prohibit negative advertising in political campaigns? Give several reasons for your position.

For use with: **Chapter 9** **Interest Groups**

For use with: Activity 17 **Putting the Right Spin on Information**

Objectives

- Review the early development and characteristics of interest groups.
- Explain the differences between various types of interest groups and between interest groups and political parties.
- Analyze the effects of interest groups on the legislative process in particular and on the political process in general.

Vocabulary

interest group   lobbying   electioneering

BACKGROUND

In 1835 Frenchman Alexis de Tocqueville wrote in his work *Democracy in America* that, "Americans of all ages, all stations in life, are forever forming associations. There are not only commercial and industrial associations in which all take part, but others of a thousand different types—religious, moral, serious, futile, general or restricted, immensely large or very minute. . . ." He could have been writing about interest groups and political parties today.

Interest groups try to provide for the particular interests of their specific groups. They provide their members with a sense of belonging to a cause, a clear goal orientation, and, often, monetary benefits. They promote specific policies that their members wish to see enacted. Some function as labor and/or professional organizations, and others serve the public interest or promote social action. Such groups also often hire and maintain lobbyists to work with members of legislative bodies to help those legislators understand the specific goals of the group.

Many politicians today wish to divorce themselves from the idea that they are servants of "special interests." However, legislators and other politicians receive a great deal of their information about the potential policy agenda and, hence, about pending legislation from interest group lobbyists.

Interest groups also have organized as political action committees (PACs). Such committees, first organized by the AFL-CIO, have become a standard way for many interests to be recognized, especially when they support candidates for office. Also, as another legacy of Watergate, PACs are regulated by federal statute.

Some scholars believe that the existence of interest groups supports the theory that the United States is a pluralist nation and that, when regulated, lobbyists and PACs serve a positive purpose. Others complain that major interest groups only serve as a front for elites, and yet others believe that the proliferation of such organized groups, especially when they achieve power, serves to divide our nation with hyperpluralism, making legislative accomplishments impossible.

Interest groups are a part of the political process and one that all citizens need to understand to truly comprehend our constitutional system of government.

Further Resources

de Tocqueville, Alexis. *Democracy in America.* New York: Vintage Books, 1990.
Wilson, James Q. *Political Organizations.* Rev. ed. Princeton, NJ: Princeton University Press, 1995.

17 | Interest Groups and PACs

For Discussion

Review

1. **What are some of the major differences between interest groups and political parties?** (Political parties serve chiefly to promote a generalized agenda and to elect candidates. Interest groups work toward achieving the specific interests of the group. Electing candidates is only important if that is the best way to achieve the group's interests.)

2. **What are the major classifications of interest groups?** (They are economic, social action and equality, and public-interest).

3. **What are some of the several strategies used by interest groups to achieve their objectives?** (Such strategies include lobbying, electioneering, and litigation.)

4. **What is a class-action lawsuit?** (It is a lawsuit brought by a person or group both on that person's/group's behalf and on the behalf of others in similar circumstances.)

Critical Thinking

1. **What do you think motivates people to join interest groups?** (Encourage students to think about interests other than economic advantages.)

2. **Why do you think that many people choose not to join interest groups?** (Have students discuss the free rider issue among possible reasons.)

3. **Do you think the "revolving door" practice of hiring lobbyists is fair?** (Encourage students to explore more than one side of the issue.)

4. **What interest groups do you or members of your family belong to?** (it might be interesting to make a list on the board of students' answers.)

Skills Development Activities

1. **WRITING:** Campaigning

   Have students write a short television or radio script encouraging people to support a particular cause or interest in which they believe strongly. Have them record their script and play it for the class.

2. **CURRENT EVENTS:** Interest Group Meetings

   Ask students to identify an interest group that holds regular meetings in their area. Have students attend a meeting and summarize the proceedings for the class.

3. **INTERNET:** Interest Group Web Sites

   Students should search the Internet and locate as many interest-group Web sites as possible, reporting a tally of the list of sites to the class. Ask them to try to classify the Web sites as they report.

4. **SPECIAL SOURCES:** Federal Election Commission

   Have students use the local library to locate a recent Federal Election Commission campaign finance report about their representative and one of their senators. Ask them to create a chart to report their findings to the class.

Study Guide

Name: _____

Complete each item as you read Chapter 9.

1. Most _____ are formed to influence public policy.

2. Three factors to consider when analyzing interest groups are _____, _____, and _____.

3. The three main types of interest groups are _____ groups, _____ and _____ groups, and _____ groups.

4. The four types of economic interest groups are _____ associations, _____ groups, _____ groups, and _____ groups.

5. Interest groups use four main strategies: _____, _____, _____, and _____.

6. _____ are the economic arms of interest groups.

7. Interest groups attempt to shape public opinion by purchasing _____, by publishing the results of their _____, and by staging media _____.

Vocabulary

Read each description, and write the letter of the correct term on the line.

1. _____ A private group formed to influence public policy

2. _____ Attempts to influence public officials

3. _____ Efforts in support of a political party or candidate

a	electioneering
b	interest group
c	lobbying

17 | Interest Groups and PACs

Multiple-Choice Test

Name: _____

Find the best answer for each item. Then completely fill in the circle for that answer.

1. When did interest groups first appear?
   a. at the beginning of the country's history
   b. during the 1830s and 1840s
   c. during the Civil War
   d. in the last 10 years

2. Interest groups vary widely in
   a. size
   b. resources
   c. intensity
   d. all of the above

3. Which is NOT an economic interest group?
   a. NAM
   b. ABA
   c. AMA
   d. MADD

4. The League of Women Voters is an example of which type of interest group?
   a. a business and trade association interest group
   b. a labor interest group
   c. a public-interest group
   d. a professional interest group

5. Ralph Nader founded
   a. early public-interest groups
   b. PACs
   c. the AFL-CIO
   d. the NAACP

6. Which term refers to attempts to influence public policy by contacting government officials?
   a. litigating
   b. lobbying
   c. interest grouping
   d. electioneering

7. Electioneering is generally conducted by
   a. PACs
   b. lobbyists
   c. interest groups
   d. professional interest groups

8. Which best describes the relationship between PACs and interest groups?
   a. PACs are a kind of interest group.
   b. PACs are members of interest groups.
   c. PACs are created by interest groups.
   d. PACs are opponents of interest groups.

9. Interest groups attempt to influence
   a. government policy
   b. public opinion
   c. election outcomes
   d. all of the above

10. An interest group that files an *amicus curiae* brief is using the tactic of _____ to achieve its goal.
    a. litigation
    b. lobbying
    c. electioneering
    d. opinion-making

	a	b	c	d
1	a	b	c	d
2	a	b	c	d
3	a	b	c	d
4	a	b	c	d
5	a	b	c	d
6	a	b	c	d
7	a	b	c	d
8	a	b	c	d
9	a	b	c	d
10	a	b	c	d

Essay Question

Do you think one interest group or one type of interest group does the most good for the people in the United States? Explain your answer.

Institutions of National Government

For use with:	**Chapter 10**	**Congress and the Legislative Branch**
For use with:	**Activity 18**	**Setting the National Agenda**

Objectives

- Explain the process of apportionment and reapportionment.
- Identify the basic qualifications for House and Senate members.
- List at least three differences between the House and the Senate.
- Explain Congress's delegated and implied powers.

Vocabulary

apportionment   reapportionment   at-large

BACKGROUND

The branch of U.S. government that is most detailed in the Constitution is the legislative branch. Congress was established as a bicameral institution with two very different houses. It is important to remember when looking at the differences that the two houses were set up to check each other as part of the checks and balances built into the Constitution.

The House of Representatives consists of 435 members, each representing about 624,000 people. To become a representative, you must be at least 25 years old, a citizen for at least 7 years, and a registered voter. There is no requirement that you live in the district you represent, but many people expect it as a matter of custom. A House member serves a 2-year term and all 435 seats are up for election every 2 years. The Senate has 100 members, two from each state regardless of the state's size. Unlike the House, if a new state is added, this number will go up. To be a senator, you must be at least 30 years old and a citizen for at least 9 years, and you must

live in the state you represent. Senators serve 6-year terms, though they are staggered so only one-third of the Senate is up for election at any time. This was done intentionally so there could never be a complete turnover in the Senate, as there could be in the House. As in the House, there are no limits on the number of terms a senator may serve, though the issue has been raised for both houses in the last 10 to 15 years.

The House is more formal than the Senate, with rigid rules and a more hierarchical structure, and it is seen as the less prestigious of the two houses. The Senate acts more slowly than the House, deals with larger constituencies, and allows unlimited debate (which probably explains why it acts more slowly). Combined, the houses have some rather impressive delegated powers, which include regulating commerce, controlling currency, setting immigration and naturalization policy, controlling territories, borrowing money, and declaring war.

Further Resources

Green, Mark. *Who Runs Congress?* New York: Viking Press, 1979.
Jones, Charles O. *The United States Congress: People, Place, and Policy.* Homewood, IL: The Dorsey Press, 1982.
U.S. House of Representatives. http://www.house.gov
U.S. Senate. http://www.senate.gov

For Discussion

Review

1. **What is reapportionment, and how does it work?** (Every 10 years a census is taken; the allocation of seats in the House is adjusted to reflect population shifts. As some states gain seats, others lose them.)

2. **What are the basic qualifications needed to run for the House and the Senate?** (To run for the House, you must be 25 or older and a citizen for 7 years. To run for the Senate, you must be 30 or older and a citizen for 9 years.)

3. **What are three differences between the House and the Senate?** (Answers could include that the House is larger, has more formal rules, is more hierarchical, and has less prestige, while the Senate is smaller, operates more slowly, allows unlimited debate, and has longer terms.)

4. **What are five of Congress's delegated powers?** (The delegated powers of Congress include borrowing money, taxing, regulating commerce, establishing and controlling currency, and declaring war. This is only a partial list.)

Critical Thinking

1. **What do you think are the advantages and disadvantages of a bicameral system?** (Advantages might include separation of powers, checks and balances, representing different constituencies, and deliberative, well-considered policies. Disadvantages might include gridlock, being too slow and deliberative, different priorities and agendas, and having different rules.)

2. **Do you think the practice of redistricting after reapportionment should take racial or ethnic factors into consideration? In other words, should there be a certain number of minority districts?** (Answers will vary, but make sure students have some support for their answers.)

3. **Do you think members of Congress should be subject to term limits?** (See the chart on page 173 for a brief list of the opposing viewpoints.)

Skills Development Activities

1. **WRITING:** Life in Congress

   Tell students they have been given a once-in-a-lifetime chance to be in Congress. Have them write a one- to two-page essay describing whether they would rather be a senator or a representative, and explain why.

2. **CURRENT EVENTS:** Budget Proposals

   The current budget surplus provides a unique opportunity for Congress. Have students pretend it is up to them to propose what to do with the surplus. Each student should make three specific proposals for a follow-up discussion.

3. **INTERNET:** Implied Powers

   Have pairs of students look up and read the *McCulloch v. Maryland* decision. Then have them explain in a one- to two-page essay how this decision established the implied powers that Congress has used freely ever since.

4. **SPECIAL SOURCES:** Reapportionment

   Have students draw a grid of 36 boxes (6 × 6). Have them randomly place 18 Ds and 18 Rs (party abbreviations) in the boxes. Then have students create a map of six districts, which are six connected (sides or top/bottom) boxes each. The goal is to have one party control four of the six newly created districts. See if they can do the same for the opposition party.

Study Guide

Name: _____

Complete each item as you read Chapter 10 (pages 138–145).

1. Congress is a _____ legislature, which means it consists of two houses.

2. The two houses of Congress are the _____ and the

   _____.

3. Membership in the House of Representatives is based on _____, while

   _____ are equally represented in the Senate.

4. An elected representative serves a _____ -year term; an elected senator serves a

   _____ -year term.

5. Congress has three main types of powers: _____ ,

   _____ , and _____ powers.

6. Borrowing money, taxing, and the ability to declare war are examples of the _____

   powers of Congress.

7. The Elastic Clause gives Congress _____ powers.

Vocabulary

Read each description, and write the letter of the correct term on the line.

1. _____ Distribution of House seats

2. _____ Periodic redistribution of House seats

3. _____ Type of election in which senators are chosen

a	apportionment
b	at-large
c	reapportionment

Mulitple-Choice Test

Name: _____

Find the best answer for each item. Then completely fill in the circle for that answer.

1. The United States has a(n) _____, or two-house, legislature.
   - **a.** apportioned
   - **b.** at-large
   - **c.** delegated
   - **d.** bicameral

2. Which statement is true?
   - **a.** The Congress is made up of the House of Representatives and the Senate.
   - **b.** The Senate is made up of the Congress and the House of Representatives.
   - **c.** The House of Representatives is made up of the Congress and the Senate.
   - **d.** none of the above

3. Which is based on population?
   - **a.** the Senate
   - **b.** the House of Representatives
   - **c.** the legislative branch
   - **d.** Congress

4. Apportionment is based on what?
   - **a.** the census
   - **b.** delegated powers
   - **c.** the Elastic Clause
   - **d.** the number of states

5. Which has 100 members?
   - **a.** the Senate
   - **b.** the House of Representatives
   - **c.** the legislative branch
   - **d.** Congress

6. Apportionment is used to determine membership in the _____.
   - **a.** Senate
   - **b.** House of Representatives
   - **c.** Congress
   - **d.** all of the above

7. Representatives serve a _____ -year term. Senators serve a _____ -year term.
   - **a.** 7, 9
   - **b.** 9, 7
   - **c.** 2, 6
   - **d.** 6, 2

8. Which is NOT a delegated power of Congress?
   - **a.** to investigate wrongdoing in the executive branch
   - **b.** to declare war
   - **c.** to establish bankruptcy laws
   - **d.** to tax citizens

9. Another name for delegated powers is _____ powers.
   - **a.** implied
   - **b.** expressed
   - **c.** at-large
   - **d.** legislative

10. The implied powers of Congress are based on
    - **a.** the Elastic Clause
    - **b.** delegated powers
    - **c.** *McCulloch v. Maryland*
    - **d.** all of the above

	a	b	c	d
1	a	b	c	d
2	a	b	c	d
3	a	b	c	d
4	a	b	c	d
5	a	b	c	d
6	a	b	c	d
7	a	b	c	d
8	a	b	c	d
9	a	b	c	d
10	a	b	c	d

Essay Question

Why do you think the Framers of the Constitution made the requirements for senators and representatives different?

For use with: | **Chapter 10** | **Congress and the Legislative Branch**

For use with: | **Activity 19** | **High Crimes and Misdemeanors**

Objectives

- Identify the major nonlegislative powers of Congress.
- List the steps in the impeachment process.
- Provide an example of Congress performing its oversight function.

Vocabulary

impeachment   oversight function   authorization   appropriation

BACKGROUND

The Constitution spelled out many different types of responsibilities for Congress. Law making is a big part of what they do, of course, but the Constitution has also spelled out a number of nonlegislative powers Congress cannot ignore. Some examples of these powers include proposing amendments, admitting new states, approving presidential appointments and treaties, and setting naturalization procedures. There are, however, two other non legislative powers that tend to get quite a bit of attention.

The powers of impeachment and investigation/oversight can lead to confrontation, embarrassment, and sometimes removal from office. The Founders saw this as a very serious undertaking, demonstrated by the requirement of a two-thirds vote for an individual's conviction and removal. The two presidential impeachments Congress has conducted thus far have both been controversial, and in both cases there was significant dispute over what exactly constituted "high crimes and misdemeanors." In both instances the Senate trial ended without a conviction. In the aftermath of President Bill Clinton's trial, there was a consensus that he had done wrong but that the crimes were not serious enough to warrant removal from office.

In a perfect world, all laws and actions of Congress would be carried out exactly as planned, and oversight would not be needed. Since that scenario is highly unlikely, Congress has been given the power to investigate the implementation stage. One organization created by Congress to help perform these investigations is the General Accounting Office (GAO). No government official likes to hear that the GAO is at the door. It usually means trouble.

Further Resources

Aberbach, Joel D. *Keeping a Watchful Eye: The Politics of Congressional Oversight.* Washington, DC: Brookings Institute, 1990.

Gerhardt, Michael J. *The Federal Impeachment Process: A Constitutional and Historical Analysis.* Princeton, NJ: Princeton University Press, 1996.

Rehnquist, William H., and Clyde Adams Phillips. *Grand Inquests: The Historic Impeachments of Justice Samuel Chase and President Andrew Johnson.* New York: William Morrow & Co., 1999.

For Discussion

Review

1. **What are five nonlegislative powers of Congress?** (Answers should include to propose amendments, admit new states, approve treaties and presidential nominations, choose a President if there is no majority in the electoral college, impeachment, and investigation or oversight.)

2. **Who is involved in the impeachment process and what is each group's role?** (The House approves charges with a simple majority vote, which impeaches the person charged. The Senate then conducts a trial based on the charges raised by the House. If the President or Vice President is the one being tried, the chief justice presides. A vote of two-thirds is needed for conviction and removal from office.)

3. **How does Congress perform oversight? Explain.** (Answers will vary, but students should be encouraged to provide specific examples.)

4. **What is the difference between authorization and appropriation?** (Authorization is the process of passing legislation that creates or allows someone to carry out a directive, while appropriation approves the money to pay for what has been authorized earlier.)

Critical Thinking

1. **Do you think there should be a less severe alternative solution to impeachment when disciplining federal officials?** (Some students may say that something less than impeachment should be available for less serious offenses.)

2. **Why do you think the oversight function is so important to the proper functioning of our government?** (The oversight function allows Congress to keep an eye on how our money is being spent and how its laws are being enforced.)

3. **During the investigation into President Clinton's activities, there was a debate to decide whether the information found should be made public or kept from the public, as with a grand jury investigation. Do you think all information uncovered in congressional investigations should be made public, or should some information be kept private?** (Answers will vary. Encourage students to think of various categories of information as they answer.)

Skills Development Activities

1. **WRITING:** Censure

   During the impeachment trial of President Clinton, one option many considered was censure. Have students pretend they are Senate staff members who have been assigned to write one paragraph in support of censure and one paragraph against it to help their boss (a senator) make up his mind.

2. **CURRENT EVENTS:** High Crimes and Misdemeanors

   Have students look up definitions for the terms *high crimes* and *misdemeanors*. After writing what each term means, have students make lists of three specific actions they think would constitute high crimes and misdemeanors.

3. **INTERNET:** Andrew Johnson's Impeachment

   Have students look up information on the impeachment and trial of Andrew Johnson. Ask them to share a list of ten interesting facts with the class.

4. **SPECIAL SOURCES:** The Clinton Impeachment

   Have students find a political cartoon dealing with President Clinton's impeachment. It can be from any stage of the process. Have students share their cartoon with the rest of the class.

Study Guide

Name: _____

Complete each item as you read Chapter 10 (pages 145–147)

1. Congress's power to propose constitutional amendments and approve treaties are examples of its _____ powers.

2. The formal procedure for removing an official from office is called _____.

3. According to the Constitution, officials can be impeached for "_____ , _____ , or other _____ and _____ ."

4. In Congress, the _____ may impeach an official, but the impeachment trial is held in the _____.

5. Two Presidents have been impeached: _____ and _____.

6. One President resigned to avoid impeachment: _____.

7. Congress's power to review policies and programs of the executive branch is called its _____.

8. Congress has the power to _____ , or issue, funds for government programs.

9. To require a person to appear in court, a _____ may be ordered.

Vocabulary

Read each description, and write the letter of the correct term on the line.

1. _____ The formal procedure for removing an official from office

2. _____ Congress's power to review programs of the executive branch

3. _____ A legislature's approval to implement or continue a program

4. _____ A grant of money by Congress

a	appropriation
b	authorization
c	impeachment
d	oversight function

Multiple-Choice Test

Name: _____

Find the best answer for each item. Then completely fill in the circle for that answer.

1. Which is a nonlegislative power of Congress?
   - **a.** the power to authorize treaties
   - **b.** the power to admit new states to the Union
   - **c.** the power to propose constitutional amendments
   - **d.** all of the above

2. Congressional removal of an official from office for "treason, bribery, or other high crimes and misdemeanors" is called
   - **a.** censure
   - **b.** impeachment
   - **c.** resignation
   - **d.** appropriation

3. Who has the power to conduct an impeachment trial?
   - **a.** the House of Representatives
   - **b.** the Senate
   - **c.** the Supreme Court
   - **d.** the cabinet

4. Who presides in an impeachment trial?
   - **a.** the President
   - **b.** the chief justice
   - **c.** an attorney
   - **d.** the Speaker of the House

5. Which of the following Presidents was NOT impeached?
   - **a.** Andrew Johnson
   - **b.** Bill Clinton
   - **c.** Richard Nixon
   - **d.** none of the above

6. Congress first executed its investigative power in?
   - **a.** 1789
   - **b.** 1792
   - **c.** 1876
   - **d.** 1973

7. Congress's power to investigate the executive branch is part of its
   - **a.** legislative power
   - **b.** appropriation function
   - **c.** authorization power
   - **d.** oversight function

8. No money for a program established by Congress may be spent until Congress passes an _____ bill.
   - **a.** oversight
   - **b.** impeachment
   - **c.** appropriation
   - **d.** authorization

9. Deficit spending is the practice of spending
   - **a.** more money than is brought in
   - **b.** money from taxes
   - **c.** money from private donors
   - **d.** none of the above

10. Congress must divide, or _____, funds among many different programs.
    - **a.** veto
    - **b.** subpoena
    - **c.** appropriate
    - **d.** impeach

1	ⓐ	ⓑ	ⓒ	ⓓ
2	ⓐ	ⓑ	ⓒ	ⓓ
3	ⓐ	ⓑ	ⓒ	ⓓ
4	ⓐ	ⓑ	ⓒ	ⓓ
5	ⓐ	ⓑ	ⓒ	ⓓ
6	ⓐ	ⓑ	ⓒ	ⓓ
7	ⓐ	ⓑ	ⓒ	ⓓ
8	ⓐ	ⓑ	ⓒ	ⓓ
9	ⓐ	ⓑ	ⓒ	ⓓ
10	ⓐ	ⓑ	ⓒ	ⓓ

Essay Question

The Constitution says an official may be impeached for "treason, bribery, or other high crimes and misdemeanors." What do all these offenses have in common? Explain your answer.

| For use with: | **Chapter 10** | **Congress and the Legislative Branch** |
| For use with: | Activity 20 | Standing Committee Work |

Objectives

- Identify the leadership positions in the House and Senate.
- List the four types of congressional legislative committees.
- Name and describe the four primary support agencies for Congress.
- Explain the value of the committee and caucus system to Congress as a whole.

Vocabulary

standing committee	select committee	majority leader
conference committee	floor leader	minority leader
Speaker of the House	joint committee	

BACKGROUND

As with any large group, Congress depends on its leadership and organization to bring order out of chaos. There are four types of structures that accomplish this: the party leadership, the committee system, caucuses, and the support agencies.

Of all the positions in Congress, the most powerful is Speaker of the House. The powers of the Speaker include channeling bills to committee, deciding who gets to speak, influencing committee assignments, and appointing other party leaders. Usually Speakers and majority and minority leaders are moderates, so they can work with all their party members.

Parties in both houses choose a majority leader and a minority leader. In the House and Senate the majority leader is the chief floor manager for all bills. The same is true for minority leaders and minority bills. To help party leaders, there are whips, who are "second-in-command" people who relay information from the leaders to the party and vice versa. Almost no vote is ever taken in Congress without the leadership knowing the outcome before the call for the vote is made.

If the leadership is key to running Congress, then the committees are key to the success of Congress. Members realize that if every member looked carefully at every bill, they wouldn't get much done. Committees divide the workload so each bill gets all the attention it deserves. Congress has even created a handful of organizations to assist it as it carries out the legislative process.

Further Resources

Deering, Christopher J., and Steven S. Smith. *Committees in Congress.* 3rd ed. Washington, DC: Congressional Quarterly Press, 1997.

Fox, Harrison W., and Susan Webb Hammond. *Congressional Staffs: The Invisible Force in American Lawmaking.* New York: Free Press, 1977.

Roll Call (the Capitol newspaper). http://www.rollcall.com

For Discussion

Review

1. ***What are the leadership positions in both the House and the Senate?*** (In the House the leadership spots are Speaker, majority and minority leaders, and chief whips for both parties. In the Senate the Vice President is technically president of the Senate, but he rarely does much. The same is true for the president *pro tempore*. The real leaders are the party leaders and the chief whips.)

2. ***What are the four types of legislative committees?*** (The four types of committees are standing, select, joint, and conference.)

3. ***What are the four primary support organizations for Congress?*** (The four main support groups for Congress are the Library of Congress, the General Accounting Office, the Congressional Budget Office, and the Government Printing Office.)

4. ***What is the franking privilege?*** (It is the perquisite, or fringe benefit that gives senators and representatives free postal service.)

Critical Thinking

1. ***What qualities do you think an effective Speaker of the House needs to have?*** (Encourage students to mention a variety of traits and to cite particular Speakers they may have heard of.)

2. ***Why do you think people from opposing parties would be willing to work together in caucuses?*** (Party issues make up only part of what interests members of Congress. Members may find they have similar concerns on issues that cross party lines—such as people from the steel caucus or members of women's caucuses, and so on.)

3. ***Why do you think the membership of Congress is not representative of the population as a whole?*** (As students offer answers, refer to the chart on page 157.)

Skills Development Activities

1. **WRITING:** Letters to Officials

   Have students choose any issue on which they hold strong beliefs. Have them find out the name of the chairman of the relevant committee and then write that person (either in the House or Senate) a letter expressing support or making a request. (You may want to look at them before sending them.)

2. **CURRENT EVENTS:** Know Your Leaders

   Have students find and list the current leaders of Congress. They should identify the Speaker of the House, majority leader, minority leader, and chief whips for each party. In the Senate they should identify the president *pro tempore,* majority and minority leaders, and chief whips for both parties.

3. **INTERNET:** Select Committees

   Have students look up and make a list of all standing and select committees and chairpersons in both houses.

4. **SPECIAL SOURCES:** Congressional Profiles

   Have students study and discuss (individually or in small groups) the chart about recent Congresses on page 530. Ask them to create a graph to reflect some of the information they find interesting. Post the graphs for all to see and discuss.

Study Guide

Name: _____

Complete each item as you read Chapter 10 (pages 148–159).

1. The two houses of Congress meet for _____ -year sessions.

2. Congress is organized through _____ leadership, the

   _____ system, _____ , and

   _____ .

3. According to who won more seats in the last congressional election, the two parties in the Senate and House are

   called the _____ party and the _____ party.

4. The Speaker of the House, always from the majority party, is the _____ .

5. Party leaders on the House floor are called _____ leaders.

6. According to the Constitution, who is president of the Senate? _____

7. The four types of Congressional committees are _____ ,

   _____ , _____ , and

   _____ committees.

8. List four important support agencies of Congress: _____ ,

   _____ , _____ , and

   _____ .

Vocabulary

Read each description, and write the letter of the correct term on the line.

1. _____ The presiding officer of the House of Representatives

2. _____ A spokesperson for a party in Congress

3. _____ The legislative leader of the majority party

4. _____ The legislative leader of the minority party

5. _____ A permanent committee

6. _____ A temporary committee

7. _____ A committee made up of members of both houses

8. _____ A temporary House–Senate committee established to find
   a compromise on conflicting versions of a bill

a	conference committee
b	floor leader
c	joint committee
d	majority leader
e	minority leader
f	select committee
g	Speaker of the House
h	standing committee

Multiple-Choice Test

Name: _____

Find the best answer for each item. Then completely fill in the circle for that answer.

1. The presiding officer of the House of Representatives is
   a. the Vice President
   b. the president *pro tempore*
   c. the Speaker of the House
   d. the majority leader

2. Who USUALLY presides over the Senate?
   a. the Vice President
   b. the president *pro tempore*
   c. the majority leader
   d. the minority leader

3. Who holds the most power in the Senate?
   a. the president *pro tempore*
   b. the floor leaders
   c. the majority whip
   d. the Speaker of the House

4. A permanent committee in Congress is called a _____ committee.
   a. standing
   b. select
   c. joint
   d. conference

5. A congressional committee established to reconcile different versions of a bill is called a _____ committee.
   a. caucus
   b. select
   c. joint
   d. conference

6. Caucus members may be
   a. both representatives and senators
   b. only senators
   c. only whips
   d. only majority party leaders

7. Appropriations, Judiciary, and Foreign Relations are all examples of
   a. standing committees
   b. House committees
   c. joint committees
   d. select committees

8. Which is considered a support agency of the U.S. Congress?
   a. the General Accounting Office
   b. the House Ways and Means Committee
   c. the cabinet
   d. joint committees

9. Which best describes the membership of Congress?
   a. Most are men.
   b. Most are white.
   c. Most are wealthier than the people they represent.
   d. all of the above

10. The thousands of people who assist senators and representatives are called
    a. support agencies
    b. congressional staff
    c. support committees
    d. legislators

	a	b	c	d
1	a	b	c	d
2	a	b	c	d
3	a	b	c	d
4	a	b	c	d
5	a	b	c	d
6	a	b	c	d
7	a	b	c	d
8	a	b	c	d
9	a	b	c	d
10	a	b	c	d

Essay Question

Compare and contrast the key leadership positions in the Senate with those in the House. Identify key positions and the job responsibilities that go with each.

For use with:	**Chapter 10**	**Congress and the Legislative Branch**
For use with:	**Activity 21**	**Getting a Bill Sponsored**

Objectives

- Identify the first stages of the lawmaking process in both the Senate and the House.
- Differentiate between a bill and a resolution.
- Explain what it means to "pigeonhole" a bill.
- Explain the role of the House Rules Committee.

Vocabulary

bill   concurrent resolution   joint resolution

BACKGROUND

The legislative process in the United States is one of the most complicated in the world. Each stage is fraught with pitfalls and dangers for supporters of any piece of legislation. The system makes it easier to stop legislation than it does to pass something. The good news is that anything that gets through the gauntlet of both houses and the President must have wide support. The bad news is that the process is so long and complicated that only some 200 of about 11,000 bills pass in a 2-year Congress.

The process of how a bill becomes a law can start in either house (unless it is a revenue bill, which means it must start in the House). Bills are introduced and then given to the clerk, who assigns them a number. From the clerk the bill is sent to the Speaker, who decides which committee will receive the proposal. He must send the bill to a committee within 2 weeks.

From the committee, the chair sends it to the appropriate subcommittee. Finally, things start to happen. Most bills are "pigeonholed," or put aside, at this point; remember: 11,000 are introduced and only 200 passed. If the subcom-

mittee decides to consider the bill, a discussion is held to hear the views of the subcommittee's members. If they like it, hearings are scheduled, with both sides having a chance to bring in witnesses. If the bill isn't tabled (put aside for later consideration), a markup, or amendment, session is held. Additions to the bill, or proposed amendments, will be voted on later by the House. All amendments must be germane (related to the subject of the bill). The subcommittee then votes. If members like the bill, they send it on to the full committee, where the whole process repeats itself. If they vote it down, the bill dies there.

The full committee repeats the process mentioned above, and, if supported, the bill is reported out and sent to the Rules Committee for a time limit and amendment rule. The process is similar in the Senate, except for these differences: the majority leader, starts the process, and amendments do not have to be germane. Also, there is no Rules Committee in the Senate. From there it goes out to the floor—but that is the next topic.

Further Resources

Fenno, Richard F., Jr. *Congressmen in Committees.* Boston: Little, Brown, 1973.
Library of Congress. "Thomas: Legislative Information on the Internet."
    http://thomas.loc.gov

For Discussion

Review

1. *Where in Congress is a bill first given serious attention?* (The first real point of consideration for legislation is the subcommittee level of either house.)

2. *What is the difference between a bill and a resolution?* (A bill is intended to become a law while a resolution is more an expression of opinion or a housekeeping matter. Also, Presidents do not sign resolutions.)

3. *What does it mean if a bill is pigeonholed?* (If a bill is pigeonholed, it has been put aside and will not move any further in the process.)

4. *What is a discharge petition?* (It's a process designed to move a bill out of committee to the House floor.)

Critical Thinking

1. *Why do you think the system is designed to make it more difficult to pass a bill than to kill a bill?* (The Constitution's Framers gave the advantage to the opposition of a bill in order to ensure legislation had wide support before it could be passed.)

2. *Do you think committee chairs have too much power in the lawmaking process?* (As students express their views, be sure they consider several of the key decisions a chair makes.)

3. *How can the Rules Committee make or break a bill by the rules it passes?* (A favorable rule—short debate and no amendments—increases a bill's chance of passage, as opposed to long debate and no limit on amendments.)

Skills Development Activities

1. **WRITING:** The Rules Committee

   Ask students to write a one- to two- page position paper about whether or not the House Rules Committee has too much power. Encourage them to do research before they start their drafts.

2. **CURRENT EVENTS:** Recent Bills

   Have students research a bill passed in a recent session of Congress. Ask students to give a short, 30-second explanation of what the bill is about, who introduced it, and when it passed.

3. **INTERNET:** A Bill's Life

   Have students look up a bill on the congressional Internet site, Thomas: http://thomas.loc.gov. Have students select a bill in process and track it over a period of time (at least 3 weeks). Afterward, have them report on the bill—the name and number of the bill, the bill's purpose, and what has happened to the bill thus far. This can be an oral report in class. Ideally, students should continue to follow the bill for the rest of the semester and turn in a two-page report at the end of the semester.

4. **SPECIAL SOURCES:** Number of Bills

   Ask students to research the number of bills introduced in each of the last five sessions of Congress. Have them work in pairs to create a graph to show their findings to the class.

Study Guide

Name: _____

Complete each item as you read Chapter 10 (pages 160–163).

1. A proposed law is called a _____.

2. Bills are introduced by _____.

3. The two types of bills are _____ bills and _____ bills.

4. In the House, a new bill is introduced when it is dropped into the _____; in the Senate it is simply announced.

5. New bills are sent first to _____.

6. Most bills _____ in committee or subcommittee.

7. A committee may hold _____ on a bill to hear testimony.

8. After the hearings, committee members" _____" the bill, or change it.

9. If it survives the committee, a bill goes to the full _____ or _____.

10. The House _____ sets the rules for debate about a bill.

Vocabulary

Read each description, and write the letter of the correct term on the line.

1. _____ A proposed law

2. _____ A statement by both houses of Congress that lacks the force of law

3. _____ A formal expression of opinion by both houses of Congress that has the force of law

> **a** bill
> **b** concurrent resolution
> **c** joint resolution

Multiple-Choice Test

Name: _____

Find the best answer for each item. Then completely fill in the circle for that answer.

1. What is a proposed law called?
   a. a joint resolution
   b. a concurrent resolution
   c. a bill
   d. a discharge petition

2. The two main types of bills are _____ and _____.
   a. joint, concurrent
   b. pigeonhole, discharge
   c. House, Senate
   d. public, private

3. When Congress wants to make an important statement without making a law, it passes
   a. a joint resolution
   b. a concurrent resolution
   c. a bill
   d. a discharge petition

4. What term refers to an opinion expressed by both houses of Congress that has the force of law?
   a. joint resolution
   b. concurrent resolution
   c. bill
   d. discharge petition

5. Bills are assigned
   a. a title
   b. a number
   c. both
   d. neither

6. Who first considers a bill?
   a. a committee
   b. the whole House or Senate
   c. the President
   d. the president *pro tempore*

7. How many bills die in committee?
   a. none
   b. some
   c. most
   d. all

8. When a committee revises a bill, it is said to
   a. pigeonhole it
   b. mark it up
   c. discharge it
   d. propose it

9. The discharge petition is
   a. often used
   b. seldom used
   c. unconstitutional
   d. used only in the Senate

10. Which statement about the House Rules Committee is true?
    a. The House Rules Committee proposes bills.
    b. The House Rules Committee sets all of the rules for the House.
    c. The House Rules Committee sets limits on debate.
    d. all of the above

	a	b	c	d
1	a	b	c	d
2	a	b	c	d
3	a	b	c	d
4	a	b	c	d
5	a	b	c	d
6	a	b	c	d
7	a	b	c	d
8	a	b	c	d
9	a	b	c	d
10	a	b	c	d

Essay Question

Passing a bill is a complex procedure. Why do you think the Framers wanted to make it so difficult to pass a new law?

For use with:	**Chapter 10**	**Congress and the Legislative Branch**
For use with:	**Activity 22**	**Casting Your Vote in Congress**

Objectives

- Review what happens to a bill during debate.
- Explain the purpose of a filibuster and a vote of cloture.
- Identify the difference between a germane amendment and a rider.
- List the three different explanations of how members of Congress vote.

Vocabulary

quorum   filibuster   cloture   germane   rider   gridlock

BACKGROUND

The second part of the legislative process doesn't involve as many different groups as the first, but it does involve both the full House and the full Senate. Everyone in both houses has the chance to review legislation before it is finally sent on to the President. The President has a number of options to complete the process.

The first part of the legislative process features many parallel processes. The same cannot be said for the second part. When the House considers a bill, the first thing its members do is vote on the proposed amendments from the committees. Once that is done, the House adjourns to a subcommittee of the full House, called the Committee of the Whole. The advantage of the Committee of the Whole is that a quorum needs only 100 members. Debate and discussion occur on the bill; amendments can be proposed, but they must be germane. The Committee of the Whole recesses back to the full House once debating time is over. There are four methods for final voting.

The Senate has no Committee of the Whole and no time limit, amendments don't have to be germane, and the chance for a filibuster exists. The Senate debate is open to all, and it allows any amendment to be added to any bill at any time.

If the House and Senate versions of the bill differ, a conference committee works out the differences. Then the bill goes back to each house for one more vote.

Assuming both houses approve the bill, it is sent to the President, who can sign it, allow it to become a law without a signature, veto it (where a two-thirds vote overrides the veto), or "pocket veto" it in the last 10 days of a congressional session.

One of the questions always asked is what influences representatives and senators to vote the way they do. There are three basic types of votes—votes based on party, votes based on constituents, and votes based on personal preference.

Further Resources

C-SPAN (Congressional-Satellite Public Affairs Network).
Cain, Bruce, John Ferejohn, and Morris Fiorina. *The Personal Vote.*
    Cambridge, MA: Harvard University Press, 1987.
Fisher, Louis. *Constitutional Conflicts Between Congress and the President.*
    4th ed. Lawrence, KS: University Press of Kansas, 1997.

For Discussion

Review

1. *What is a filibuster, and why do senators use it?* (A filibuster involves a senator talking non-stop to delay action on some piece of legislation.)

2. *Is it possible to end a filibuster? Explain.* (To end a filibuster, a vote of cloture must pass the Senate. It requires 60 votes to pass.)

3. *What is the difference between a rider and a germane amendment?* (A rider is an amendment in the Senate that has no relation to the substance of the bill; a germane amendment can be added in either house and is related to the subject of the bill.)

4. *What are the three influences on how members of Congress vote?* (Three factors influencing congressional votes are constituents' views, party membership, and personal views.)

Critical Thinking

1. *Why do you think filibusters are not allowed in the House?* (Given the larger membership in the House, filibusters and delays would be too disruptive.)

2. *You either are of voting age or will be soon. Of the three types of influences on congressional votes, which would you want your elected officials to follow?* (Answers will vary, but students should try to explain why they feel the way they do.)

3. *Some political scientists have said the threat of a presidential veto is more effective than a veto. Explain why you agree or disagree with this position.* (The threat of a veto alerts Congress to potential problems and allows time for adjustments that prevent the confrontation a veto often creates.)

4. *"Christmas tree" bills are seen either as wasteful spending or as members of Congress just doing their job, bringing federal money back home. With which view do you most agree, and why?* (Answers will vary.)

Skills Development Activities

1. **WRITING:** Constituents' Views

   Have students pretend they are members of the House of Representatives. They have decided to base their votes on constituents' views. Their task is to find out what their constituents think. Have them write a one- to two-page report on how they would accomplish their task and any problems they might have.

2. **CURRENT EVENTS:** Pork Barrel Legislation

   Have students research recent examples of pork barrel legislation. Have them write a brief summary of what the bill entailed and how much cost was involved. Have students share what they find with the class. The class can vote on the most outlandish.

3. **INTERNET:** Line-Item Veto

   Have students look up the Supreme Court decision in *Clinton v. City of New York* (1998) that nullified the line-item veto. They should write a two-page summary of the case and the basis for the decision. Then discuss how the line-item veto could have helped keep down wasteful spending.

4. **SPECIAL SOURCES:** "Christmas Tree" Bill

   Have students draw their own "Christmas tree" bill political cartoon, placing special ornaments on the tree to represent different types of projects that might be included in a bill like this. Have the students explain their different "ornaments" to the class.

Study Guide

Name: _____

Complete each item as you read Chapter 10 (pages 164–170).

1. For the House or Senate to conduct official business, a _____ must be present.

2. To create a quorum, the House calls a _____ of the _____ .

3. House debate is conducted under strict _____ ; Senate debate has fewer restrictions.

4. Senators sometimes try to "talk a bill to death" by using a _____ .

5. A filibuster can be stopped through _____ .

6. In the House, amendments to a bill must be _____ .

7. In the Senate, nongermane amendments to a bill are called _____ .

8. What four voting options on a bill do representatives and senators have? _____ ; _____ ; _____ ; _____ .

9. When enough riders are attached to a bill in the Senate, the bill is called a " _____ " bill.

10. _____ is said to have occurred when disagreements between the Congress and the President result in little or no action.

Vocabulary

Read each description, and write the letter of the correct term on the line.

1. _____ Presence of a sufficient number to conduct business

2. _____ "Talking a bill to death" in the Senate

3. _____ Procedure for ending a filibuster

4. _____ Relevant

5. _____ Amendment irrelevant to the purpose of a bill

6. _____ Conflict between the legislative and executive branches that commonly results in inaction

a cloture
b filibuster
c germane
d gridlock
e quorum
f rider

Multiple-Choice Test

Name: _____

Find the best answer for each item. Then completely fill in the circle for that answer.

1. Which term means a sufficient number of House or Senate members are present to conduct business?
   - **a.** cloture
   - **b.** constituent
   - **c.** filibuster
   - **d.** quorum

2. A filibuster can occur
   - **a.** in the Senate
   - **b.** in the House
   - **c.** in a Committee of the Whole
   - **d.** in all of the above

3. What is cloture?
   - **a.** a way to start gridlock
   - **b.** a way to exchange political favors
   - **c.** a way to call a quorum
   - **d.** a way to end a filibuster

4. In the House, amendments must be _____; in the Senate, many amendments are _____.
   - **a.** constituent; filibusters
   - **b.** filibustered, quorums
   - **c.** germane, riders
   - **d.** logrolled, riders

5. Members of Congress can
   - **a.** kill a bill
   - **b.** amend a bill
   - **c.** pass a bill
   - **d.** any of the above

6. When a bill has many riders, what is it called?
   - **a.** a "Christmas tree" bill
   - **b.** a rider bill
   - **c.** a logrolling bill
   - **d.** a pork barrel bill

7. Different versions of House and Senate bills are resolved through
   - **a.** the Committee of the Whole
   - **b.** a conference committee
   - **c.** a pocket veto
   - **d.** presidential action

8. Which statement is true?
   - **a.** Congress can override a veto.
   - **b.** A veto kills a bill forever.
   - **c.** The President no longer has the power of veto.
   - **d.** Vetoes are a way to end gridlock.

9. Members of Congress vote with their party _____ of the time.
   - **a.** almost none
   - **b.** some
   - **c.** most
   - **d.** all

10. What term refers to legislation created chiefly to bring benefits to a lawmaker's home district and constituents?
    - **a.** logrolling legislation
    - **b.** pork barrel legislation
    - **c.** home legislation
    - **d.** benefit legislation

1	a	b	c	d
2	a	b	c	d
3	a	b	c	d
4	a	b	c	d
5	a	b	c	d
6	a	b	c	d
7	a	b	c	d
8	a	b	c	d
9	a	b	c	d
10	a	b	c	d

Essay Question

Explain how the veto is related to the system of checks and balances.

For use with:	**Chapter 10**	**Congress and the Legislative Branch**
For use with:	**Activity 23**	**Congressional Term Limits**

Objectives

- Identify both sides of the three controversial issues described.
- Explain why incumbents are so often re-elected.
- Analyze recent Supreme Court decisions concerning gerrymandering.

Vocabulary

seniority system   malapportionment   gerrymandering

BACKGROUND

The U.S. public has never understood its Congress very well. It has been full of "those politicians in Washington," who go about making decisions for the rest of us! We have never thought much of Congress as a whole, but strangely enough we keep re-electing our representatives because we know they are doing their absolute best to fix things. Given how popular "our" representative is, there must be some explanation of why Congress as a group is looked down upon. The last section of this chapter provides three explanations (and perhaps there is a fourth) for why Congress is not viewed favorably. These include the seniority system, incumbency and term limits, and apportionment. A fourth factor that could be considered is congressional ethics, or perhaps the lack thereof.

The seniority system has both good and bad points. On the positive side, the system rewards longevity and expertise that should come with years of service. On the down side, if chair positions are automatically awarded, it breeds invincibility and arrogance, which is why

seniority is no longer the guaranteed road to those positions. Another concern is that those who have been in Congress the longest may be least in touch with the people they serve.

As the chart on page 173 indicates, the second factor, incumbency and term limits, is a double-edged sword. Term limits would offer advantages and alleviate some concerns. Incumbents clearly have a huge electoral edge, and that is not likely to change as long as the incumbents are making the rules.

Malapportionment and gerrymandering are not as much a congressional issue as a state issue, but the related problems still seem to reflect poorly on Congress. Any time an advantage is gained, the disadvantaged will find someone to blame.

One final "black eye" to Congress has been the periodic ethics violations in which members have been involved. Writing bad checks, taking bribes, and bending the rules on outside income are only a few of the problems members have had in recent years.

Further Resources

Burke, Christopher M. *The Appearance of Equality: Racial Gerrymandering, Redistricting, and the Supreme Court.* Westport, CT: Greenwood Press, 1999.

Caro, Robert. *Path to Power.* New York: Alfred Knopf, 1982.

Grofman, Bernard, ed. *Legislative Term Limits: Public Choice Perspectives.* Boston: Kluwer Academic Publishers, 1996.

For Discussion

Review

1. *What are the three controversial issues that affect the public's perception of Congress?* (The three controversial issues are seniority, incumbency and term limits, and apportionment.)

2. *What is the seniority system?* (The seniority system is a congressional tradition in which the majority member with the longest continuous service on a committee is automatically given the chair position. This is no longer guaranteed.)

3. *How would you define gerrymandering?* (Gerrymandering is the process of dividing voting districts to give an unfair advantage to one candidate, party, or group.)

4. *Who was Elbridge Gerry?* (He was the early governor of Massachusetts who redrew legislative districts to favor the Democratic-Republicans.)

Critical Thinking

1. *Do you think Congress has been seen negatively over the years?* (Answers will vary.)

2. *Why do you think the seniority system went unchallenged for so long?* (As long as the system was in place, chairmen were kings in their own kingdom [their committee]. Since many hoped one day to become a chair, no one challenged this power for many years.)

3. *Why do you think term limits have such wide support in the general public and are so opposed by those in Congress?* (Outsiders see the benefits of a more responsive Congress that pays more attention to constituents, while insiders see term limits as forcing the best and most experienced members to step aside, which will increase the inefficiency of the organization.)

Skills Development Activities

1. **WRITING:** Presidential Commission

   Have students pretend that they have been appointed to a special presidential commission that is charged with fixing one problem of Congress. You can either assign issues to groups or let each group choose its own, so long as they are different. Each group must come up with three solutions and a benefit from each solution. Have groups of three or four present their recommendations to the class.

2. **CURRENT EVENTS:** Scandals and Ethics

   Have students research recent congressional scandals and/or ethics violations. Students should find reports of misconduct and write a newspaper story that summarizes what happened and the outcome. Use the stories to start a discussion on congressional ethics.

3. **INTERNET:** Incumbents

   Have students find results for incumbents over the last ten congressional elections. Have them make a chart that shows the electoral success of incumbents and then have them include one paragraph that explains why this percentage is so high.

4. **SPECIAL SOURCES:** Civics Lesson

   Have students work in pairs to analyze the cartoon on page 172. Ask each group to create a one-sentence statement of the message of the cartoon. After students share their statements, discuss why some interpretations might differ from others.

Study Guide

Name: _____

Complete each item as you read Chapter 10 (pages 171–175).

1. The chairmanship of congressional committees is based on the _____.

2. Voters tend to re-elect _____.

3. Incumbency became the rule, rather than the exception, in the _____.

4. Incumbents have the advantages of getting more donations from _____ than challengers and of widespread _____ among voters.

5. Restricting the number of terms representatives can serve is called _____.

6. _____ results from creating districts of unequal size.

7. The creation of oddly shaped districts give one party an advantage is called _____.

8. Creating political districts to increase the influence of minorities is called _____.

Vocabulary

Read each description, and write the letter of the correct term on the line.

1. _____ Congressional tradition of giving committee chairmanships to the longest-serving members

2. _____ Distribution of representatives among congressional districts that is unequal proportionally to the population

3. _____ Creating illogically shaped districts to give one party an advantage

a	gerrymandering
b	malapportionment
c	seniority system

Multiple-Choice Test

Name: _____

Find the best answer for each item. Then completely fill in the circle for that answer.

1. What factor determines who will get a committee chairmanship in Congress?
   a. expertise on the committee's purpose
   b. the number of years served
   c. the number of popular votes won
   d. the number of congressional votes won

2. The seniority system exists
   a. in the House
   b. in the Senate
   c. in both the House and Senate
   d. in neither the House nor Senate

3. Incumbents are re-elected _____ of the time.
   a. none
   b. some
   c. most
   d. all

4. What advantages do incumbents have over challengers?
   a. fund-raising ability
   b. name recognition
   c. the ability to logroll and add pork
   d. all of the above

5. Which is a common argument AGAINST term limits?
   a. Term limits keep competent people out of office.
   b. Term limits maintain democracy.
   c. Term limits are unconstitutional.
   d. Term limits reinvigorate Congress.

6. Districts of unequal size are a result of
   a. term limits
   b. the seniority system
   c. incumbency
   d. malapportionment

7. What is the origin of the term *gerrymandering*?
   a. It comes from an old Latin word.
   b. It comes from the debate over term limits.
   c. It comes from a resolution of Congress.
   d. It comes from the name of a governor.

8. What is the meaning of the term *gerrymandering*?
   a. maintaining incumbency by banning term limits
   b. assigning committee chairmanships based on seniority
   c. redrawing districts to increase minority participation
   d. creating oddly shaped districts to gain political advantage

9. The Supreme Court addressed malapportionment and gerrymandering in the "one man, one vote" case of
   a. *Shaw v. Reno*
   b. *Wesberry v. Sanders*
   c. *Bush v. Vera*
   d. *McCulloch v. Maryland*

10. Which term refers to reapportioning districts to increase the political power of minorities?
    a. racial polling
    b. racial gerrymandering
    c. malapportioning
    d. incumbency

	a	b	c	d
1	a	b	c	d
2	a	b	c	d
3	a	b	c	d
4	a	b	c	d
5	a	b	c	d
6	a	b	c	d
7	a	b	c	d
8	a	b	c	d
9	a	b	c	d
10	a	b	c	d

Essay Question

Explain how pork barrel legislation might be related to the drive to set term limits.

For use with:	**Chapter 11**	**The Presidency**
For use with:	**Activity 24**	**Questioning the Electoral College**

Objectives

- Identify the constitutional qualifications for becoming President of the United States.
- Define and identify the reasons for the existence of the electoral college.
- Explain the pay and benefits the President receives.

Vocabulary

elector   electoral college   electoral vote

BACKGROUND

When the Founders of the United States were writing the Constitution, they wanted to avoid the problems of a weak executive that had occurred with the Articles of Confederation. They wished to create a strong executive, but not so strong that such a person would gain dictatorial powers and thwart the "consent of the governed" outlined in the Declaration of Independence.

At the same time, the authors of the Constitution wished to avoid demagoguery, which they feared might develop if the people directly elected the head of the executive branch of the government. So they invented the electoral college.

The college was designed to allow more reasoned heads the time to reflect and to elect a President indirectly. Thus, so the reasoning went, the dangers of a "mobocracy" could be avoided, and the government could exist under another check on the directly elected lower house—the House of Representatives.

However, the role the President would eventually assume was unclear, as is evidenced by the brevity of Article II in the Constitution. As history records, the electoral college has often been in contention as an institution. Also, the person who has held the office of the presidency has often determined the way it is perceived by the people and the system. Sometimes Congress seems to have more power; at other times the presidency holds sway.

Certainly in times of crisis, the individual occupying the presidency, whether Abraham Lincoln or Franklin Roosevelt, has helped define the office. When a Warren G. Harding or a Ulysses S. Grant becomes President, Congress seems to have the upper hand.

However, the power of the office comes from the people and provides the focal point for national leadership. Citizens view the President as theirs, warts and all. Therein may lie the real power and effectiveness of the presidency.

Further Resources

Barber, James David. *The Presidential Character.* 3rd ed. Englewood Cliffs, NJ: Prentice-Hall, 1985.

Burns, James Macgregor. *Roosevelt: The Lion and the Fox.* New York: Harcourt Brace, 1956.

Jackson, John S., and William Crotty. *The Politics of Presidential Selection.* New York: Longman, 1996.

The White House.
http://www2.whitehouse.gov/WH/Welcome.html

For Discussion

Review

1. *What qualifications does a person have to meet in order to become President of the United States?* (He or she must be 35 years of age, a natural-born citizen, and a resident of the United States for at least 14 years.)

2. *What are some of the benefits a person can receive by becoming President of the United States?* (They include a salary of $200,000 per year, a private plane, and excellent health care.)

3. *What limitations exist on how long a President may serve?* (Due to the 22nd Amendment, a President may serve only two terms and a portion of another term.)

4. *Who won the presidency in the critical election of 1800?* (Thomas Jefferson became President.)

Critical Thinking

1. *Why do you think that the 22nd Amendment, limiting the number of presidential terms, was added to the Constitution?* (It was added because the Republicans feared the advent of another Franklin Roosevelt, who was elected to four terms.)

2. *Why do you think that a person who becomes President must be at least 35 years old when people as young as 18 may vote to elect the President?* (One argument may be the value of maturity and experience; another may focus on a potential distrust of youth.)

3. *Do you believe, as many do, that an amendment should be added to the Constitution to eliminate the electoral college so that we may directly elect our Presidents? Why or why not?* (Encourage the students to answer this question using specific supporting evidence.)

4. *Congress periodically considers raising the President's salary. Do you think he should be given more money?* (Have students consider the CEO chart on page 180 before they answer.)

Skills Development Activities

1. **WRITING:** Honor and Responsibility

   Have students write a paragraph in response to William McKinley's quote (page 179) about the honor and responsibility of the presidency. Ask them to clarify what McKinley might have meant.

2. **CURRENT EVENTS:** Presidential Candidates

   Ask students to find articles about recent or potential candidates for President (such as George W. Bush, Steve Forbes, Elizabeth Dole, Al Gore, Bill Bradley, or Ross Perot). Help students offer and then evaluate generalizations about education and previous experience of presidential candidates.

3. **INTERNET:** Chief Executives

   Encourage students to use Web sites to locate data about the personal and political backgrounds of one or more heads of government in such countries as the United Kingdom and France. Ask them to compare these backgrounds with several past Presidents of the United States and to present their findings to the class.

4. **SPECIAL SOURCES:** The Election of 1960

   Have students locate a map showing the electoral vote results of the 1960 Nixon-Kennedy election. Ask them to prepare a chart to show how many states each man carried.

Study Guide

Name: _____

Answer each question as you reach Chapter 11 (pages 176–186)

1. To be President, a person must be a _____ citizen, have lived in the United States at least _____ years, and be at least _____ years old.

2. The President serves a _____-year term. He or she may serve a maximum of _____ full terms.

3. What annual salary does the President earn? _____

4. _____ suggested the electoral college in 1787.

5. Members of the electoral college are called _____.

6. Originally, the Constitution required that the person receiving the most electoral votes would become _____, while the person with the second-most votes would become _____.

7. In 1804 the _____ Amendment changed the electoral college so that _____ cast separate ballots for _____ and _____.

8. Voters don't vote for the President directly; they actually vote for _____.

9. To become President, a candidate must have at least _____ electoral votes.

10. Two criticisms of the electoral college are that the division of votes among the _____ is not fair; and, most seriously, that the electoral college might not elect as President the person who won the _____ vote.

Vocabulary

Read each description, and write the letter of the correct term on the line.

1. _____ A member of the electoral college

2. _____ Group of people selected in each state to formally cast the votes for President and Vice President

3. _____ Vote cast for President and Vice President by the electoral college

a	elector
b	electoral college
c	electoral vote

Multiple-Choice Test　　　　　　　　　　**Name:** _____

Find the best answer for each item. Then completely fill in the circle for that answer.

1. What is the length of the presidential term?

   a. 2 years　　　　　　　**c.** 6 years

   b. 4 years　　　　　　　**d.** 8 years

2. To become President, a person must be all of the following EXCEPT

   a. 35 years old　　　　　**c.** a resident of the United States at least 14 years

   b. a natural-born citizen of the United States　　**d.** an elector

3. The 22nd Amendment limits a President to _____ term(s).

   a. one　　　　　　　　　**c.** three

   b. two　　　　　　　　　**d.** four

4. The President is elected by

   a. the House of Representatives　　**c.** the electoral college

   b. the Senate　　　　　　**d.** the popular vote

5. Originally, the person receiving the second-highest number of electoral votes became the

   a. President　　　　　　**c.** elector

   b. Vice President　　　　**d.** secretary of state

6. The total number of electors is based on

   a. the total number of members of Congress　　**c.** the total number of candidates for President

   b. the population of the United States　　**d.** the total electoral vote

7. Today, the President and the Vice President are selected on separate ballots. This is a result of

   a. the election of 1800　　**c.** Aaron Burr's death

   b. the election of 1808　　**d.** a joint resolution

8. To win a presidential or vice presidential election, a candidate must win

   a. a majority of the electoral votes　　**c.** a majority of the popular vote

   b. all of the electoral votes　　**d.** all of the popular vote

9. "A presidential candidate who won the popular vote won the electoral vote." This statement is

   a. always true　　　　　**c.** sometimes true and sometimes false

   b. always false　　　　　**d.** part of the 12th Amendment

10. The electoral college has how many total votes?

    a. 100　　　　　　　　**c.** 695

    b. 538　　　　　　　　**d.** none of the above

1	a	b	c	d
2	a	b	c	d
3	a	b	c	d
4	a	b	c	d
5	a	b	c	d
6	a	b	c	d
7	a	b	c	d
8	a	b	c	d
9	a	b	c	d
10	a	b	c	d

Essay Question

Should the President be elected through a direct, popular vote, instead of through the electoral college? Identify the main flaws of the electoral college in your answer.

For use with:	**Chapter 11**	**The Presidency**
For use with:	**Activity 25**	**Choosing the Vice President**

Objectives

- Outline and describe the process and personnel in presidential succession.
- Describe the role played by the Vice President, both constitutionally and in practice.
- Analyze contributions, using examples, made by Vice Presidents during the course of American history.

Vocabulary

presidential succession   cabinet   administration

BACKGROUND

People have often asked just what it is that the Vice President of the United States actually does. The role is certainly secondary to the President's. When John Nance Garner, a Vice President from Texas during the Great Depression, purportedly stated that the vice presidency "wasn't worth a warm bucket of spit," few disagreed.

Many Presidents have failed to include their Vice Presidents in the most basic workings of their administrations. When Vice President Harry Truman was forced into the presidency upon the death of Roosevelt in 1945, he knew little or nothing about the inside administrative operations of the war and certainly nothing about the development of the atomic bomb.

However, with Truman, the nation was lucky. Even though he was an "accidental" President, he was up to the task of ending U.S. involvement in World War II. In fact, today many historians rate him as one of our best Presidents. Often Vice Presidents are chosen to balance the party's ticket for either regional or ideological purposes, or both.

During the latter half of the twentieth century, Presidents have had their Vice Presidents play more active roles in governing. When Dwight Eisenhower sent Vice President Richard Nixon to South America and to the Soviet Union during the 1950s, he used Nixon as a representative of the administration in more than just a symbolic role. When Jimmy Carter included Vice President Walter Mondale in cabinet and Security Council meetings, he relied on Mondale to provide him with sound advice. And finally, when Bill Clinton assigned Vice President Al Gore to develop an environmental plan for the administration and to work on eliminating waste in the bureaucracy, he gave Gore greater responsibility than the vast majority of Vice Presidents have had throughout history.

Certainly, as the role of the Vice President gains in prestige and substance, more qualified people will wish to seek the office. While its constitutional powers are limited, its potential for responsibility is great.

Further Resources

George, Alexander. "Assessing Presidential Character." *World Politics* 26 (January 1974):10–30.

Neustadt, Richard E. *Presidential Power and Modern Presidents.* New York: Free Press, 1990.

For Discussion

Review

1. *If the President dies while in office, what is the official order of succession to become President?* (It progresses from the Vice President to the Speaker of the House, to the president *pro tempore* of the Senate, and then to the cabinet members in order of the seniority of the department.)

2. *What is supposed to occur if the President becomes severely disabled while in office?* (Encourage students to carefully examine the 25th Amendment to the Constitution.)

3. *What are the official constitutional duties of the Vice Presidents?* (They are assigned to preside over the Senate, to assume the duties of the President should he or she leave office, and to help decide about the President's disability.)

4. *What are some of the roles played by Vice Presidents other than the assigned constitutional ones?* (Vice Presidents have worked as official representatives of Presidents, have acted as confidants, and have performed specifically assigned tasks important to various administrations.)

Critical Thinking

1. *Why do you think that the Speaker of the House and the president* pro tempore *of the Senate were chosen in the line of presidential succession?* (They are elected officials, although not by the entire nation.)

2. *Why do you think that many potential candidates for Vice President have chosen not to run for the office?* (Even though several former Vice Presidents have become President, the office has historically been viewed as a dead end for many politicians.)

3. *If you were a presidential candidate faced with choosing a vice presidential running mate, what are some of the personal and professional qualities you would look for before making your selection?* (Encourage students to examine the qualities they would wish for in a President and perhaps those of successful past Vice Presidents who have become President.)

Skills Development Activities

1. **WRITING:** Vice Presidents

Ask students to do some research before writing a short position paper naming the five best Vice Presidents in U.S. history. Have them debate their choices with others in the class.

2. **CURRENT EVENTS:** Vice-Presidential Roles

Have students use a newspaper or a news magazine to search for articles about the recent activities of the current Vice President. Have these articles copied and place several on display in the classroom.

3. **INTERNET:** Women Candidates

Have students search for Web sites about women who have been put forward as potential presidential candidates or vice-presidential candidates (such as Elizabeth Dole and Dianne Feinstein). Ask them to assess the chances of these women becoming either President or Vice President.

4. **SPECIAL SOURCES:** Vice-Presidential Cartoons

Ask students to use the Internet, the *Reader's Guide,* or possibly their librarian's clippings file to locate one or more cartoons addressing the vice presidency. Have them present their cartoons to the class and explain their messages.

Study Guide

Name: _____

Complete each item as you read Chapter 11 (pages 186–190).

1. There are four ways in which the presidency may be vacated: by _____ , _____ , _____ , or _____ .

2. The order in which a presidential vacancy is filled is _____ .

3. The order of presidential succession was established by the 1947 _____ .

4. The order of presidential succession is as follows: 1) _____ ;
   2) _____ ;
   3) _____ of the Senate;
   4) _____ ;
   and 5) other members of the President's _____ , according to seniority.

5. The _____ provides for filling a vacancy in the vice presidency.

6. If both the presidency and vice presidency are vacant at the same time, who becomes President? The

   _____

   Who becomes Vice President? The _____

   _____

7. According to the Constitution, the Vice President has but two duties: One is to preside over the

   _____ ; the other is to help decide questions of _____ .

Vocabulary

Read each description, and write the letter of the correct term on the line.

1. _____ The procedure by which a vacancy in the presidency is filled

2. _____ The heads of the executive departments in their capacity as advisers to the President

3. _____ The executive branch

a	administration
b	cabinet
c	presidential succession

Multiple-Choice Test

Name: _____

Find the best answer for each item. Then completely fill in the circle for that answer.

1. Which of the following results in a vacancy in the presidency?

   a. disability

   b. resignation

   c. impeachment

   d. all of the above

2. When did the practice of vice presidential succession begin?

   a. 1789

   b. 1841

   c. 1947

   d. 1967

3. The order of presidential succession was established by

   a. a law

   b. tradition

   c. the original constitution

   d. a constitutional amendment

4. Who is SECOND in the order of presidential succession?

   a. the president *pro tempore* of the Senate

   b. the Vice President

   c. the Speaker of the House

   d. the secretary of state

5. How many times in history has the United States had no Vice President?

   a. 8

   b. 2

   c. 19

   d. 0

6. The 25th Amendment concerns what?

   a. the order of presidential succession

   b. vacancies in the vice presidency

   c. the establishment of the cabinet

   d. all of the above

7. Who can declare the President unable to fulfill presidential duties?

   a. the Vice President alone

   b. the Vice President and a majority of Congress

   c. the president *pro tempore* of the Senate

   d. a majority of the President's cabinet

8. The administration is people and organizations that make up the

   a. cabinet

   b. federal government

   c. executive branch

   d. legislative branch

9. Which of the following is a constitutional duty of the Vice President?

   a. to consult with the President

   b. to preside over the Senate

   c. to head up commissions

   d. to lead the cabinet

10. Who or what called the vice presidency "the most insignificant office" ever devised?

    a. the 25th Amendment

    b. the Presidential Succession Act

    c. John Adams

    d. Gerald Ford

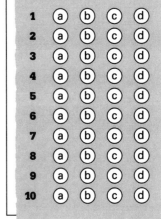

Essay Question

Do you think the Vice President should have more power? Why or why not?

For use with:	**Chapter 11**	**The Presidency**
For use with:	Activity 26	**Preparing the State of the Union Address**

Objectives

- Identify and define the major constitutional powers assigned to the President of the United States.
- Explain the War Powers Act.
- Explain the President's veto power.

Vocabulary

legislative veto   treaty   executive agreement   executive order

BACKGROUND

Many nations separate the office of the Head of State from the office of the Head of Government, for the official holding each office is expected to perform different duties. For example, the Head of State in most countries performs most of the ceremonial functions within the country and usually represents the country in symbolic and ceremonial ways in foreign lands. In the United Kingdom, the Queen performs as Head of State and the Prime Minister performs as Head of Government. Recently this distinction has been blurring.

In the United States, the President has always held the official roles of both Head of State and Head of Government. His constitutional duties prescribe such roles. The President may assign specific duties to the Vice President or to a member of the cabinet, but the individuals who gain such assignments are representing the President.

In defining both roles, Presidents have had greater or lesser success. Still, people in the United States often see their President as the embodiment of the nation. He (or she) is our President. We can criticize him, we can even denigrate him, but he is our President and he represents us.

When "our" President is at his best, he leads us through inspiration and persuades us that we are, or can be, the best nation in the world. Even at times in history when the Congress appeared to have more power than the executive, the President was still the President and something special—our elected and chosen leader.

Some scholars and politicians believe that the presidency of the late twentieth century has become an "imperial presidency"—one with too much power and too little accountability. Perhaps. However, the resignation of Richard Nixon in 1974 and the impeachment of Bill Clinton in 1998 should lay to rest the idea that the President can act with impunity or that his power is so great that he is above criticism. True, he holds the offices of Head of Government and of Head of State of currently the most powerful nation on Earth. Thanks to our Constitution and to our ability to operate the system created by the Constitution, that power is far from unchecked.

Further Resources

Blumenthal, Sidney. "Marketing the President." *New York Times Magazine,* 13 Sept. 1981, 110–111.

Burke, John P. *The Institutional Presidency.* Baltimore: Johns Hopkins University Press, 1992.

Schlesinger, Arthur. *The Imperial Presidency.* Boston: Houghton Mifflin, 1973.

For Discussion

Review

1. *What are three of the major powers assigned to the presidency by the Constitution?* (They include chief legislator, chief negotiator, chief executive, and commander in chief.)

2. *What is the major constitutional check on Congress provided for the President, and how does it work?* (It is the veto, and it provides the President with a great deal of input over many kinds of legislation.)

3. *What is a legislative veto?* (It is the power of Congress to void an action of the executive branch.)

4. *What is an example of a President's legislative powers?* (Answers may include veto power or calling special sessions.)

Critical Thinking

1. *Why do you think that the authors of the Constitution did not define the President's "executive power" more specifically?* (Help students to think about the Elastic Clause as they answer.)

2. *Do you think that the President's constitutional role as commander in chief gives the President too much power? Why or why not?* (Encourage students to consider how Presidents have used this power and to examine the timeline on pages 194 and 195.)

3. *Do you think that Presidents really need to claim the power of executive privilege? Why or why not?* (Have students consider the appropriate need for confidentiality in the executive. You may wish to have them debate this question.)

4. *Which presidential power do you believe is the most important for the presidency and for the nation?* (Encourage students to examine the powers in depth and to imagine what might happen if the President lost some of them.)

Skills Development Activities

1. **WRITING**: Presidential Appointments

   Have students research one of the well-publicized appointments described on page 198. Ask students to write a two-page essay explaining why the appointment was so controversial.

2. **CURRENT EVENTS**: Presidential Performance

   Ask students to locate and present to the class one or more public opinion polls that show a rating of the President's performance during the past 2 months.

3. **INTERNET**: Military Power

   Have students use one or more of the White House URLs to locate a Web site showing ways that the President has used his power as commander in chief during the past year. Ask them to present their findings to the class.

4. **SPECIAL SOURCES**: Presidential Veto Power

   Have students create a graph to show how various Presidents have used vetoes over the years. They can use the chart on pages 200–201, but encourage them to do additional research.

Study Guide

Name: _____

Complete each item as you read Chapter 11 (pages 191–201).

1. The constitutional powers of the presidency are described in Article _____ of the Constitution.

2. The President is _____ of the armed forces.

3. The _____ limits the amount of time a President can commit U.S. troops without congressional approval.

4. The President is the country's chief _____, or negotiator with other countries.

5. All _____ negotiated by the President with other countries must be approved by the Senate.

6. The President has the power to enter into _____, which are pacts between heads of state.

7. Presidential directives called _____ have the force of law.

8. The President can grant _____ and _____ to federal criminals.

9. The President is required to deliver a _____ message to Congress "from time to time."

10. A President can _____, or reject, any bill passed by Congress.

Vocabulary

Read each description, and write the letter of the correct term on the line.

1. _____ The power of Congress to void executive branch actions

2. _____ A formal agreement between nations

3. _____ An agreement between the President and another head of state

4. _____ Directive issued by the President that defines new policies or carries out existing laws

a	executive agreement
b	executive order
c	legislative veto
d	treaty

Multiple-Choice Test   Name: _____

Find the best answer for each item. Then completely fill in the circle for that answer.

1. The power to authorize money for military forces is given to
   a. the President
   b. Congress
   c. the cabinet
   d. all of the above

2. What did the War Powers Act overturn?
   a. presidential leadership of the armed forces
   b. the Gulf of Tonkin Resolution
   c. Article II of the Constitution
   d. the legislative veto

3. Any treaty negotiated by the President must be confirmed by
   a. the Congress
   b. the secretary of state
   c. the House of Representatives
   d. the Senate

4. The Congress voids a presidential action. What is this called?
   a. advice and consent
   b. a line-item veto
   c. a legislative veto
   d. a pocket veto

5. The President has the power to enter into an executive agreement with
   a. the House of Representatives
   b. the Senate
   c. the people of the U.S.
   d. other heads of state

6. An executive order is most similar to what?
   a. a treaty
   b. a law
   c. an executive agreement
   d. a pardon

7. A person who is convicted of a federal crime can permanently escape penalties if the President grants
   a. a pardon
   b. amnesty
   c. a reprieve
   d. an executive order

8. How often does the Constitution say the President must report on the state of the Union?
   a. every month
   b. every year
   c. after each general election
   d. from time to time

9. The President refuses to sign a bill passed by the legislative branch. What is this called?
   a. an executive order
   b. a legislative veto
   c. a line-item veto
   d. a veto

10. The Supreme Court ruled that the line-item veto is
    a. required by the Constitution
    b. the legal equivalent of an executive order
    c. unconstitutional
    d. a power of the President as commander in chief

1	a b c d
2	a b c d
3	a b c d
4	a b c d
5	a b c d
6	a b c d
7	a b c d
8	a b c d
9	a b c d
10	a b c d

Essay Question

Do you think the Congress should have less power and the President more power? Explain your answer.

For use with: | **Chapter 11** | **The Presidency**

For use with: | **Activity 27** | **The Press and the President**

Objectives

- List and describe the evolutionary nature of presidential powers.
- Define and apply such terms as *impoundment, executive privilege,* and *powers of persuasion* to the evolution of presidential powers.
- Analyze the ways in which Presidents use the media and develop different leadership styles.

Vocabulary

executive privilege   impoundment   bipartisan

BACKGROUND

During the twentieth century, the American presidency has undergone profound changes. Except for the tenure of Abraham Lincoln, no eighteenth- or nineteenth-century President has held as much power as many of those who served during the twentieth century. In fact, it can be argued that no Presidents in U.S. history have held as much potential power in their hands as those who succeeded Herbert Hoover.

Some of these powers have come, of course, from the greatly expanded powers of the U.S. military. Since World War II, the United States has been one of, if not the, preeminent military power in the world. However, many of these powers have been assumed as Presidents have learned to use the mass media effectively. The President's potential powers of persuasion are second to none.

Some White House occupants have been more effective in their use of the media than others. Most observers and political pundits agree that both Ronald Reagan and Bill Clinton have been the most effective Presidents in history at using the media to rally U.S. citizens around whatever cause each happened to espouse. And even if people failed to support a particular presidential proposal, they still tended to rally around the individual.

Much of this effectiveness depends on the particular style of the President. Many people remember the time during the 1972 presidential debates when President George Bush glanced at his watch while candidate Bill Clinton talked to the audience in a seemingly personal way. Bush certainly came across as impatient, while Clinton appeared to care.

How effective Presidents will be depends upon how well they communicate with the people in the United States and how well they are willing to make hard decisions. Presidential style—press conferences, photo ops, and sound bites—goes a long way toward helping a President make such decisions and then selling them to an often skeptical public.

Further Resources

Edwards III, George C. *Presidential Approval.* Baltimore: Johns Hopkins University Press, 1990.

Thomas, Norman C., and James A. Pika. *The Politics of the Presidency.* Washington, DC: Congressional Quarterly Press, 1996.

Wills, Garry. *The Kennedy Imprisonment.* Boston: Atlantic-Little, Brown, 1982.

For Discussion

Review

1. **On what basis does the concept of executive privilege rest?** (It rests mainly on the Constitution's principle of separation of powers.)

2. **What do people mean when they refer to "presidential impoundment"?** (They mean the refusal of the President to spend monies appropriated by Congress.)

3. **What do we mean when we refer to "presidential style"?** (We refer to the way Presidents relate to the public and to the media and to such things as frequency of public appearances and leadership qualities.)

4. **Why do Presidents hold press conferences?** (They want to gain media attention and to attempt to build bipartisan support for policies they favor.)

Critical Thinking

1. **Do you think that news leaks by administration officials—sometimes the President—are appropriate in a democratic society? Why or why not?** (Encourage students to think about attribution and about fairness as they develop their answers.)

2. **Do you think that the use of sound bites endangers the flow of information in a democratic society? Why or why not?** (Have students consider accessibility to the media and the costs versus the attention needed to gain all the necessary information to make an intelligent decision.)

3. **Which twentieth-century Presidents do you think have been the most effective leaders?** (Have students consider the criteria for effective leadership listed on page 209.)

4. **Do you agree with Woodrow Wilson's statement (page 209) about a President's sympathy?** (As students respond, encourage them to discuss particular Presidents.)

Skills Development Activities

1. **WRITING: Executive Privilege**

   Have students write short position papers defending or critiquing presidential use of executive privilege.

2. **CURRENT EVENTS: Sound Bites and Photo Ops**

   Have students view current television news programs to locate evidence of the presidential use of sound bites and/or photo ops. If appropriate, encourage them to videotape their findings to present to the class.

3. **INTERNET: First Lady**

   Have the students visit a Web site such as www2.whitehouse.gov/WH/EOP/First_Lady/html/talking.html/ to find data about the activities of the First Lady. Encourage them to report their findings to the class.

4. **SPECIAL SOURCES: Presidential Images**

   Have students read the feature on page 206 on "The President in the Movies." Have them view one or more of the films and then critique them for fairness and accuracy. Have them present their findings to the class. If possible, ask students to find and report on a review of the film.

Study Guide

Name: _____

Complete each item as you read Chapter 11 (pages 201–209).

1. Since the Constitution was ratified, four types of powers have strengthened the presidency:

_____, _____,

_____, and _____.

2. President _____ established the President as the chief

economic planner of the country.

3. What law directed the President to submit an annual economic report to Congress and created the Council of

Economic Advisers? _____

4. _____ is the President's right to withhold information from Congress or the courts.

5. Executive privilege was first questioned during the administration of President _____

in 1974.

6. _____ is the refusal of a President to spend money appropriated by Congress.

7. Congress sought to stop presidential impoundment by passing the _____ of 1974.

8. Presidents exercise their power of persuasion through the mass media in five main ways:

_____, _____,

_____, _____,

and _____.

9. The three Presidents who are widely considered "great" are _____,

_____, and _____.

Vocabulary

Read each description, and write the letter of the correct term on the line.

1. _____ The President's right to refuse to supply information to a
court or Congress

2. _____ The President's power to refuse to spend money allocated by Congress

3. _____ Marked by cooperation between the two major political parties

a	bipartisan
b	executive privilege
c	impoundment

Multiple-Choice Test

Name: _____

Find the best answer for each item. Then completely fill in the circle for that answer.

1. Which does NOT identify an "evolutionary power" of the President?
   a. impoundment
   b. executive privilege
   c. commander in chief
   d. economic planning

2. The President is required by _____ to submit an annual economic report to Congress.
   a. the Employment Act of 1946
   b. the Constitution
   c. *The United States v. Nixon*
   d. impoundment

3. When President Richard Nixon froze wages and prices, he was exercising his _____ power.
   a. economic
   b. executive privilege
   c. impoundment
   d. persuasion

4. What weakened executive privilege?
   a. *The United States v. Nixon*
   b. the Employment Act of 1946
   c. bipartisanship
   d. the Federal Reserve Board

5. What issue did the Supreme Court address in *Clinton v. Jones?*
   a. the power of impoundment
   b. executive privilege
   c. presidential–media relations
   d. presidential pay

6. A President refuses to spend money appropriated by Congress. What is this called?
   a. executive privilege
   b. impoundment
   c. a veto
   d. a freeze

7. What is a "leak"?
   a. a news conference
   b. an unofficial statement to the press
   c. a sound bite
   d. a staged media event

8. The first televised presidential debate was between which two candidates?
   a. Kennedy and Eisenhower
   b. Kennedy and Nixon
   c. Nixon and Johnson
   d. none of the above

9. *Bipartisanship* refers to
   a. presidential persuasion
   b. executive privilege
   c. party cooperation
   d. presidential leadership

10. According to most surveys, who is NOT consistently considered a "great" President?
    a. Thomas Jefferson
    b. Abraham Lincoln
    c. Franklin Roosevelt
    d. George Washington

	a	b	c	d
1	a	b	c	d
2	a	b	c	d
3	a	b	c	d
4	a	b	c	d
5	a	b	c	d
6	a	b	c	d
7	a	b	c	d
8	a	b	c	d
9	a	b	c	d
10	a	b	c	d

Essay Question

Compare and contrast the powers a twentieth-century President has with those of a nineteenth-century President.

For use with:	**Chapter 12**	**The Executive Branch and the Bureaucracy**
For use with:	**Activity 28**	**Education: In the Cabinet?**

Objectives

- Define and demonstrate an understanding of bureaucracy.
- Describe the work of the agencies of the EOP.
- Differentiate the two primary roles of Cabinet members.

Vocabulary

bureaucracy   public policy   federal budget

BACKGROUND

When most of us think of the executive branch and the federal bureaucracy, one of two images comes to mind. The most common image is the President. We have always seen that he is chief legislator and that he is also the country's chief law enforcement officer. Richard Neustadt has called the President a "glorified clerk" because he is head of the large federal bureaucracy. He is the boss over all of those bureaucrats.

The other image we have is of a "sea of people" sitting at desks shuffling papers, and doing it all somewhat inefficiently. Bureaucratic errors and excesses tend to make headlines when uncovered, but that "sea of people" really is performing valuable functions. Without those people, social security checks might not be delivered, meat could make it to the public uninspected, and work sites could be dangerous and deadly places to work.

Both images are true. The President, along with a number of other assistants, does make a lot of decisions. He has the advantage of not having to make those decisions all by himself. Going way back to George Washington, who realized the office required more than he was capable of by himself, there have been advisers to help the President. Today there are many groups that surround and advise the President; among those are the Office of Management and Budget (OMB), the National Security Council (NSC), the National Economic Council (NEC), and the White House Office. These organizations are relatively new.

The cabinet currently consists of 14 department heads, each of whom is responsible for bringing the President's point of view to his or her agency or department. The cabinet appointments have become very political over the years, with certain numbers of women or minorities expected to get appointments. Often the President appoints people he doesn't even know but who are friends of friends or recommended by friends. As a result, the cabinet is not as vital to the President as in the past.

Further Resources

Federal World Information Network.
        http://www.fedworld.gov
Reich, Robert B. *Locked in the Cabinet*. New York: Random House, 1998.
Wilson, James Q. *Bureaucracy: What Government Agencies Do and Why They
        Do It*. New York: Basic Books, 1989.

For Discussion

Review

1. *What is a bureaucracy?* (A bureaucracy is a large and complex group of people and agencies whose purpose it is to manage government and implement policy.)

2. *What function does the Office of Management and Budget (OMB) perform?* (OMB works with the President to create a budget for the upcoming fiscal year. This version of the budget contains the President's preferences and is sent to Congress for consideration.)

3. *What are the two primary roles of the President's cabinet?* (The two roles cabinet members play are adviser to the President and head of a government department.)

4. *Besides the heads of the 14 executive departments, what other top officials have sometimes been asked to join a President's cabinet?* (They include the Vice President, the OMB director, the trade representative, the chief of staff, and chief domestic policy adviser.)

Critical Thinking

1. *Where else besides the government do you find bureaucracies?* (Answers will vary. There are lots of possibilities, such as schools and corporations.)

2. *Why do you think it is important for Presidents to have a balanced or diverse cabinet?* (One possible answer is that diverse cabinets may be used to demonstrate to party members faith in the different groups that make up the party's membership.)

3. *Many people believe the National Security Council has replaced the Department of State as the most influential adviser to the President on foreign policy. Why do you think that might have happened?* (Answers may vary, but the Department of State has a multitude of tasks, and its focus is clearly outside the White House. The NSC's only real task is to keep the President informed.)

Skills Development Activities

1. **WRITING:** Bureaucracy

   Bureaucracies are very common in large organizations. Have students pick one bureaucracy—the school or the government—and have them write a one- to two-page essay on what they would change to make that bureaucracy more user-friendly. Remind students to be as specific as possible.

2. **CURRENT EVENTS:** White House Office

   The White House Office is about 400 strong under President Clinton. Have students make a list of the types of jobs these people have. What do they do for the President? They don't need to list 400 jobs, but they should think of the wide range of things a President does.

3. **INTERNET:** The Cabinet

   Have students research one of the cabinet departments and make a two- to three-minute report to the class on what each agency does for the nation and for them. Since there are only 14 cabinet posts, students may have to work in pairs or groups. Ask them to include the name of the current head.

4. **SPECIAL SOURCES:** The EOP

   Have students look over the chart on page 212 of the Executive Office of the President. Then have students pick one of those groups and find information on its recent programs and budget. Ask them to present some of the information to the class in the form of a graph, chart, or table.

Study Guide

Name: _____

Complete each item as you read Chapter 12 (pages 210–222).

1. The executive branch of the federal government consists of the President, the Vice President, the

   _____, the _____ departments, and the

   _____ agencies.

2. Franklin Roosevelt created the _____ in 1939.

3. The largest office in the EOP is the _____.

4. The _____ prepares the federal budget for the coming

   _____.

5. How many executive departments are there? _____

6. The cabinet is made up of the heads of the 14 _____, although other

   officials often join.

7. The head of a cabinet department is called a _____, with the exception of the head

   of the Department of Justice, whose title is _____.

8. The two basic roles of cabinet members are as _____ to the President and as

   _____ of their respective agencies.

9. The first woman cabinet member was appointed in _____.

Vocabulary

Read each description, and write the letter of the correct term on the line.

1. _____ The complex combination of people, procedures, and agencies of the
   federal government

2. _____ All of a government's actions and programs that work toward
   a national goal

3. _____ Document detailing the federal government's income and spending

a	bureaucracy
b	federal budget
c	public policy

Multiple-Choice Test

Name: _____

Find the best answer for each item. Then completely fill in the circle for that answer.

1. What makes up the federal bureaucracy?

   a. officials

   b. procedures

   c. agencies

   d. all of the above

2. Which is NOT a part of the EOP?

   a. the White House Office

   b. the cabinet

   c. the National Security Council

   d. the Office of Management and Budget

3. Which prepares the federal budget?

   a. the NSC

   b. the NEC

   c. the EOP

   d. the OMB

4. What did President Harry Truman create?

   a. the Office of Administration

   b. the National Security Council

   c. the National Economic Council

   d. the White House Office

5. The Office of National Drug Control Policy is part of all of the following EXCEPT

   a. the cabinet

   b. the bureaucracy

   c. the executive branch

   d. the Executive Office of the President

6. How many leaders of executive departments form the cabinet?

   a. 6

   b. 12

   c. 14

   d. 16

7. Who does NOT hold the title of "secretary"?

   a. the head of the Department of State

   b. the head of the Department of the Treasury

   c. the head of the Department of Agriculture

   d. the head of the Department of Justice

8. Which cabinet department protects public lands?

   a. the Department of Agriculture

   b. the Department of Commerce

   c. the Department of Energy

   d. the Department of the Interior

9. Which cabinet department includes the Secret Service?

   a. the Department of the Interior

   b. the Department of State

   c. the Department of Justice

   d. the Department of the Treasury

10. The Department of Defense supervises

    a. the Marine Corps

    b. U.S. embassies

    c. the FBI

    d. all of the above

	a	b	c	d
1	ⓐ	ⓑ	ⓒ	ⓓ
2	ⓐ	ⓑ	ⓒ	ⓓ
3	ⓐ	ⓑ	ⓒ	ⓓ
4	ⓐ	ⓑ	ⓒ	ⓓ
5	ⓐ	ⓑ	ⓒ	ⓓ
6	ⓐ	ⓑ	ⓒ	ⓓ
7	ⓐ	ⓑ	ⓒ	ⓓ
8	ⓐ	ⓑ	ⓒ	ⓓ
9	ⓐ	ⓑ	ⓒ	ⓓ
10	ⓐ	ⓑ	ⓒ	ⓓ

Essay Question

Explain the two, often conflicting, roles of a cabinet member and how those roles can present problems for a President.

For use with:	**Chapter 12**	**The Executive Branch and the Bureaucracy**
For use with:	**Activity 29**	EPA Assessment

Objectives

- Define and give examples of an independent regulatory commission.
- List at least two examples of government corporations.
- Describe an independent executive agency.

Vocabulary

independent regulatory commission   government corporation

independent executive agency

BACKGROUND

Generally when we think of executive departments and agencies, we think immediately of the President's cabinet. Cabinet departments were created to help the President manage and run the country. As the nation became more complicated, additional cabinet posts were added to meet the new demands. At times, however, demands were made on the government that seemed inappropriate for a cabinet-type organization to deal with. Enter the independent agencies.

Independent agencies come in three different flavors: independent regulatory commissions, government corporations, and independent executive agencies. Each has a slightly different function from the other, but all are ultimately tied back to the executive in some manner. Also, the nature of these groups has allowed them to be established with fewer political influences, which explains why they are not "cabinet" agencies.

Independent regulatory commissions regulate different aspects of the nation's economy. They are headed by groups of between 5 and 11 commissioners, who serve long terms (often around 7 years); thus, the influence of politics is minimal. Some examples are the Securities and Exchange Commission, the Federal Trade Commission, and the National Labor Relations Board.

Government corporations are like private corporations, except that they are run by the government. Ideally, these organizations turn a profit, but if they don't, the government will make up the difference to keep them solvent. Some examples of government corporations are the U.S. Postal Service and Amtrak.

Independent executive agencies make up the third type of agency. Their functions are varied and their sizes are too, but each specializes in one area. Some examples of these agencies include the Central Intelligence Agency, the Citizens' Stamp Advisory Committee, and the National Aeronautics and Space Administration (NASA).

Further Resources

Federal World Information Network.
     http://www.fedworld.gov
Heymann, Philip. *The Politics of Public Management.* New Haven: Yale
     University Press, 1988.
Vranich, Joseph. *Derailed: What Went Wrong and What to Do About America's
     Passenger Trains.* New York: St. Martin's Press, 1997.

For Discussion

Review

1. *What is an independent regulatory commission?*
(An independent regulatory commission is a federal agency whose purpose is to protect the public interest.)

2. *What are two examples of government corporations?* (Two examples of government corporations are the U.S. Postal Service and Amtrak.)

3. *How would you describe an independent executive agency?* (These are executive branch agencies outside the cabinet departments that oversee a single area.)

4. *About how many independent agencies has Congress created?* (Congress has created nearly 150.)

Critical Thinking

1. *Why do you think independent regulatory commissioners have unusually long terms?* (The long terms make it more difficult to apply political pressure one way or the other. It also allows the directors to stay for more than one presidential term since their appointments are staggered; thus, the loyalty to one party is diminished.)

2. *Amtrak is a money-losing government corporation. What do you think would happen to rail service if Amtrak was privatized?* (Chances are that unprofitable connections would be ended, which would cost jobs. Prices would probably go up, though quality of service might improve. A final option, of course, is that passenger rail service would go out of existence.)

3. *The C.I.A. has indicated it would not be able to function as well if it were more closely monitored. How much independence should independent agencies be given?* (Encourage students to offer specific reasons or identify possible problems as they formulate their answers.)

Skills Development Activities

1. **WRITING:** Regulatory Commissions

Have students reread the section in the text about regulatory commissions. Then have students write a one- to two-page essay that addresses either of the following statements: "Regulatory commissions are important because . . ." or "Regulatory commissions are not really needed because. . . ." Have students provide specific examples, real or made up, in their essays.

2. **CURRENT EVENTS:** Amtrak

Have students research Amtrak and make a chart of the benefits and drawbacks of privatization, as is being suggested by a number of people in Congress.

3. **INTERNET:** Government Corporations

Have students pick a government corporation and research its activities and history. Ask students to summarize the corporation's mission statement and list a number of specific areas it manages. Have students work in pairs or small groups.

4. **SPECIAL SOURCES:** The National Security Council

Have students find and read Part IV, Section B, of the *Tower Commission Report,* which is the section on "Failure of Responsibility." The National Security Council, though part of the Executive Office of the President, was operating as an independent agency. Have students read the passage and summarize the concerns about how the NSC operated.

Study Guide

Name: _____

Complete each item as you read Chapter 12 (pages 223–224).

1. About how many independent agencies are there? _____

2. Are most independent agencies free from presidential control? _____

3. There are three primary reasons for the existence of independent agencies: 1) They don't fit well within executive _____; 2) they are protected from _____ politics; and 3) they serve as _____ over other parts of the government.

4. The three types of independent agencies are _____ _____, and _____.

5. The ten _____ are independent agencies that police various aspects of the economy.

6. The largest government corporation is the _____.

7. About 60 independent agencies are _____, which are businesses run by the federal government.

Vocabulary

Read each description, and write the letter of the correct term on the line.

1. _____ Independent agency that polices industry and protects the public interest

2. _____ Independent agency that takes the form of a business run by the federal government

3. _____ Independent agency that falls outside of a cabinet department

a	government corporation
b	independent executive agency
c	independent regulatory commission

Multiple-Choice Test

Name: _____

Find the best answer for each item. Then completely fill in the circle for that answer.

1. About how many independent agencies are there?

    a. 20   **c.** 150

    b. 100   **d.** 500

2. Which statement about independent agencies is true?

    a. Some don't fit well within the purposes of particular executive departments.

    b. Some serve as watchdogs for other parts of the government.

    c. Some are independent to protect them from party politics.

    d. all of the above

3. Which is the MOST independent?

    a. independent regulatory commissions

    b. government corporations

    c. independent executive agencies

    d. an executive department

4. How many independent regulatory commissions exist?

    a. 1   **c.** 50

    b. 10   **d.** 150

5. The Federal Trade Commission is an example of

    a. an independent regulatory commission

    b. a government corporation

    c. an independent executive agency

    d. an executive department

6. Which is an independent regulatory commission?

    a. Amtrak

    b. the Central Intelligence Agency

    c. the Securities and Exchange Commission

    d. the National Aeronautics and Space Administration

7. The U.S. Postal Service is an example of

    a. an executive department

    b. a government corporation

    c. an independent regulatory commission

    d. an independent executive agency

8. Which is an independent executive agency?

    a. Amtrak

    b. the U.S. Postal Service

    c. the Federal Trade Commission

    d. the Migratory Bird Conservation Commission

9. About how many government corporations are there?

    a. 20   **c.** 60

    b. 40   **d.** 80

10. The Interstate Commerce Commission is

    a. an independent agency

    b. an independent regulatory commission

    c. an agency of the executive branch

    d. all of the above

	a	b	c	d
1	a	b	c	d
2	a	b	c	d
3	a	b	c	d
4	a	b	c	d
5	a	b	c	d
6	a	b	c	d
7	a	b	c	d
8	a	b	c	d
9	a	b	c	d
10	a	b	c	d

Essay Question

Do you think government corporations that don't make a profit but provide a public service should be abolished? Explain your answer.

For use with:	**Chapter 12**	**The Executive Branch and the Bureaucracy**
For use with:	**Activity 30**	**The Food and Drug Administration**

Objectives

- Trace the development of civil service and give examples of civil service jobs and hiring procedures.
- Explain how an iron triangle works.
- Discuss the various influences on the bureaucracy.

Vocabulary

civil service   bureaucrat   iron triangle

BACKGROUND

So far, most of Chapter 12 has dealt with the big picture of bureaucracy: agencies, commissions, and offices. This section looks at the workers behind the agencies, the bureaucrats themselves.

The federal bureaucracy has undergone a number of changes since the first positions were created in the late 1700s. Those early government workers usually received their jobs through patronage. Patronage was a system in which elected officials appointed their supporters to government jobs. As elected officials changed, so did bureaucrats. Andrew Jackson gave the system a new name—the spoils system—but the practice was the same. The problems with this sort of system were corruption and inefficiency. Since appointments were political and not based on qualifications, more often than not jobs were filled by unqualified workers who were ready to do favors for friends.

All this changed in the 1880s, when President James Garfield, a reformer, was assassi-nated by a dissatisfied office seeker. This event so discredited the spoils system that reform was demanded by all. Congress responded by passing the Pendleton Act, which created the civil service and began the process of testing to find qualified workers for government jobs. Although only 10 percent of government jobs were designated as civil service jobs at the time, over the years that percentage has increased to about 90 percent. Today, civil service is controlled by the Office of Personnel Management (OPM), which administers the tests. There are now protections against using government workers for political advantage (the Hatch Act).

Bureaucrats today have unprecedented responsibility. Congress has found it easier to pass generally worded laws and allow bureaucrats to fill in the details. This has increased the influence of the iron triangles and made bureaucrats key players in the lawmaking process.

Further Resources

Hill, Michael. *The Policy Process in the Modern States.* Englewood Cliffs, NJ: Prentice-Hall, 1998.

Kerwin, Cornelius M. *Rulemaking: How Government Agencies Write Law and Make Policies.* Washington, DC: Congressional Quarterly Press, 1994.

Stillman, Richard. *The American Bureaucracy.* Chicago: Nelson-Hall, 1987.

For Discussion

Review

1. *What is the civil service?* (The civil service is the name given to federal employees who are hired and promoted based on merit.)

2. *What was the impact of the Pendleton Act?* (The Pendleton Act changed the way people got government jobs. Prior to this, the spoils system was used; after the Act, hiring was based on merit, though it was years before more than 50 percent of government employees were hired this way.)

3. *Who is involved in an iron triangle?* (An iron triangle consists of three participants: congressional committees, interest groups, and government agencies.)

4. *What impact did the Hatch Act have on bureaucrats?* (Once the Hatch Act was passed, it prohibited federal employees from working on campaigns and running for office themselves, and it prevented politically motivated firings.)

Critical Thinking

1. *Why do you think Congress has given the bureaucracy more responsibility in the lawmaking process?* (Bureaucrats are experts in their field and they have been trusted to fill in the details when Congress passes vaguely worded laws. Congress does this to make it easier to pass the law in the first place—fewer details, fewer opponents.)

2. *Why do you think the courts have played a more active role in getting the bureaucracy to carry out laws?* (Individuals and interest groups use the courts to make sure laws are carried out fairly and all guidelines are being followed.)

3. *Which of the three participants do you think benefits the most from an iron triangle?* (Answers may vary, but the most logical beneficiaries are members of the interest group because it makes them part of the government and gives them access they wouldn't have otherwise.)

4. *Do you agree that the bureaucracy holds the real power in government?* (Encourage students to explain their answers by citing specific situations.)

Skills Development Activities

1. **WRITING:** Red Tape

   The bureaucracy has come a long way, but many people are still critical of its inefficiency and the "red tape" it creates. Have students write an essay that identifies three problems of the bureaucracy. Then pick one of those problems and propose at least three solutions or improvements.

2. **CURRENT EVENTS:** Government Workers

   Have students study the chart on Characteristics of Federal Civilian Employees in the text. Then have them list at least three valid conclusions about government workers.

3. **INTERNET:** The Central Intelligence Agency

   Have students look up the CIA Web site on the Internet and find out how to apply for a job at the CIA. Then have them select one of the job descriptions and summarize in their own words what the job responsiblities are.

4. **SPECIAL SOURCES:** Reinventing Government

   Have students look at and analyze the political cartoon on page 231. Have them write a paragraph explaining the meaning of the cartoon and whether more than one interpretation is possible. Who or what is being criticized?

Study Guide

Name: _____

Complete each item as you read Chapter 12 (pages 225–231).

1. Before the civil service was created, government jobs were given out as patronage, in the

   "_____ system."

2. The civil service was established by the _____ in 1883.

3. There are about 3 million _____, or federal employees.

4. The vast majority of government employees are hired by the _____.

5. Instead of patronage, federal hiring is based on the _____ principle. The

   _____ exists to protect this principle.

6. The _____ prohibits federal employees from being political party activists.

7. Bureaucracy's funding is controlled by _____.

8. The President can influence executive agencies' budgets through the Office of

   _____ and _____.

9. The three points of an iron triangle are _____,

   _____, and _____.

Vocabulary

Read each description, and write the letter of the correct term on the line.

1. _____ An employee of a federal agency

2. _____ Name given to federal government employees who are hired and promoted based on merit

3. _____ Close relationship between agencies, interest groups, and congressional committees

a	bureaucrat
b	civil service
c	iron triangle

Multiple-Choice Test

Name: _____

Find the best answer for each item. Then completely fill in the circle for that answer.

1. Before the civil service was created, government jobs were awarded under
   - **a.** the spoils system
   - **b.** the Hatch Act
   - **c.** the Pendleton Act
   - **d.** the merit principle

2. Charles Guiteau
   - **a.** issed the first injunction
   - **b.** was a Vice President
   - **c.** directed the OPM
   - **d.** shot President Garfield

3. What created the federal civil service?
   - **a.** the spoils system
   - **b.** the Hatch Act
   - **c.** the Pendleton Act
   - **d.** the merit principle

4. What does the OPM do?
   - **a.** hire civil service workers
   - **b.** promote patronage
   - **c.** enforce the Hatch Act
   - **d.** link the bureaucracy to Congress

5. What does GS stand for?
   - **a.** government standing
   - **b.** general service
   - **c.** government salary
   - **d.** general standing

6. Which of the following can a civil service employee NOT do?
   - **a.** hold a position in a political party
   - **b.** be a member of a political party
   - **c.** help a political party raise funds
   - **d.** run as a candidate of a political party

7. Which best describes the way the bureaucracy wields power?
   - **a.** The bureaucracy is powerful because it administers public policy.
   - **b.** The bureaucracy is powerful because it approves the budget.
   - **c.** The bureaucracy is powerful because it isn't checked and balanced.
   - **d.** The bureaucracy is powerful because it has many employees.

8. How can the President influence the bureaucracy?
   - **a.** by ordering an agency to take an action
   - **b.** by using the Office of Management and Budget
   - **c.** by replacing an agency head
   - **d.** by all of the above

9. _____ of the cases in federal court involves the U.S. government.
   - **a.** None
   - **b.** A few
   - **c.** About half
   - **d.** Nearly all

10. Which is NOT part of an iron triangle?
    - **a.** an interest group
    - **b.** a congressional committee
    - **c.** a federal court
    - **d.** an executive agency

	a	b	c	d
1	ⓐ	ⓑ	ⓒ	ⓓ
2	ⓐ	ⓑ	ⓒ	ⓓ
3	ⓐ	ⓑ	ⓒ	ⓓ
4	ⓐ	ⓑ	ⓒ	ⓓ
5	ⓐ	ⓑ	ⓒ	ⓓ
6	ⓐ	ⓑ	ⓒ	ⓓ
7	ⓐ	ⓑ	ⓒ	ⓓ
8	ⓐ	ⓑ	ⓒ	ⓓ
9	ⓐ	ⓑ	ⓒ	ⓓ
10	ⓐ	ⓑ	ⓒ	ⓓ

Essay Question

Explain why "iron triangles" are called by that name and how they work to shape policy.

| For use with: | **Chapter 13** | **Courts and the Judicial Branch** |
| For use with: | **Activity 31** | **Term Limits for Justices** |

Objectives

- Identify what the Constitution says about the judicial system.
- Explain and clarify the differences between civil and criminal law and between appellate and original jurisdiction.
- Analyze the effects of varying interpretations of the Constitution, such as strict constructionism and loose constructionism, on the law.

Vocabulary

jurisdiction	original jurisdiction	appellate jurisdiction
judicial review	loose constructionist	strict constructionist

BACKGROUND

When asked about the major job of the Supreme Court, a significant body of Americans would say that it is to interpret the law. Of course, the Court does interpret the law. However, the U.S. judicial system—one of the most, if not the most, complicated in the world—takes its roots from English common law.

English common law traditionally developed to help Norman kings settle disputes among their subjects. Judges traveled about the kingdom settling those disputes, keeping records in yearbooks. Eventually they referred to these yearbooks to see how previous cases had been settled, creating the use of precedents.

In the United States we have added to the common law the idea of constitutional law, creating a system of courts based on the Constitution. The common law combined with constitutional and statute law has become the basis for our legal system.

Arguably, U.S. citizens have developed the most complicated legal system in the world. The U.S. legal system has gone beyond settling disputes—although such settlement is a very important part of the system—to interpretation through precedent. Many believe today that the courts have become the final arbiters of what the law means and, in fact, what it is. Others would say that if the courts have such power, then they are operating beyond the boundaries originally designed by the Framers of the Constitution.

From this argument comes the current dispute between those who favor a strict constructionist approach to the law and the Constitution and those who favor a loose constructionist approach. As we will see, the outcome of that dispute at any given time in history will determine how the laws are interpreted by the courts.

Further Resources

Baum, Laurence. *American Courts: Process and Policy.* 3rd ed. Boston: Houghton Mifflin, 1994.

Hamilton, Alexander. *"The Federalist 78." The Lanahan Readings in the American Polity,* eds. Ann G. Gerow and Everett C. Ladd. Baltimore: Lanahan Publishers, 1994.

Woodward, Bob, and Scott Armstrong. *The Brethren.* New York: Simon and Schuster, 1979.

For Discussion

Review

1. *What do scholars mean when they refer to a dual court system in the United States?* (They refer to state and federal systems existing side by side.)

2. *What does* jurisdiction *mean? What is the difference between original and appellate jurisdiction?* (It means that a certain court will hear the case, either originally or on appeal.)

3. *What are some basic differences between criminal law and civil law?* (Civil law deals with disputes between parties over, say, money or property, while criminal law deals with crimes in which laws have been broken.)

4. *What does the Supreme Court do when it exercises its power of judicial review?* (It interprets the law and establishes whether or not it is constitutional.)

Critical Thinking

1. *Why do you think that some cases involve concurrent jurisdiction between both state and federal courts?* (Encourage students to think about the nature of the case in terms of the location in which the act was committed.)

2. *Which should prevail in a court deciding a constitutional issue: strict constructionist opinions or loose constructionist opinions?* (Suggest that students think about how the laws may be interpreted by each position in a particular case.)

3. *Do you think federal judges have too much independence from the President and Congress?* (Be certain students understand the guidelines for terms of office as they express their views.)

Skills Development Activities

1. **WRITING:** Dual Sovereignty

   Have students refer to the feature on Dual Sovereignty on page 235. Have them write a short, three- to five-paragraph essay explaining why they agree or disagree with the way dual sovereignty operated in the two Rodney King cases.

2. **CURRENT EVENTS:** Criminal Law

   Have students locate a news article or a television news report about a recent criminal conviction or acquittal in your area. Have them report the facts of the case and the reasons (if available) for the court's decision.

3. **INTERNET:** Supreme Court

   Have students use a Web site (such as http://supct.law.cornell.edu/supct/) to learn about Supreme Court decisions of the last year. Ask them to report briefly on several of those recent decisions.

4. **SPECIAL SOURCES:** *The Federalist* No. 78

   Have students read *The Federalist* No. 78 and summarize in modern language Hamilton's basic attitudes about the powers he believed the Supreme Court should be able to exercise.

Study Guide

Name: _____

Complete each item as you read Chapter 13 (pages 232–238).

1. The Supreme Court is created by Article _____ of the Constitution, which also gives _____ the power to create "_____."

2. A court's authority is called its _____.

3. There are three main types of law in the United States: _____ law, _____ law, and _____ law.

4. The authority of the federal courts alone to hear and rule in certain cases is called _____.

5. The Supreme Court's power to interpret the constitutionality of a law is called _____.

6. What landmark Supreme Court case established the principle of judicial review? _____.

Vocabulary

Read each description, and write the letter of the correct term on the line.

1. _____ The right of a court to hear a case

2. _____ A court's authority to first hear a case

3. _____ A court's authority to hear a case on appeal

4. _____ The power of a court to determine the constitutionality of an act of government

5. _____ View that judges should interpret the Constitution narrowly

6. _____ View that judges should interpret the Constitution broadly

a	appellate jurisdiction
b	judicial review
c	jurisdiction
d	loose constructionist
e	original jurisdiction
f	strict constructionist

Multiple-Choice Test

Name: _____

Find the best answer for each item. Then completely fill in the circle for that answer.

1. Which court or courts was/were directly established by the Constitution?
   - **a.** state courts
   - **b.** appeals courts
   - **c.** the Supreme Court
   - **d.** federal courts

2. Who establishes inferior federal courts?
   - **a.** the Supreme Court
   - **b.** the Constitution
   - **c.** the President
   - **d.** the Congress

3. In concurrent jurisdiction,
   - **a.** only the Supreme Court hears the case
   - **b.** either federal or state courts might hear the case
   - **c.** a case is heard on appeal
   - **d.** a case is heard in federal court

4. In legal cases "arising under the Constitution, the laws of the United States, and treaties," _____ has/have exclusive jurisdiction.
   - **a.** state courts
   - **b.** constitutional courts
   - **c.** federal courts
   - **d.** the Supreme Court

5. A man is arrested for selling narcotics. What type of law is involved?
   - **a.** civil law
   - **b.** criminal law
   - **c.** constitutional law
   - **d.** all of the above

6. A woman sues a company for failure to perform an advertised service. What type of law is involved?
   - **a.** civil law
   - **b.** criminal law
   - **c.** constitutional law
   - **d.** all of the above

7. A man claims that the federal government doesn't have the authority to confiscate his property. What kind of law is involved?
   - **a.** civil law
   - **b.** criminal law
   - **c.** constitutional law
   - **d.** all of the above

8. Who holds the ultimate authority to interpret the Constitution?
   - **a.** state courts
   - **b.** inferior courts
   - **c.** federal courts
   - **d.** the Supreme Court

9. Someone who believes that the federal government should only exercise powers specifically mentioned in the Constitution is called a
   - **a.** loose constructionist
   - **b.** strict constructionist
   - **c.** judicial reviewer
   - **d.** plaintiff or defendant

10. What did *Marbury v. Madison* establish?
    - **a.** writs of *mandamus*
    - **b.** judicial review
    - **c.** inferior courts
    - **d.** strict constructionism

	a	b	c	d
1	a	b	c	d
2	a	b	c	d
3	a	b	c	d
4	a	b	c	d
5	a	b	c	d
6	a	b	c	d
7	a	b	c	d
8	a	b	c	d
9	a	b	c	d
10	a	b	c	d

Essay Question

How is judicial review related to checks and balances?

For use with:	**Chapter 13**	**Courts and the Judicial Branch**
For use with:	**Activity 32**	**The Selection of Federal Judges**

Objectives

- Define and identify the different kinds of federal courts.
- Describe how judges are selected for the federal court system.
- Analyze the process of selection of federal judges in terms of qualifications, background, and ideology.

Vocabulary

constitutional courts   legislative courts   senatorial courtesy

BACKGROUND

People in the United States generally believe that the U.S. judicial system exists to protect their rights by law in disputes with others and with the state. As a result, citizens have long used the courts in this country to find relief for their grievances. In fact, as Alexis de Tocqueville stated in the early nineteenth century, "Scarcely any question arises in the United States that is not resolved, sooner or later, into a judicial question."

Clearly, the judiciary is important to most U.S. citizens. Next to the bureaucracy, the courts may be the main contact most citizens have with the government, and perhaps the most popular, given the plethora of television programs related to the courts. From the 1950s, with *Perry Mason,* to the 1980s and 1990s, with *Court TV, The People's Court, L.A Law, Law and Order,* and *Matlock.* Americans have clearly demonstrated an interest in the system.

However, that does not mean that people fail to sit in judgment on court decisions. U.S. citizens want the courts to rule in their own interests, either directly or indirectly. Many U.S. citizens feel that the court ruled incorrectly in cases such as *Roe v. Wade* and *Miranda v. Arizona.* Even Presidents use self-interest as a factor when appointing people to the courts whom they believe will rule in ways favorable to the administration. Often, those same appointees rule differently than expected.

When President Eisenhower appointed Earl Warren to the Supreme Court, he had every reason to believe that Warren would be a conservative jurist. As we know today, the Warren court became known as one of the most liberal on record. Similarly, President Nixon was surprised by many of the decisions made by Warren Burger, a justice Nixon nominated. In the end, judges tend to be very independent.

The structure of the judicial system promotes such independence. While the selection process would seem to favor politicization of the courts, lifetime tenure leads often to the ability of judges to rule not only from precedent but also from personal belief tempered with an extensive knowledge of the law.

Further Resources

Savage, David. *Turning Right.* New York: John Wiley and Sons, 1992.
Supreme Court oral arguments. http://oyez.at.nyu.edu/oyez.html
Walker, Thomas G., and Deborah J. Barrow. "The Diversification of the Federal Bench: Policy and Process Ramifications." *Journal of Politics* 47 (May, 1985):596–617.

For Discussion

Review

1. **What specific qualifications exist for judges occupying the federal bench?** (None, although criteria for their selection have developed through the years.)

2. **What kinds of cases do most federal district courts try?** (They try cases involving federal offenses, either civil or criminal, and sometimes appeals from state courts.)

3. **How many judicial circuits is the United States divided into?** (There are 12 judicial circuits.)

4. **How does the selection process work for gaining a seat on a federal court?** (The President appoints people, and the Senate confirms them.)

Critical Thinking

1. **Why do you think that a President appoints individuals to federal judgeships who share the President's ideology?** (Encourage students to think about this question in terms of both ideology and legacy.)

2. **Do you believe that the practice of senatorial courtesy in the selection of federal judges is an advisable one? Why or why not?** (Ask students to think about this question as both a political question and one of pragmatism.)

3. **Do you think that some of the Senate criticisms of presidential court appointees, such as those of Robert Bork or of Clarence Thomas, have been justified?** (Have students think about the reasons each man was criticized in light of the past makeup of the court as well as the particular issues of the times. You may want to suggest that students do more research on the confirmation hearings described on page 250.)

Skills Development Activities

1. **WRITING: Impeached Judges**

   Have students research the impeachment and trial of one of the seven judges listed in the feature on page 248. Ask them to write a one-page paper summarizing the key details.

2. **CURRENT EVENTS: Appeals**

   Have students use the Internet, the library, or another news source to locate reasons for a recent appeal of a federal court decision. Have them develop a one-paragraph summary of both sides' positions.

3. **INTERNET: Supreme Court Justices**

   Have students find out about the background of one of the current justices on the Supreme Court. Ask them to give a brief speech to the class about the justice they chose.

4. **SPECIAL SOURCES: Selection Gridlock**

   Ask students to reread pages 250–251 on selection gridlock. Then have them work in pairs to create a political cartoon that expresses Chief Justice Rehnquist's frustration. Ask each group to present its cartoon to the class.

Study Guide

Name: _____

Complete each item as you read Chapter 13 (pages 239–251).

1. The _____ of 1789 created _____ courts.
   Congress has since created many _____ courts. Most federal cases go to
   _____ courts.

2. Constitutional courts include _____ courts, the courts of
   _____, and the U.S. Court of _____.

3. District courts regularly use _____ to determine if a person should have a trial.

4. There are _____ federal courts of appeal.

5. Six important legislative courts are the Court of _____;
   the U.S. _____ Court; the Courts of the District of
   _____, _____ courts, the Courts of
   _____ Appeals, and the U.S. _____ Court.

6. The _____ appoints all federal judges. Criteria considered in the selection process
   include _____, _____ affiliation, political
   _____, race and _____, and
   _____, which is related to "advice and consent."

7. The _____ must confirm all persons appointed to federal judgeships.

8. Selection _____ occurs when the Senate is slow to confirm appointees to federal
   judgeships.

Vocabulary

Read each description, and write the letter of the correct term on the line.

1. _____ Federal courts whose power is based in the Constitution, including the
   Supreme Court, district courts, and the courts of appeals

2. _____ Specialized courts established to hear cases about the powers
   of Congress

3. _____ Practice of submitting a judicial nominee's name to the senators from
   the nominee's state

a	constitutional courts
b	legislative courts
c	senatorial courtesy

Multiple-Choice Test

Name: _____

Find the best answer for each item. Then completely fill in the circle for that answer.

1. The Judicial Act of 1789 created _____ courts.
   - **a.** legislative
   - **b.** constitutional
   - **c.** state
   - **d.** Senate

2. Most federal cases go to _____ courts.
   - **a.** legislative
   - **b.** constitutional
   - **c.** state
   - **d.** Senate

3. Which is NOT a constitutional court?
   - **a.** a district court
   - **b.** a court of appeals
   - **c.** the Court of International Trade
   - **d.** the U.S. Tax Court

4. Which hears the majority of federal cases?
   - **a.** the courts of appeals
   - **b.** the district courts
   - **c.** the U.S. Claims Court
   - **d.** the Courts of the District of Columbia

5. The courts of appeal _____ have original jurisdiction.
   - **a.** never
   - **b.** sometimes
   - **c.** always
   - **d.** rarely

6. How many courts of appeal are there?
   - **a.** 3
   - **b.** 13
   - **c.** 25
   - **d.** 50

7. Which is NOT a legislative court?
   - **a.** the Court of International Trade
   - **b.** the U.S. Claims Court
   - **c.** the Court of Veterans Appeals
   - **d.** the U.S. Tax Court

8. The _____ appoints all federal judges and the _____ must confirm them.
   - **a.** President, Senate
   - **b.** President, Congress
   - **c.** House, President
   - **d.** Senate, Judiciary Committee

9. A senator rejects a name submitted for a federal judgeship before the whole Senate considers it. Based on what you know of senatorial courtesy, what is most likely to be true?
   - **a.** the Senator is majority leader
   - **b.** the Senator is from the appointee's state
   - **c.** the Senator is from a different party than the President
   - **d.** the Senator is chairman of the Rules Committee

10. Who influences the President's selection of judiciary appointees?
    - **a.** Congress
    - **b.** the American Bar Association
    - **c.** sitting judges
    - **d.** all of the above

1	a	b	c	d
2	a	b	c	d
3	a	b	c	d
4	a	b	c	d
5	a	b	c	d
6	a	b	c	d
7	a	b	c	d
8	a	b	c	d
9	a	b	c	d
10	a	b	c	d

Essay Question

Explain what selection gridlock is, identify what causes it, and propose one solution to lessen the problem.

For use with:	**Chapter 13**	**Courts and the Judicial Branch**
For use with:	**Activity 33**	**Getting to Know the Supreme Court**

Objectives

- Analyze the process through which the Supreme Court decides to hear cases.
- Describe the process used by the Supreme Court when deciding to hear a case.
- Identify the kinds of opinions the Court can issue.

Vocabulary

majority opinion   dissenting opinion   concurring opinion

BACKGROUND

No absolute right exists for an individual or group to appeal a case to the Supreme Court. The cases heard by the Court must have some kind of constitutional standing and certainly must be subject to judicial review. Although the Constitution did not grant the court the right of judicial review, Alexander Hamilton argued for something like it in *The Federalist* No. 78, and the Court assumed the right in *Marbury v. Madison* in 1803. In that ruling the Court said, "It is emphatically the province and duty of the judicial department to say what the law is. Those who apply the rule to a particular case must of necessity expound and interpret that rule."

Given the Court's assumed right to interpret the law, once the law is stated and becomes precedent, how is it enforced? Of course, the immediate answer must be that it is the duty of the executive branch to do the enforcing, and that's not always so easy. In their book *Judicial Policies: Implementation and Impact*, Charles Johnson and Bradley Canon indicate that different populations are involved in implementing court decisions.

First, there is an *interpreting population*, made up of lawyers and judges who need to understand the intent of the ruling in order for action to follow in the lower courts. Federal and state judges, and bureaucrats in particular, must interpret the ruling so that implementation can follow the Court's intent.

Then, there is the *implementing population*, those charged with actually implementing the decision. Decisions such as *Brown* and *Roe* had to be implemented by school districts and by states, often in the face of existing state statutes to the contrary.

Finally, there is the *consumer population*, who is affected by the ruling. African Americans seeking the same opportunities as white people, or women wanting legal abortions, found relief through the *Brown* and *Roe* rulings. Others found themselves without a legal basis for their beliefs about segregation or abortion. Once the Court rulings are implemented fully—and this often takes years—the way laws are enforced is irrevocably changed.

Further Resources

Savage, David G. *Turning Right: The Making of the Rehnquist Supreme Court.* New York: John Wiley and Sons, 1992.

Totenberg, Nina. "Behind the Marble, Beneath the Robes." *New York Times Magazine,* 16 March 1975, 37.

Ulman, Sidney. "The Supreme Court's *Certiorari* Decisions: Conflict as a Predictive Variable." *American Political Science Review* (December, 1984):901–911.

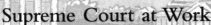

For Discussion

Review

1. *What is the writ of **certiorari**?* (It is an order to send up a case record from a lower court due to a claim that the lower court had mishandled the case.)

2. *Name two reasons why the Supreme Court decides to hear a case.* (Answers may include that lower courts may disagree about the case, it may have constitutional significance, or the lower court ruling conflicts with an existing Supreme Court ruling.)

3. *How many Supreme Court justices are there?* (There are eight associate justices and a chief justice.)

4. *What is the difference between a majority opinion and a concurring opinion?* (A majority opinion reflects the actual opinion of the court, while a concurring opinion agrees but makes a point not emphasized by the majority.)

Critical Thinking

1. *Why do you think that the justices never explain why they choose to hear the cases that they do?* (Ask students to think about the multitude of cases that the justices never choose to hear.)

2. *Why do you think that many people consider the justices on the court to be "above politics"?* (Encourage students to consider lifetime appointments and secret deliberations, among other factors.)

3. *Do you think that the executive branch should be required to implement immediately Court decisions? Why or why not?* (Have students consider the balance of powers and the often unclear direct meanings of some of the decisions.)

4. *Do you agree with the Court's decision in **United States v. Virginia?*** (Encourage students to consider both sides.)

Skills Development Activities

1. **WRITING:** Chief Justices

   Have the students locate data about two former chief justices of the U.S. Supreme Court. Then have them write an analytical essay comparing the judicial philosophies and major decisions.

2. **CURRENT EVENTS:** Privacy

   Have students locate one or more recent news articles addressing the continuing controversy over the *Roe v. Wade* decision. Ask them to prepare a two- to three-minute oral presentation summarizing the information they located.

3. **INTERNET:** Judicial Decisions

   Have students locate information about one of the important cases listed on pages 554–557. Ask them to summarize the issues and the Court's decision in a brief oral presentation.

4. **SPECIAL SOURCES:** Roosevelt and the Court

   Have students read the information on page 551 about Franklin Roosevelt's court-packing plan. Ask them to find and then share with the class a 1937 editorial, cartoon, or speech about Roosevelt's efforts.

Study Guide

Name: _____

Complete each item as you read Chapter 13 (pages 251–256).

1. How many justices sit on the Supreme Court? _____

2. What is the head justice called? _____

3. Most cases are brought before the Supreme Court by a _____ of
   _____, which is an order to send the case record to the Court because of a claim
   that a lower court mishandled the case.

4. Chief Justice William Rehnquist cited three factors the Court considers when deciding whether to review a case.
   These are 1) whether the _____ has been decided
   differently by lower courts, 2) whether a lower-court ruling conflicts with a _____
   ruling, and 3) whether the case will have significance beyond the two _____
   involved in it.

5. Are Supreme Court sessions open to the public? _____
   Are Court discussions and deliberations? _____

6. The official decision of the Supreme Court is written in the _____, although
   dissenting justices may issue a _____.

7. A _____ may be issued by justices who agree with the majority opinion but want
   to emphasize other legal points.

8. New Supreme Court sessions begin each _____.

Vocabulary

Read each description, and write the letter of the correct term on the line.

1. _____ Opinion issued by Supreme Court justices who agree with a ruling

2. _____ Opinion issued by Supreme Court justices who disagree with a ruling

3. _____ Opinion issued by Supreme Court justices who agree with a ruling but
   for reasons other than those offered by the majority

a	concurring opinion
b	dissenting opinion
c	majority opinion

Multiple-Choice Test

Name: _____

Find the best answer for each item. Then completely fill in the circle for that answer.

1. Most cases come before the Supreme Court as a result of what?
   a. original jurisdiction
   b. writs of *certiorari*
   c. executive orders
   d. judicial activism

2. What do justices consider when deciding whether to hear a case?
   a. whether the legal question involved has been decided differently by lower courts
   b. whether a lower court has issued a decision that conflicts with a previous Supreme Court ruling
   c. neither a nor b
   d. both a and b

3. Which Supreme Court matter is private?
   a. hearings of cases
   b. deliberations of justices
   c. dissenting opinions
   d. all of the above

4. When the Supreme Court rules, how many opinions can it issue about this one ruling?
   a. one
   b. two
   c. three
   d. four

5. A ruling of the Supreme Court is explained in a
   a. majority opinion
   b. dissenting opinion
   c. concurring opinion
   d. precedent

6. A justice agrees with a Supreme Court ruling but for unique reasons. He or she might issue a
   a. majority opinion
   b. dissenting opinion
   c. concurring opinion
   d. brief

7. Most of the Court's decisions are
   a. unanimous
   b. split
   c. overturned
   d. appealed

8. Which statement is true about the *Brown v. Topeka* case?
   a. It was in 1954.
   b. It was enforced immediately.
   c. Brown was the defendant.
   d. none of the above

9. Who assists the Supreme Court in its work?
   a. members of Congress
   b. lower court judges
   c. law clerks
   d. members of the President's staff

10. If a decision is split, who writes the dissenting opinion?
    a. the chief justice
    b. a law clerk
    c. the senior justice on the losing side
    d. anyone who volunteers

	a	b	c	d
1	ⓐ	ⓑ	ⓒ	ⓓ
2	ⓐ	ⓑ	ⓒ	ⓓ
3	ⓐ	ⓑ	ⓒ	ⓓ
4	ⓐ	ⓑ	ⓒ	ⓓ
5	ⓐ	ⓑ	ⓒ	ⓓ
6	ⓐ	ⓑ	ⓒ	ⓓ
7	ⓐ	ⓑ	ⓒ	ⓓ
8	ⓐ	ⓑ	ⓒ	ⓓ
9	ⓐ	ⓑ	ⓒ	ⓓ
10	ⓐ	ⓑ	ⓒ	ⓓ

Essay Question

Supreme Court justices are not required to explain why they accept or reject a case. Should they be required to do so? Why or why not?

| For use with: | **Chapter 13** | **Courts and the Judicial Branch** |
| For use with: | **Activity 34** | **You Be the Justice** |

Objectives

- Analyze the importance of precedents. List and describe some ways
- Define and explain major differences between judicial activism and judicial restraint.
- Analyze the power of the judiciary to make policy and explain the checks on its power.

Vocabulary

precedent   judicial activism   judicial restraint

BACKGROUND

As the Supreme Court settles disputes and engages in judicial review, it also solves problems. When one party in a dispute seeks relief from the Court, each wishes to have a particular problem solved. As the Court takes on such cases, it is dealing not only with the law but also with personal and public values. As such, the Court makes policy.

The Court will make major policy more rapidly if it takes on an activist role. Judicial activists believe that it is the judiciary's job to discover the underlying principles embedded in the Constitution and then to act upon those underlying principles when making a ruling. Those who advocate judicial restraint believe that interpretations of the Constitution should only come from direct or implied statements in the Constitution.

Whichever position the justices take, they are setting precedent for future rulings and are addressing problems that occur today. In the process, the justices also rule to either uphold the contemporary public norms, reflect the public norms, or try to change the normative behaviors of the society. For example, in *Miller v. California, Miranda v. Arizona,* and *Mapp v. Ohio,* the Court caused changes to be made in the ways police and the public viewed obscenity, defendant's rights, and admissible evidence.

While many citizens may not always approve of the Court's decisions, the Court defines the law, and it has to rely on others to enforce it. Sometimes that can take a long time. Congress may pass laws to implement Court decisions, which require further interpretation because some laws are vague.

However, the Court may not seek laws on which to rule. It cannot and does not create hypothetical situations for its rulings. When the Courts choose to rule, they rule in an activist way, discovering some underlying principles, or they rule in a more restrained pattern, relying on the actual language of the Constitution. Either way, their rulings certainly affect, and often make, policy.

Further Resources

Garrow, David J. "The Rehnquist Rein." *New York Times Magazine,*
        6 Oct. 1996, 65.
Rodhe, David W., and Harold J. Spaeth. *Supreme Court Decision Making.*
        San Francisco: W. H. Freeman, 1976.
Rosenberg, Gerald N. *The Hollow Hope: Can the Courts Bring About Social
        Change?* Chicago: The University of Chicago Press, 1991.

For Discussion

Review

1. ***What do the terms*** precedent ***and*** stare decisis ***mean?*** (*Precedent* refers to a decision that is used as a basis for deciding similar cases, and *stare decisis* means "let the decision stand," with precedents from similar cases.)

2. ***What are some major differences between judicial restraint and judicial activism?*** (The differences revolve around whether or not the Court should or should not actively make policy.)

3. ***Does judicial activism imply judicial liberalism?*** (Not necessarily. Judicial activists can be conservative as well.)

4. ***List at least two instances in which the Court has reversed a ruling it had set earlier?*** (*Minersville School District v. Gobitis* reversed *West Virginia State Board of Education v. Barnette* and *Brown v. Board of Education* reversed *Plessy v. Ferguson*.)

Critical Thinking

1. ***Which position do you favor, judicial activism or judicial restraint?*** (Encourage students to examine the arguments listed on page 262.)

2. ***Why do you think that justices such as Earl Warren, who seemed a conservative before he was appointed to the Supreme Court, made liberal rulings after he assumed the role of chief justice?*** (Encourage students not to simplify the beliefs of conservatives and liberals as they answer this question.)

3. ***Do you think that public opinion is, or should be, a factor in the Court's decisions? Why or why not?*** (Students may respond that it depends on the era of the ruling and the situation surrounding the decision. Ask them to be specific.)

4. ***Do you agree with Alexander Hamilton's statement in the*** The Federalist ***No. 78 that the "judiciary is beyond comparison the weakest of the three (branches) . . . "?*** (Encourage students to review how each branch makes decisions and the roles of each as they respond.)

Skills Development Activities

1. **WRITING:** Thoughts on the Court

   Have students respond to one of the quotes on page 264 about the Supreme Court. Ask them to paraphrase the quote and then to state whether they agree or disagree with what was said.

2. **CURRENT EVENTS:** Guns and Cigarettes

   Have students locate news articles concerning current state and class-action lawsuits over guns and/or cigarettes. Have them present oral statements to the class about the issues and whether or more of these cases might reach the U.S. Supreme Court.

3. **INTERNET:** Dissenting Opinions

   Have students locate and read the majority and dissenting opinions written in a case that interests them. Ask them to summarize the key differences between the two and indicate with which view they agree.

4. **SPECIAL SOURCES:** Activist Rulings

   Have students create a graph or chart comparing the activism of the Supreme Court and the ideological rulings of the Court over the last half century. Suggest that they research selected cases from their text and also use Web sites to locate additional information.

Study Guide

Name: _____

Complete each item as you read Chapter 13 (pages 257–265).

1. The cornerstone of the Court's power is _____.

2. *Stare decisis* decisions use _____ as their basis.

3. Factors influencing Court decisions include _____ of the justices, the influence of one _____ on another, and changes in the U.S. _____ and _____.

4. _____ calls for bold policy making by justices.

5. _____ is the belief that the Supreme Court should not actively make public policy.

6. The Warren Court was the most _____ Court in recent times.

7. Four checks on the Supreme Court's power are its limited power of _____, the _____, the _____, and public opinion.

8. Congress may _____ the Constitution.

Vocabulary

Read each description, and write the letter of the correct term on the line.

1. _____ Judicial decision used as a standard in later cases

2. _____ Belief that courts should shape policy and actively redefine the Constitution

3. _____ Belief that courts should not actively shape policy or redefine the Constitution

a	judicial activism
b	judicial restraint
c	precedent

Multiple-Choice Test

Name: _____

Find the best answer for each item. Then completely fill in the circle for that answer.

1. *Stare decisis* means
   a. "the ruling must change"
   b. "friend of the court"
   c. reasoned decision
   d. "let the decision stand"

2. Which term refers to a judicial decision that is used as a standard in later cases?
   a. brief
   b. concurring opinion
   c. precedent
   d. judicial restraint

3. A justice believes that the Supreme Court should issue rulings that result in bold policy changes. He or she might best be called
   a. a liberal
   b. a dissenter
   c. a judicial activist
   d. a supporter of judicial restraint

4. A justice believes that the Supreme Court should NOT issue rulings that result in bold policy changes. He or she might best be called
   a. a conservative
   b. a precedent-setter
   c. a believer in judicial restraint
   d. a moderate

5. Consider the case *Brown v. Board of Education of Topeka*. What is it an example of?
   a. judicial restraint on the Supreme Court
   b. judicial activism on the Supreme Court
   c. a congressional check of Supreme Court power
   d. gridlock on the Supreme Court

6. Which term is sometimes used to describe the outlook of the Supreme Court at a particular point in time?
   a. conservative
   b. moderate
   c. divided
   d. all of the above

7. Which court is considered most activist?
   a. the Rehnquist Court
   b. the Burger Court
   c. the Warren Court
   d. It is impossible to tell.

8. Which is NOT a way Congress can check the power of the federal judiciary?
   a. by nominating judges and justices
   b. by amending the Constitution
   c. by impeaching judges and justices
   d. by reorganizing the court system

9. How can the President affect the Supreme Court?
   a. by vetoing its decisions
   b. by nominating justices
   c. by appealing cases
   d. all of the above

10. Which statement is true?
    a. Public opinion has no effect on Supreme Court decisions.
    b. Supreme Court decision making is based largely on public opinion.
    c. The Supreme Court is not completely independent of public opinion.
    d. all of the above

	a	b	c	d
1	a	b	c	d
2	a	b	c	d
3	a	b	c	d
4	a	b	c	d
5	a	b	c	d
6	a	b	c	d
7	a	b	c	d
8	a	b	c	d
9	a	b	c	d
10	a	b	c	d

Essay Question

Identify and explain what you see as the three major checks on judicial power.

Civil Liberties and Civil Rights

For use with:	**Chapter 14**	**1st Amendment Freedoms**
For use with:	**Activity 35**	**Tinker and the Bill of Rights**

Objectives

- Review the content of the Bill of Rights.
- Define and demonstrate an understanding of civil liberties.
- Explain the concept of civil rights and give examples.
- Trace the process of incorporation.

Vocabulary

civil rights   civil liberties   incorporation

BACKGROUND

The Constitution of the United States was a document with which no one was completely satisfied at the time it was written. As part of the ratification debate, a promise was made to add amendments that would address concerns raised by those opposed to a strong central government. Not long after the government began, the Bill of Rights was passed and sent out to the states for approval. It was pretty clear at the time the Bill of Rights was ratified that it was aimed at the national government. There was never any discussion about whether these should be applied to the states because the individual states had their own bills of rights. This prevailing attitude was made "official" by *Barron v. Baltimore* (1833), which ruled that the Bill of Rights applied only to the national government.

This opinion would, of course, gradually change. The big impetus for this change was the 14th Amendment, which said the states "shall not deprive any person of life, liberty, or property without due process. . . ." This seemed to change the outlook on how far the Bill of Rights should go, and over time more and more of the first amendments were applied to the states. The process of applying the national Bill of Rights to the states is called *incorporation*.

One area in which incorporation has made a big impact is in 1st Amendment rights. This Amendment is seen as protecting individual freedoms and rights against government interference. These protections are known as *civil liberties*, a term often confused with *civil rights*, which generally refers to positive acts of government protection against group discrimination. Today civil rights are often thought of in terms of which groups are being protected. Civil liberties prevent government interference while civil rights rely on government enforcement.

Civil liberties do protect against government involvement, but they do not prevent "dueling rights." One area that keeps courts hopping is rights in conflict, because in many cases you can argue that both sides are right.

Further Resources

American Civil Liberties Union. "Freedom Network."
http://www.aclu.org

Ivers, Gregg. *Redefining the First Freedom: The Supreme Court and the Consolidation of State Power.* New Brunswick, NJ: Transaction Press, 1993.

For Discussion

Review

1. *What is incorporation?* (Incorporation is the process of gradually applying the Bill of Rights to the states.)

2. *What are civil liberties?* (Civil liberties are constitutionally based freedoms guaranteed to individuals.)

3. *How would you explain civil rights?* (Civil rights are rights belonging to a citizen or member of society regardless of race, sex, or national origin. The idea is to make sure that all receive equal treatment under the law.)

Critical Thinking

1. *What do you think would happen in this country if there were no incorporation?* (There would be no uniform standard in terms of how the protections of the Constitution are applied, and as a result, there would be variety in how people were treated, depending on the state in which they lived.)

2. *Why is it important to protect the civil liberties of such groups as the Ku Klux Klan or the Nazi party?* (By protecting the civil liberties of the most abhorrent groups, the courts are also protecting the rights of all people.)

3. *Do you agree with the Court's ruling in the* Tinker *case? Why or why not?* (Encourage students to refer to page 273 as they state their views.)

Skills Development Activities

1. **WRITING:** The Right to Bear Arms

   One of the more controversial parts of the Bill of Rights is the 2nd Amendment, which says people have the right to bear arms. Have students write a one- to two-page essay that either supports or opposes gun ownership. This can be based on opinion alone or students can be allowed to research to find support.

2. **CURRENT EVENTS:** The Right to Know

   One civil liberty, freedom of the press, allows considerable access to the lives of public figures. Some believe the press goes too far. Have students write a one-page essay exploring whether the press has gone too far when reporting on private lives of public figures. If they can, they should refer to particular people and situations.

3. **INTERNET:** Incorporation

   Have students look up *Gideon v. Wainwright*. Have students write a brief of the case—the basic facts, the key issue, the outcome, and the opinion that supported the verdict. Then have students write a one-paragraph summary of how this decision was an example of incorporation.

4. **SPECIAL SOURCES:** Rights in Conflict

   Have students reread the information on the *Tinker* case in their textbook (if possible, have them read the actual Supreme Court decision). Divide the class into thirds. One third has to argue the case for Tinker, one third has to argue the case for the school district, and one third is the jury. Let each side make their case, and then the jury must decide who made a better case in class. The jury may ask questions to clarify issues or statements.

Study Guide

Name: _____

Complete each item as you read Chapter 14 (pages 268–273).

1. Briefly identify the rights associated with each constitutional amendment:

1st: _____

2nd: _____

3rd: _____

4th: _____

5th: _____

6th: _____

7th: _____

8th: _____

9th: _____

10th: _____

2. Constitutionally based freedoms guaranteed to individuals are _____.

3. _____ refer to the positive acts of government protection against group discrimination.

Vocabulary

Read each description, and write the letter of the correct term on the line.

1. _____ The gradual process by which the Bill of Rights is applied to the states

2. _____ Protections against government

3. _____ Protections created by government against group discrimination

a	civil liberties
b	civil rights
c	incorporation

Multiple-Choice Test

Name: _____

Find the best answer for each item. Then completely fill in the circle for that answer.

1. Which amendment to the Constitution guarantees freedoms of religion, speech, press, and assembly?
   a. the 1st Amendment
   c. the 6th Amendment
   b. the 2nd Amendment
   d. the 10th Amendment

2. Which amendment to the Constitution guarantees the right to bear arms?
   a. the 1st Amendment
   c. the 9th Amendment
   b. the 2nd Amendment
   d. the 10th Amendment

3. Which amendment to the Constitution guards against excessive bail?
   a. the 1st Amendment
   c. the 5th Amendment
   b. the 4th Amendment
   d. the 8th Amendment

4. Which amendment to the Constitution reserves certain powers for the states?
   a. the 5th Amendment
   c. the 10th Amendment
   b. the 9th Amendment
   d. none of the above

5. Incorporation extended what to the states?
   a. the 1st Amendment
   c. the 5th Amendment
   b. the 4th Amendment
   d. all of the above

6. Which statement is most accurate?
   a. The entire Bill of Rights is now incorporated.
   c. Parts of the Bill of Rights that have not been incorporated relate to freedoms that are otherwise protected.
   b. The Bill of Rights was incorporated by the 14th Amendment.
   d. The 14th Amendment halted incorporation.

7. Which term is best used to describe citizens' individual freedoms?
   a. civil rights
   c. incorporation
   b. civil liberties
   d. due process

8. Which term refers to protected freedoms of minority groups against discrimination?
   a. civil rights
   c. incorporation
   b. civil liberties
   d. due process

9. Which constitutional amendment was at issue in *Tinker v. Des Moines School District?*
   a. the 1st Amendment
   c. the 5th Amendment
   b. the 2nd Amendment
   d. the 10th Amendment

10. Thomas Jefferson considered liberty to be a(n)
    a. right
    c. incorporation
    b. civil liberty
    d. duty

1	ⓐ	ⓑ	ⓒ	ⓓ
2	ⓐ	ⓑ	ⓒ	ⓓ
3	ⓐ	ⓑ	ⓒ	ⓓ
4	ⓐ	ⓑ	ⓒ	ⓓ
5	ⓐ	ⓑ	ⓒ	ⓓ
6	ⓐ	ⓑ	ⓒ	ⓓ
7	ⓐ	ⓑ	ⓒ	ⓓ
8	ⓐ	ⓑ	ⓒ	ⓓ
9	ⓐ	ⓑ	ⓒ	ⓓ
10	ⓐ	ⓑ	ⓒ	ⓓ

Essay Question

Explain the differences between rights and liberties, making specific reference to at least three of the amendments in the Bill of Rights.

For use with:	**Chapter 14**	**1ˢᵗ Amendment Freedoms**
For use with:	**Activity 36**	**School Prayer**

Objectives

- Define and demonstrate an understanding of the Establishment and Free Exercise Clauses.
- Explain and give examples of limits on the freedom of speech and the press.
- Identify key issues concerning the freedom of assembly and petition.

Vocabulary

Establishment Clause   Free Exercise Clause   sedition

BACKGROUND

Freedom of religion, freedom of speech, freedom of the press, freedom to assemble, and freedom to petition are all part of the 1ˢᵗ Amendment. These are probably the best known of all amendments, and they form the key to what most Americans consider our liberty. These rights provide powerful protections against government restrictions.

Freedom of religion, as a right, is usually broken into two separate areas, the Establishment Clause and the Free Exercise Clause. The Establishment Clause prevents the government from establishing or supporting a religion. In practice this has come to mean no praying in schools, which demonstrates a clear separation of church and state. The Free Exercise Clause has allowed most religions to practice as they wish, though the government has restricted some activities, such as polygamy and animal sacrifice (as practiced by some satanic cults).

Freedom of speech has also been divided into subsets: pure speech, speech plus, and symbolic speech. Pure speech is spoken words only, while speech plus involves spoken words along with some activity, such as marching or demonstrating. Symbolic speech is the most controversial because it involves no speech at all. Burning flags and wearing armbands are protected, but these protections are not unlimited. The least regulated by the courts is pure speech.

A significant issue is the area of freedom of the press and prior restraint. Can papers be prevented from printing something before it is printed? The answer has been no, but they can be sued if what they print is malicious and intended to harm. Recently the issue receiving lots of attention has been the Internet. Should the Internet be regulated or censored? This is a question currently being decided by the courts and Congress.

Related to the freedom of speech are the rights of assembly and petition. The right of assembly, or the right to gather, has been upheld regularly by the courts, but some restrictions have been allowed. Recent cases involving the rights of groups to assemble and demonstrate outside abortion clinics demonstrate the difficulty in establishing guidelines for the freedom to assemble.

Further Resources

American Civil Liberties Union. "Freedom Network."
    http://www.aclu.org
Leonard, Levy, et al. *The First Amendment*. New York: Macmillan, 1986.
O'Brien, David M. *The Public's Right to Know: The Supreme Court and the First Amendment*. New York: Praeger, 1982.

For Discussion

Review

1. *What does the Establishment Clause prevent the government from doing?* (It prevents the government from establishing a national religion, and it provides assistance to religious groups.)

2. *How is symbolic speech different from pure speech?* (Symbolic speech involves gestures or activities, such as stepping on a flag or wearing armbands in protest. No actual verbal sound need be made.)

3. *What are shield laws?* (Shield laws protect journalists from having to reveal their sources of confidential information.)

4. *What is treason?* (Treason is the betrayal of one's own country by acting to aid its enemies.)

Critical Thinking

1. *If a journalist has information from an informant whose identity he vowed to keep secret, do you think he should be forced to divulge that source if the information will lead to a murder conviction?* (Answers will vary.)

2. *Why do you think the courts have ruled that prayer should not be allowed in school?* (Answers will vary but should include some mention of offending atheists or violating the Establishment Clause, which prohibits any government organization from being involved with religion in any way.)

3. *Do you think the states and Congress should pass a constitutional amendment prohibiting desecration of the flag?* (Encourage students to refer to the *Texas v. Johnson* case as they respond.)

4. *Do you think the Internet should be censored or controlled in some manner? Explain.* (As students answer, have them try to align their views with those in the feature on page 287.)

Skills Development Activities

1. **WRITING:** Ku Klux Klan

   The Ku Klux Klan wants to hold a rally and march in your town. Have students write a one- to two-page position paper on whether or not this group should be allowed to march. Be sure students explain their positions in detail.

2. **CURRENT EVENTS:** Holiday Displays

   One debate that comes up every winter is whether or not to allow religious displays on government property. Have students pretend they are in charge of making the case for the community either in support of or against a religious display in front of city hall. They should make a one-minute speech to relay their position.

3. **INTERNET:** Censorship

   Have students use a Web site, such as that of the American Civil Liberties Union, to find a case related to a censorship issue in the chapter. Have them write a summary of the case that includes the basic facts and the ruling (if there is one). Have them write a paragraph on whether or not they agree with the decision.

4. **SPECIAL SOURCES:** Freedom of Religion

   Have students work in groups to develop a poll about freedom of religion. They should choose one of the "difficult questions" listed on page 277 as their topic. Suggest that they formulate their questions carefully to avoid bias. Have them poll at least 25 people and then report on their results.

Study Guide

Name: _____

Complete each item as you read Chapter 14 (pages 274–291).

1. Write the Establishment Clause. _____

2. The _____ of church and state is required by the Constitution.

3. True or false: The Free Exercise Clause allows any religious practice. _____

4. Identify six important Supreme Court cases related to religion: 1) _____;
   2) _____; 3) _____;
   4) _____; 5) _____; and
   6) _____.

5. The three types of speech are _____ speech, _____,
   _____, and _____ speech.

6. In *Texas v. Johnson,* what type of speech did the Supreme Court rule flag burning to be?
   _____.

7. The first sedition act was passed in _____.

8. Identify four important Supreme Court cases related to the freedom of speech:
   1) _____; 2) _____;
   3) _____; and 4) _____.

9. Identify four important Supreme Court cases related to the freedom of the press:
   1) _____; 2) _____;
   3) _____; and 4) _____.

10. Identify four important Supreme Court cases related to the freedom of assembly: 1) _____;
    2) _____; 3) _____; and 4) _____.

Vocabulary

Read each description, and write the letter of the correct term on the line.

1. _____ Part of the 1st Amendment that prohibits the establishment
   of a national religion

2. _____ Part of the 1st Amendment that guarantees freedom of religion

3. _____ Actions or language that incite rebellion

a	Establishment Clause
b	Free Exercise Clause
c	sedition

Multiple-Choice Test

Name: _____

Find the best answer for each item. Then completely fill in the circle for that answer.

1. "Congress shall make no law respecting an establishment of religion." This statement is known as
   a. the 1st Amendment
   b. the Establishment Clause
   c. symbolic speech
   d. the Free Exercise Clause

2. In _____, the Supreme Court ruled that a state law requiring the saying of the Lord's Prayer is unconstitutional.
   a. *Engle v. Vitale*
   b. *Abington School District v. Schempp*
   c. *Stone v. Graham*
   d. *Wallace v. Jaffre*

3. Under the 1st Amendment,
   a. people have the right to hold any religious belief they choose
   b. people have the right to follow any religious practice they choose
   c. both a and b are true
   d. neither a nor b is true

4. A group of people march in front of a state capitol building, carrying signs and shouting slogans. According to the Supreme Court, this is
   a. pure speech
   b. speech plus
   c. symbolic speech
   d. treason

5. A man publicly burns an American flag to protest American involvement in a war. According to *Texas v. Johnson,* this is an example of
   a. pure speech
   b. sedition
   c. treason
   d. symbolic speech

6. Which speech is not permitted, even under the 1st Amendment?
   a. sedition
   b. treason
   c. slander
   d. all of the above

7. What are shield laws designed to do?
   a. protect confidential sources
   b. protect individuals from slander
   c. convict people of treason
   d. shield children from obscenity on the Internet

8. When is prior restraint allowed?
   a. never
   b. always
   c. when the content involves national security
   d. when the content is broadcast on airwaves

9. Which case resulted in the passage of shield laws?
   a. *Near v. Minnesota*
   b. *Yates v. United States*
   c. *Branzburg v. Hayes*
   d. *Miller v. California*

10. The government can enforce rules about
    a. the time and content of assemblies
    b. the time and place of assemblies
    c. both a and b
    d. neither a nor b

Answer grid:
1 ⓐ ⓑ ⓒ ⓓ
2 ⓐ ⓑ ⓒ ⓓ
3 ⓐ ⓑ ⓒ ⓓ
4 ⓐ ⓑ ⓒ ⓓ
5 ⓐ ⓑ ⓒ ⓓ
6 ⓐ ⓑ ⓒ ⓓ
7 ⓐ ⓑ ⓒ ⓓ
8 ⓐ ⓑ ⓒ ⓓ
9 ⓐ ⓑ ⓒ ⓓ
10 ⓐ ⓑ ⓒ ⓓ

Essay Question

How is the freedom of association necessary for the freedoms of speech and religion to exist?

| For use with: | **Chapter 15** | **Rights of Due Process** |
| For use with: | **Activity 37** | **The Rights of Aliens** |

Objectives

- Explain due process, its significance, and its constitutional basis.
- Explain naturalization.
- Summarize the rights of aliens.

Vocabulary

due process   naturalization   alien

BACKGROUND

At the time the Constitution was written, U.S. citizens had certain ideals they felt should be protected by the new government. A number of states considered withholding ratification until they had a guarantee that certain protections would be included. One of the promises made by supporters was to add a bill of rights as soon as the Constitution was ratified. The supporters lived up to their promise by passing the first ten amendments, better known as the Bill of Rights.

One of the rights it protects is the right of due process. Due process is the principle that state and federal governments must not deprive an individual of life, liberty, or property by unfair or unreasonable actions. For the first 80 years or so, this was not a big issue, but as the Civil War came and went, it was clear to some that the 5th Amendment did not provide enough protection, especially for the newly freed slaves. As a result of the concerns raised about how African Americans would be treated, especially in the South, Congress and the states passed and ratified the 14th Amendment, which defined citizenship and called for equal protection of the law, or due process. Today, many of citizens' local protections are based on the 14th Amendment and the many federal guidelines for protection that have been incorporated to the states by the Supreme Court.

As mentioned above, the 14th Amendment also defines citizenship. There are three basic ways to become a citizen: you are born here, you are born elsewhere to U.S. citizens, or you go through a naturalization process. The final process applies to those that have immigrated and wish to become U.S. citizens. It is also possible to move here but choose not to become a citizen. The person who makes that choice has the status of legal alien, gets a "green card" (which isn't actually green), and has most of the privileges of citizenship, except voting and holding public office. Last, aliens may be subject to deportation if they break the law.

Further Resources

Neuman, Gerald R. *Strangers to the Constitution: Immigrants, Borders, and Fundamental Law.* Princeton: Princeton University Press, 1996.

Shklar, Judith N. *American Citizenship: The Quest for Inclusion.* Cambridge, MA: Harvard University Press, 1991.

U.S. Immigration and Naturalization Service. "Welcome to the INS." http://www.ins.usdoj.gov

For Discussion

Review

1. *How would you define due process?* (Due process is a principle, guaranteed by the Constitution, that federal and state governments must not deprive an individual of life, liberty, or property by unfair or unreasonable actions.)

2. *What two constitutional amendments are key to protecting due process rights?* (The 5th and 14th Amendments are key.)

3. *What is the function of naturalization?* (Naturalization is a process that allows immigrants to become citizens after they have met all the requirements.)

4. *What is the legal term for those whom most people call* immigrants? (The term is *resident aliens*.)

Critical Thinking

1. *Why do you think the concept of due process was and is so important to U.S. citizens?* (Due process protects individual citizens from potential abuses by the government, and it guarantees that the laws will be applied the same way to all people, especially minorities or other disadvantaged people.)

2. *Do you think it should be harder or easier for immigrants to become citizens?* (Answers will vary.)

3. *Why do you think so many immigrants choose to come to the United States?* (Answers may vary but will probably include greater political freedom or better economic opportunities.)

4. *Do you agree with the Supreme Court's decision in* New Jersey v. T.L.O *(described on page 294)?* (Urge students to be specific as they try to define what "reasonable grounds" for a search are.)

Skills Development Activities

1. **WRITING**: Due Process

   Have students choose a minority group (such as people with disabilities, senior citizens, or African Americans). Then have them write a research essay that explores when that group might, in the past, have been denied due process (equal treatment) and how those inequalities have been remedied.

2. **CURRENT EVENTS**: Immigration Trends

   Ask students to construct a table (similar to the one on page 297) about where immigrants to their state come from. Suggest that they work in groups and stress that they should find two reliable sources for their information.

3. **INTERNET**: The INS

   Have students look up the Immigration and Naturalization Service Web site at http://www.ins.usdoj.gov. Once there, have students look up the current guidelines for naturalization and have them make a list of what is required to become a citizen. Have them include who is eligible according to INS standards.

4. **SPECIAL SOURCES**: *Dred Scott v. Sandford*

   Ask students to find and read the original majority decision written in the *Dred Scott v. Sandford* case. Have them identify two or three difficult or confusing sentences and ask them to write paraphrases of them in readable, modern English.

Study Guide

Name: _____

Complete each item as you read Chapter 15 (pages 292–298).

1. The principle that the government must not deprive a person of life, liberty, or property by unfair actions is called

   _____.

2. Due process related to how laws are carried out is called _____.

3. Due process related to the laws themselves is called _____.

4. There are three ways to become a citizen of the United States: _____,

   _____, or _____.

5. About how many immigrants become citizens each year? _____

6. The Immigration Act sets a ceiling of _____ immigrants to the

   United States each year.

7. The federal government uses five categories to classify people who come to the United States. These categories

   are 1) _____, 2) _____,

   3) _____, 4) _____, and

   5) _____.

8. Aliens in the United States legally can own _____, run a business, and

   _____ schools.

Vocabulary

Read each description, and write the letter of the correct term on the line.

1. _____ A principle that the government must not deprive a person of life, liberty, or property by unfair actions

2. _____ Process of becoming a citizen

3. _____ Person who is not a citizen of the country in which he or she lives

a	alien
b	due process
c	naturalization

Multiple-Choice Test

Name: _____

Find the best answer for each item. Then completely fill in the circle for that answer.

1. The principle that the government must not deprive a person of life, liberty, or property unreasonably is called
   - **a.** civil rights
   - **b.** procedural due process
   - **c.** substantive due process
   - **d.** due process

2. The phrase "due process of law" is found where in the Constitution?
   - **a.** the Preamble
   - **b.** 5th and 14th Amendments
   - **c.** the 1st Amendment
   - **d.** Article III

3. Who is a citizen of the United States?
   - **a.** most people born in the United States
   - **b.** someone born to U.S. citizens while traveling abroad
   - **c.** someone who has completed the naturalization process
   - **d.** all of the above

4. A child is born in the United States to foreign diplomats. The child is a(n)
   - **a.** citizen of the United States
   - **b.** illegal alien
   - **c.** alien
   - **d.** refugee

5. What qualifications must a person have to begin the naturalization process?
   - **a.** must have lived in U.S. for the 10 years
   - **b.** must speak English
   - **c.** must be at least 21 years old
   - **d.** all of the above

6. About how many aliens complete the naturalization process and become citizens each year?
   - **a.** less than 100
   - **b.** about 250,000
   - **c.** about 5.8 million
   - **d.** 675,000

7. Which is true about the *Dred Scott v. Sandford* Supreme Court case?
   - **a.** Scott won.
   - **b.** Scott lost.
   - **c.** It was in 1807.
   - **d.** Sandford was a slave.

8. Which statement is most accurate?
   - **a.** Aliens have no constitutional rights.
   - **b.** Aliens have one constitutional right.
   - **c.** Aliens have many constitutional rights.
   - **d.** Aliens have all constitutional rights.

9. A woman enters the United States from Mexico without a passport, visa, or entry permit. She is a(n)
   - **a.** non-resident alien
   - **b.** illegal alien
   - **c.** refugee
   - **d.** enemy alien

10. Which statement is true?
    - **a.** All resident aliens are immigrants.
    - **b.** All refugees are illegal aliens.
    - **c.** All illegal aliens are enemy aliens.
    - **d.** All naturalized citizens are resident aliens.

	a	b	c	d
1	a	b	c	d
2	a	b	c	d
3	a	b	c	d
4	a	b	c	d
5	a	b	c	d
6	a	b	c	d
7	a	b	c	d
8	a	b	c	d
9	a	b	c	d
10	a	b	c	d

Essay Question

How has U.S. immigration policy changed through the years? Explain key changes and identify current policies.

For use with:	**Chapter 15**	**Rights of Due Process**
For use with:	**Activity 38**	**Rewriting the 4th Amendment**

Objectives

- Define and give examples of the writ of *habeas corpus, ex post facto* laws, and bills of attainder.
- Identify the basic protections of the 4th, 5th, 6th, and 8th Amendments.
- Explain rights of property and privacy.

Vocabulary

writ of *habeas corpus*   *ex post facto*   bill of attainder   exclusionary rule

BACKGROUND

The U.S. Constitution is a document based on the beliefs of the people who wrote it. Over the years, certain understandings have emerged from that document. One of those understandings is that we would rather free from jail someone who might be guilty of something than punish someone who is innocent. As a result, there are many protections for the accused that some say go too far and make it too hard to convict anyone of a crime. Others argue that these protections ensure fairness and justice and prevent abuses by the government.

These protections are detailed in a number of amendments passed as part of the Bill of Rights. The 4th Amendment limits the nature of searches and seizures, making sure there truly is evidence of something to search for. It also protects us from illegally obtained evidence being used against us. The 5th Amendment protects us from being tried twice for the same offense (double jeopardy), and it protects the right to remain silent.

Another major understanding, even though it is not spelled out in the Constitution, is the right to privacy. Through various court decisions, the right to privacy has developed as being implied by the wording and intention of the Founders. This right was first "recognized" in the early 1960s and, most significantly, has led to the nationalizing of abortion rights. Many scholars and citizens saw this ruling as a stretch constitutionally and have continued to work for a reversal of this decision.

The 6th Amendment provides the right to an attorney even if people can't afford one, and it guarantees a fair trial with an unbiased jury and the right to change venue if it is likely that the trial will not be fair. Finally, the 8th Amendment deals with cruel and unusual punishment, usually seen in reference to the death penalty. The issue before the courts has not been whether the death penalty should be legal, but whether it has been applied fairly.

Further Resources

Cole, George F. *Criminal Justice: Law and Politics.* 6th ed. Belmont, CA: Wadsworth Publishers, 1993.

Craig, Barbara Hinkson, and David M. O'Brien. *Abortion and American Politics.* Chatham, NJ: Chatham House Publishers, 1993.

———. *Constitutional Law for a Changing America: Rights, Liberties, and Justice.* 3rd ed. Washington, DC: Congressional Quarterly Press, 1997.

For Discussion

Review

1. *What does* habeas corpus *mean?* (*Habeas corpus* basically means authorities have to have a formal charge in order to detain or hold you.)

2. *What are the two basic protections provided by the 4th Amendment?* (The 4th Amendment protects individuals from illegal searches and seizures, and it prohibits illegally obtained evidence from being admitted in a court.)

3. *On TV you often hear people "plead the Fifth." What does that mean?* (Pleading the Fifth means you refuse to testify against yourself, though you may testify if you want.)

4. *Abortions are legal but states have imposed some restrictions. Can you name three?* (Three restrictions on abortions in various states include a 24-hour waiting period, the requirement that teens under a certain age have the approval of at least one parent, and a requirement that abortion alternatives be explained.)

Critical Thinking

1. *What do you think should happen if a murder case is proven, and guilt is established beyond a shadow of doubt, but it is later revealed that the evidence was obtained under questionable circumstances?* (Ask students to cite specific situations.)

2. *Do you think it is possible for someone who is involved in a famous case (such as O.J. Simpson's murder trial or the trial of Timothy McVeigh for the Oklahoma City bombing) to receive a fair trial by an unbiased jury in the jurisdiction where the crime was committed?* (Answers will vary, but if the judge feels there is a problem, there can be a change in venue, which would move the case to a different jurisdiction.)

3. *What do you think the death penalty is supposed to accomplish, and do you think it achieves those goals?* (The reasons for the death penalty are usually a deterrent and/or punishment, but answers will probably vary.)

Skills Development Activities

1. **WRITING:** Abortion

   Have students write a position paper for either side of the abortion issue. Make sure they support their opinions and detail their reasons, perhaps providing examples to support their opinions. This should be one to two pages in length.

2. **CURRENT EVENTS:** Death Penalty

   Have students find a story related to a death penalty case from the last 2 years. Have students rewrite the story in simpler form as if it were for a student newspaper. It shouldn't take more than a page. Have the students read their stories to the class. A discussion should follow. Suggest that students try to distinguish facts from opinions.

3. **INTERNET:** Rights of the Accused

   Have students look up one Supreme Court decision mentioned in Chapter 15 that dealt with the rights of the accused. Ask them to write a brief that includes the basic facts of the case, the constitutional issue, and the decision detailed in the majority opinion. This should be one to two pages.

4. **SPECIAL SOURCES:** Capital Punishment

   Ask students to research current laws and practices of various states concerning the death penalty. Ask them to present their findings in a map, chart, or graph. Post students' work for all to see.

Study Guide

Name: _____

Complete each item as you read Chapter 15 (pages 299–311).

1. Three important civil liberties safeguards in the original Constitution are the right to a writ of

   _____, the protection against _____ laws, and the

   ban on bills of _____.

2. The _____ Amendment protects persons from "unreasonable searches

   and seizures."

3. As a rule, searches are considered "reasonable" if the police have a _____ or the

   person searched has been _____.

4. According to the _____, evidence gathered illegally cannot be used in a trial.

5. The 5th Amendment prohibits _____, or being tried twice for the same crime.

6. A legal statement charging a person with a crime or other offense is an _____.

7. The 6th Amendment guarantees accused persons the right to _____ and the right

   to a _____.

8. The 8th Amendment prohibits "_____ punishment."

9. Is the "right to privacy" specifically mentioned in the Constitution? _____

10. The landmark 1973 case _____ allowed for the

    constitutionality of abortions.

Vocabulary

Read each description, and write the letter of the correct term on the line.

1. _____ Court order requiring custody to be explained and justified

2. _____ A law that makes an act criminal after the fact

3. _____ A law that pronounces a person guilty of a crime without a trial

4. _____ Rule that states illegally obtained evidence cannot be used in a trial

a	bills of attainder
b	*ex post facto*
c	exclusionary rule
d	writ of *habeas corpus*

Multiple-Choice Test

Name: _____

Find the best answer for each item. Then completely fill in the circle for that answer.

1. A law that pronounces a person guilty of a crime without a trial is called a(n) _____.
   - **a.** writ of *habeas corpus*
   - **b.** *ex post facto* law
   - **c.** exclusionary rule
   - **d.** bill of attainder

2. *Ex post facto* means
   - **a.** "a second trial"
   - **b.** "without a trial"
   - **c.** "after the fact"
   - **d.** "without facts"

3. In the United States, people are "secure in their persons, houses, papers, and effects, against unreasonable searches" under the _____ Amendment.
   - **a.** 4th
   - **b.** 5th
   - **c.** 6th
   - **d.** 8th

4. In general, police can conduct a search if
   - **a.** they have a search warrant
   - **b.** the individual has been lawfully arrested
   - **c.** either a or b
   - **d.** both a and b

5. Evidence obtained illegally cannot be used in trial. This describes
   - **a.** the exclusionary rule
   - **b.** an *ex post facto* law
   - **c.** civil rights
   - **d.** probable cause

6. Police are required to inform people they arrest of their rights. This is a result of
   - **a.** *Mapp v. Ohio*
   - **b.** *Terry v. Ohio*
   - **c.** *Ex parte Milligan*
   - **d.** *Miranda v. Arizona*

7. Which amendment protects people from "cruel and unusual" punishment?
   - **a.** the 4th Amendment
   - **b.** the 5th Amendment
   - **c.** the 6th Amendment
   - **d.** the 8th Amendment

8. According to the Supreme Court, is capital punishment currently considered "cruel and unusual" punishment?
   - **a.** yes
   - **b.** no
   - **c.** only if the criminal is under 18
   - **d.** only if the criminal is under 21

9. _____ is the government's right to take private property for public purposes.
   - **a.** *Ex post facto*
   - **b.** Eminent domain
   - **c.** The Miranda Rule
   - **d.** none of the above

10. What is the significance of *Roe v. Wade*?
    - **a.** During an arrest, it required police to read people their rights.
    - **b.** It required the courts to provide legal counsel to people who cannot afford it.
    - **c.** It declared a ban on all abortions unconstitutional.
    - **d.** It declared that the exclusionary rule applies to states.

Answer grid:

	a	b	c	d
1	a	b	c	d
2	a	b	c	d
3	a	b	c	d
4	a	b	c	d
5	a	b	c	d
6	a	b	c	d
7	a	b	c	d
8	a	b	c	d
9	a	b	c	d
10	a	b	c	d

Essay Question

Do you think the Constitution should be amended to include specific mention of a "right to privacy"? Explain your answer.

For use with:	**Chapter 16**	**Civil Rights**
For use with:	**Activity 39**	**Bilingual Education**

Objectives

- Trace key developments in the struggle for equality for African Americans.
- Differentiate between *de facto* and *de jure* segregation.
- Analyze the history and key issues in the civil rights struggles of Hispanic Americans. Asian-Pacific Americans, and Native Americans.

Vocabulary

discrimination   segregation   separate-but-equal

BACKGROUND

Civil rights, as an issue worthy of national attention, has gone through various stages. At the time of the nation's founding, civil rights were pushed behind civil liberties in importance. Minorities were neither considered nor consulted when the Constitution was written. As a result, the second-class status of African Americans was never questioned. As the Civil War drew near, the debate over the place of African Americans in society intensified. The issue was not completely addressed until the 13th, 14th, and 15th Amendments were passed. It was one thing to provide legal equality; it was quite another to get the rest of the country to go along.

Two types of segregation developed: *de jure* segregation, which was segregation based on the law (as a result of Jim Crow laws); and *de facto* segregation, which was segregation "in fact" (based on settlement patterns, such as in places where African Americans lived on one side of town and whites on the other). The idea of segregation was further enhanced by the Civil Rights Cases in the 1870s and finally by *Plessy v.*

Ferguson (1896), which legalized the doctrine of "separate but equal."

Many consider that the modern Civil Rights Movement had its start with the formation of the National Association for the Advancement of Colored People (NAACP). This group began a series of court challenges that would lead the way to the reversal of *Plessy* with the *Brown* decision. Activist efforts culminated in the civil rights laws of the 1960s, the Civil Rights Acts of 1964 and 1968, and the Voting Rights Act of 1965. These were seen as major steps toward social equality for all.

Although most of the attention regarding civil rights has focused on African Americans, other racial and ethnic minorities have recently sought fair treatment as well, including Hispanics, Asians, Pacific Islanders, and Native Americans. These groups have the benefit of the laws already in place, but their small numbers have made it harder for them to obtain recognition.

Further Resources

Kenworthy, Tom. "Native Americans Denounce Race Panel."
         The Washington Post, 25 Mar 1998, A3.
National Association for the Advancement of Colored People.
         http://www.naacp.org
National Congress of American Indians.
         http://www.ncai.org

For Discussion

Review

1. *What does the term* discrimination *mean?* (Discrimination is unfair treatment of any individual based on group membership, such as race, alone.)

2. *What is the difference between* de facto *and* de jure *segregation?* (*De facto* segregation is the result of residential settlement patterns, as opposed to *de jure* segregation, which is segregation authorized by the government and the law.)

3. *Why was the* Plessy v. Ferguson *decision so important?* (It established the principle of separate-but-equal as being legally acceptable.)

4. *What was known as the "policy of termination"?* (It was the reduction of government-provided services to Native-American reservations.)

Critical Thinking

1. *Why do you think segregation lasted so long after the Civil War?* (Adding amendments and freeing slaves did not change people's attitudes about segregation. African Americans may have been liberated from slavery, but attitudes concerning the races did not change for quite a while.)

2. *Why do you think the Supreme Court moved to end segregation before Congress did?* (The courts have only the law to consider while Congress has to consider the politics of both segregation and re-election.)

3. *Do you think the relocation of Japanese Americans during World War II was justifiable as a wartime measure?* (Answers will vary.)

Skills Development Activities

1. **WRITING:** Du Bois and King

   Have students read at least part of a biography of W.E.B. Du Bois or Martin Luther King or a chapter about their involvement in civil rights struggles. On the basis of what they read, have students write a one-paragraph review of the book.

2. **CURRENT EVENTS:** Bilingual Education

   Have students review the feature on bilingual education on page 323. Ask them to prepare a 2–3 minute speech that they could make in front of the school board that either supports or opposes bilingual classes in their school. Encourage students to go beyond the text for more information.

3. **INTERNET:** The NAACP

   Have students sign on to the NAACP Web site at http://www.naacp.org. After they explore the site, have them write a report (one-half to one page long) on one of the areas in which the NAACP is currently involved. The "Programs" button may yield some helpful information.

4. **SPECIAL SOURCES:** Discrimination

   Ask students to locate a political cartoon that concerns the topic of discrimination. Some may look for a current example; others may want to research past newspapers or magazines. Have students bring in copies of their cartoons for a class discussion.

Study Guide

Name: _____

Complete each item as you read Chapter 16 (pages 312–327).

1. Three constitutional amendments passed in the wake of the Civil War are the

   _____, _____, and

   _____ Amendments.

2. Laws that were passed to discriminate against African Americans were called

   _____ laws.

3. The separate-but-equal doctrine came from the landmark case _____.

4. In 1954 the landmark case _____

   declared segregated schools to be unconstitutional.

5. Two key civil rights laws are the _____ of 1964 and the

   _____ of 1965.

6. About what percentage of the population is Hispanic American? _____

7. About how many Asian Americans are there in the United States today? _____

8. Ben Nighthorse Campbell is the first _____ to serve as a U.S.

   _____.

Vocabulary

Read each description, and write the letter of the correct term on the line.

1. _____ Unfair treatment of an individual based on group membership alone

2. _____ Separation of people by race or ethnicity in schools, housing,
   and industry

3. _____ Established by *Plessy v. Ferguson*

a	discrimination
b	segregation
c	separate-but-equal doctrine

Multiple-Choice Test

Name: _____

Find the best answer for each item. Then completely fill in the circle for that answer.

1. Which constitutional amendment abolished slavery?

    a. the 13ᵗʰ Amendment

    b. the 14ᵗʰ Amendment

    c. the 15ᵗʰ Amendment

    d. the 16ᵗʰ Amendment

2. What did the 15ᵗʰ Amendment do?

    a. guarantee "equal protection of the law"

    b. abolish slavery

    c. protect voting rights for African Americans

    d. all of the above

3. What did *Plessy v. Ferguson* establish?

    a. *de facto* segregation

    b. Jim Crow laws

    c. the separate-but-equal doctrine

    d. discrimination

4. Jim Crow laws resulted in

    a. slavery

    b. segregation

    c. *de facto* segregation

    d. *Brown v. Board of Education of Topeka*

5. *Brown v. Board of Education of Topeka*

    a. overturned *Plessy v. Ferguson*

    b. was a victory for the Civil Rights Movement

    c. declared segregated schools to be unconstitutional

    d. all of the above

6. *Plessy v. Ferguson* was decided in _____; *Brown v. Board of Education of Topeka* was decided in _____.

    a. 1896; 1954

    b. 1950; 1991

    c. 1954; 1964

    d. 1964; 1965

7. Discrimination by private businesses and in public places was outlawed by

    a. *Plessy v. Ferguson*

    b. *Brown v. Board of Education of Topeka*

    c. The Civil Rights Act of 1964

    d. The Voting Rights Act of 1965

8. Approximately what percentage of the U.S. population is Hispanic American?

    a. 1 percent

    b. 9 percent

    c. 15 percent

    d. 25 percent

9. Who were placed in internment camps during World War II?

    a. Hispanic Americans

    b. Asian Americans

    c. Japanese Americans

    d. Native Americans

10. The Native American Rights Fund is

    a. a congressional caucus

    b. a reservation

    c. a political party

    d. a legal defense firm

	a	b	c	d
1	ⓐ	ⓑ	ⓒ	ⓓ
2	ⓐ	ⓑ	ⓒ	ⓓ
3	ⓐ	ⓑ	ⓒ	ⓓ
4	ⓐ	ⓑ	ⓒ	ⓓ
5	ⓐ	ⓑ	ⓒ	ⓓ
6	ⓐ	ⓑ	ⓒ	ⓓ
7	ⓐ	ⓑ	ⓒ	ⓓ
8	ⓐ	ⓑ	ⓒ	ⓓ
9	ⓐ	ⓑ	ⓒ	ⓓ
10	ⓐ	ⓑ	ⓒ	ⓓ

Essay Question

Historians refer to a group of constitutional amendments as "the Civil War Amendments." Identify them, explain what each one does, and tell why they are given that name.

For use with:	**Chapter 16**	**Civil Rights**
For use with:	**Activity 40**	**Comparable Worth**

Objectives

- Explain the four stages in the struggle for women's rights.
- Explain the Equal Rights Amendment—its purpose and history.
- Define *feminist* and demonstrate an understanding of current feminist issues.

Vocabulary

comparable worth   Title IX   feminist

BACKGROUND

The fight to secure women's rights is as old as the nation. When John Adams was at the Continental Congress, his wife Abigail wrote him to remind him, "Don't forget the ladies." Women in our early history were denied the vote, legal rights, and education, and they could not sign contracts. Things began to change in the 1800s.

In 1848 the women's rights movement began with a meeting in Seneca Falls, New York, where the ladies who attended rewrote the Declaration of Independence with a feminist slant. Although there were no immediate results, the leaders at this meeting went on to lead the suffrage movement in the late 1800s.

Once suffrage was achieved, the next significant development was a book published in 1963. Betty Friedan's *The Feminine Mystique* challenged women to throw off stereotypical roles and put themselves first for a change. It also encouraged women to get an education and have a career. All this led to the formation of the National Organization for Women (NOW), and it helped motivate women to become politically active.

Congress started to pay attention. It passed Title IX of the Education Act of 1972, and it sent the Equal Rights Amendment out to the states for ratification. Title IX has sparked controversy because it forced colleges to spend evenly on men's and women's activities, which often meant cutting back on men's programs. Needless to say, this caused some resentment on many campuses.

The courts have stepped in and created guidelines (the reasonableness standard) to establish whether different treatment based on gender is appropriate. The courts have also helped establish the doctrine of comparable worth, which guarantees men and women will be paid based on the value of the job they are performing, not who is performing the job. Another key issue is the "glass ceiling." This is the concept that women will only rise to a certain point in corporations, and no further. This is not written as corporate policy, but statistics support it as reality.

Further Resources

McGlen, Nancy E., and Karen O'Connor. *Women, Politics, and American Society.* 2nd ed. Englewood Cliffs, NJ: Prentice-Hall, 1998.

National Organization for Women. http://www.now.org

Rhode, Deborah L. *Speaking of Sex: The Denial of Gender Inequality.* Cambridge, MA: Harvard University Press, 1997.

For Discussion

Review

1. *What are the requirements of Title IX?* (Title IX requires that all schools receiving federal funds offer male and female students equal classroom and extracurricular activities.)

2. *Is it possible for a man to be a feminist? Explain.* (Feminists are persons who advocate political, social, and economic rights for women, so gender doesn't matter as long as they have these views.)

3. *Who was Lucretia Mott?* (She was a leader in the early days of the woman's suffrage movement and an organizer of the Women's Rights Convention of 1848.)

4. *What is the concept of comparable worth?* (Comparable worth is the principle that women should be paid salaries equal to those of men for equivalent jobs and skills.)

Critical Thinking

1. *Do you think it is fair that women would not be drafted if the draft were reinstated?* (Answers will vary, but students should provide reasons.)

2. *Why do you think the Equal Rights Amendment was not ratified when it was sent to the states?* (Answers will vary, but they may include that most state legislatures were made up of men who did not want to approve it, that the nation was not ready for the ERA, or that the impact on society was exaggerated by groups opposed, most of which were led by women.)

3. *Do you think the United States will elect a woman President in the next 20 years?* (Be sure students explain their answers.)

Skills Development Activities

1. **WRITING:** Title IX

   Have students write a letter to the school board (not to be sent) that explains the benefits and drawbacks of having co-educational physical education classes based on Title IX. As part of their letters, students need to include a recommendation to either keep the classes the way they are or propose an alternative. Whichever point of view they take, they must support the position.

2. **CURRENT EVENTS:** Women Leaders

   Have students work in pairs to research powerful women in government and political positions throughout the world. Suggest they choose five women and list several facts about each.

3. **INTERNET:** National Organization for Women

   Have students log on to the Web site of the National Organization for Women at http://www.now.org. They should click on the "Issues" button and then select one of the issues. Ask students to summarize NOW's position on the issue and explain why they agree or disagree. This should take one or two pages.

4. **SPECIAL SOURCES:** Seneca Falls

   Have students find a complete copy of the Seneca Falls *Declaration of Sentiments*; it can be found on the Internet or in many books on women's rights. Have students read the *Declaration* and write their reaction to it in a two-paragraph essay stating what surprised them in the document and why.

Study Guide

Name: _____

Complete each item as you read Chapter 16 (pages 328–331).

1. Women's rights activists met at _____, New York, in 1848.

2. Two key leaders of the early women's rights movement were_____ and

   _____.

3. The _____ Amendment gave women the right to vote in the year

   _____.

4. Who wrote *The Feminine Mystique?* _____.

5. _____ of the Education Act of 1972 forbids sex discrimination in federally subsidized schools.

6. Two standards the Supreme Court uses when considering sexual equality are the

   _____ standard and the _____ standard.

7. The _____, or ERA, was passed by Congress in

   _____.

8. It fell just three states short of ratification in _____.

Vocabulary

Read each description, and write the letter of the correct term on the line.

1. _____ Advocates of women's rights

2. _____ Requires equal funding of male and female activities in federally subsidized educational programs

3. _____ Principle that men and women should be paid equally for equivalent work

a comparable worth
b feminists
c Title IX

Multiple-Choice Test

Name: _____

Find the best answer for each item. Then completely fill in the circle for that answer.

1. When was the Seneca Falls meeting held?

    a. 1840
    b. 1848
    c. 1920
    d. 1963

2. For what did Lucretia Mott and Elizabeth Cady Stanton fight?

    a. abolition
    b. women's rights
    c. women's suffrage
    d. all of the above

3. Which amendment gave women the right to vote?

    a. the 16th Amendment
    b. the 17th Amendment
    c. the 18th Amendment
    d. the 19th Amendment

4. Who wrote *The Feminine Mystique?*

    a. National Organization for Women
    b. Betty Friedan
    c. Lucretia Mott
    d. none of the above

5. What are feminists?

    a. female advocates of women's rights
    b. members of the National Organization for Women
    c. advocates of women's rights
    d. women

6. Educational programs subsidized by the federal government must provide males and females equal activities under

    a. *Reed v. Reed*
    b. Title IX
    c. comparable worth
    d. the 19th Amendment

7. The Supreme Court applies the _____ standard and the _____ standard when considering issues of sexual equality.

    a. political, economic
    b. equal protection, Seneca Falls
    c. reasonableness, equality
    d. reasonableness, strict scrutiny

8. What is the ERA?

    a. a proposed constitutional amendment
    b. part of Title IX
    c. the Equal Rights Act
    d. a feminist interest group

9. Comparable worth is most directly related to the world of

    a. the courts
    b. business
    c. government
    d. education

10. The *Reed v. Reed* decision involved

    a. the draft
    b. pregnancy leaves
    c. estate administrators
    d. drinking ages

	a	b	c	d
1	a	b	c	d
2	a	b	c	d
3	a	b	c	d
4	a	b	c	d
5	a	b	c	d
6	a	b	c	d
7	a	b	c	d
8	a	b	c	d
9	a	b	c	d
10	a	b	c	d

Essay Question

Should the ERA be ratified? Provide at least two specific reasons for your position.

For use with:	**Chapter 16**	**Civil Rights**
For use with:	Activity 41	The Timeline of Affirmative Action

Objectives

- Identify key equality concerns of older Americans, disabled Americans, and homosexuals.
- Explain affirmative action and reverse discrimination.
- Discuss the significance of the *Bakke* decision.

Vocabulary

affirmative action   quota   reverse discrimination

BACKGROUND

The issue of civil rights has historically involved the rights of African Americans. Recently, however, other groups have stepped forward to demand fair treatment and recognition as well.

Senior citizens have become one of the most powerful groups in America today. As their numbers have increased, they have demanded more attention from those in Washington. In recent years, seniors' issues have included Social Security, Medicare, age discrimination, and mandatory retirement. This final issue is the one that has received the most attention thus far: a mandatory retirement age of 65. Social Security has also received a lot of attention from the American Association of Retired Persons (AARP), and, as a result, from Washington too.

With the Americans with Disabilities Act (ADA), people with disabilities have been granted significant protection. Accommodations for those with disabilities have caused resentment. The most visible signs of ADA have been the ramps and parking places for the handicapped, but it has also meant adjustments in the workplace as well. The issue for business is the phrase "reasonable accommodation." How far must an employer go to enable an employee with disabilities?

Another group that has sought equal treatment has been gay men and lesbians. In recent times issues for gays have included access to housing, being able to adopt children, gay marriages, and the right to serve in the military. A number of communities have passed laws forbidding discrimination based on sexual orientation.

Racial minorities, seniors, individuals with disabilities, and homosexuals have fought for equal treatment for years. The government has tried to step in and help with a program called affirmative action. This program stems from an executive order by President Lyndon Johnson. The order was to guarantee that minorities would be hired, promoted, etc., according to set proportions, often based on race and/or gender. Recent Court rulings have increasingly limited affirmative action.

Further Resources

American Civil Liberties Union. "Freedom Network."
    http://www.aclu.org
Bronner, Ethan. "Black and Hispanic Admissions off Sharply at
    U. of California." *The New York Times,* 1 Apr 1988, Al.
Roemer, John E. *Equality of Opportunity.* Cambridge, MA: Harvard
    University Press, 1998.

For Discussion

Review

1. *What are four rights guaranteed to disabled individuals by the ADA?* (Answers should include four of the following: employment [people with disabilities cannot be denied jobs or promotions], access to government programs, public accommodations [people with disabilities must have access to all public buildings], public transportation, and telephones [special devices must be provided to those in need, where possible].)

2. *What is affirmative action?* (Affirmative action is a program of government and private policies designed to provide equal opportunity for minority groups who have suffered from discrimination in the past.)

3. *What is reverse discrimination?* (This is a situation in which affirmative action policies benefit one group and result in the loss of opportunity for the majority group.)

4. *Why was the* Bakke *case ruling important?* (The ruling stated that a college admissions program based solely on racial preference was illegal, but race may be considered as a factor in a set-aside program that looks at multiple factors.)

Critical Thinking

1. *Do you think there should be a mandatory retirement age?* (Before students answer, ask them to imagine they are 64 years of age.)

2. *Do you agree with Justice Kennedy's opinion in* Romer v. Evans? (As students answer, encourage them to recognize the assumptions various arguments rest upon.)

3. *To make public transportation truly accessible for persons with disabilities, some cities would have to buy new buses. What do you think is a reasonable accommodation for a city to make? Can you think of an alternative?* (Answers will vary.)

4. *Do you believe colleges should set admissions quotas?* (Students may want to refer to the* Bakke *case as they answer.)

Skills Development Activities

1. **WRITING:** Affirmative Action

   Have students write a two- to three-page formal research essay analyzing one of the affirmative action Supreme Court decisions cited on pages 337–339. Suggest that students use at least five reliable sources and require that they use MLA documentation. Essays should provide background of the issue and a summary of both sides. Ask students not to disclose their own views in their papers.

2. **CURRENT EVENTS:** Don't Ask, Don't Tell

   One of President Bill Clinton's campaign promises was a pledge to allow gays to serve openly in the military, but he backed off and went to a "don't ask, don't tell" position. Have students write short editorials that support one side of this question.

3. **INTERNET:** The AARP's Issues

   Ask students to log on to the Web site of the American Association of Retired Persons (AARP) at http://www.aarp.org, and have them search for an issue or go to the legislative issues link on the home page. Ask students to find the AARP's position on that issue and write a one- to two-paragraph summary of the issue and the AARP's position. Students can work in groups or individually.

4. **SPECIAL SOURCES:** Proposition 209

   Have students reread the feature on Proposition 209 in the textbook. Also have students look at http://vote96.ss.ca.gov/BP/209.htm (and the links at the bottom of the page). Then have them make a chart with one side listing the benefits and the other side listing the concerns or impacts of the proposition. Once students bring in information, the class can debate the issues surrounding Proposition 209.

Study Guide

Name: _____

Complete each item as you read Chapter 16 (pages 332–339).

1. Today, the general compulsory retirement age is _____.

2. One of the most powerful interest groups that lobbies for older Americans is the

   _____, or AARP.

3. About _____ percent of the U.S. population is made up of people with disabilities.

4. In 1990 the _____ passed, extending many protections to people with disabilities.

5. In _____,

   the Supreme Court ruled that laws against homosexual relations are constitutional.

6. The " _____ " policy applies to gays in the

   military.

7. Various policies designed to provide equal opportunity for groups that have suffered discrimination are called

   _____.

8. _____ refers to discrimination against a majority group.

9. Who won the *Bakke* case? _____

10. Four important court decisions about affirmative action are:

    1) _____,

    2) _____,

    3) _____, and

    4) _____.

Vocabulary

Read each description, and write the letter of the correct term on the line.

1. _____ Policies designed to provide equal opportunity for groups that have
   suffered discrimination

2. _____ Minimum numbers of minority group members that must be hired,
   promoted, or admitted

3. _____ Discrimination against a majority group

a	affirmative action
b	quotas
c	reverse discrimination

Multiple-Choice Test

Name: _____

Find the best answer for each item. Then completely fill in the circle for that answer.

1. What is today's general compulsory retirement age?
   - **a.** 50
   - **b.** 55
   - **c.** 65
   - **d.** 70

2. About how many people are members of AARP?
   - **a.** 1 million
   - **b.** 3 million
   - **c.** 10 million
   - **d.** 30 million

3. In 1990 Congress passed the
   - **a.** Americans with Disabilities Act
   - **b.** Rehabilitation Act
   - **c.** U.S. Education of All Handicapped Children Act
   - **d.** Age Discrimination in Employment Act

4. Which case stated that laws forbidding homosexual relations are constitutional?
   - **a.** *Romer v. Evans*
   - **b.** *Reed v. Reed*
   - **c.** *Fullilove v. Klutznick*
   - **d.** *Hardwick v. Georgia*

5. Various policies that promote equality are called
   - **a.** quotas
   - **b.** affirmative action
   - **c.** reverse discrimination
   - **d.** all of the above

6. A legal requirement to hire at least a certain number of minority members in a certain industry is called a(n)
   - **a.** quota
   - **b.** injunction
   - **c.** civil right
   - **d.** "undue hardship"

7. Which best describes one result of the *Bakke* case?
   - **a.** Quotas are unconstitutional.
   - **b.** Race can be considered when admitting students.
   - **c.** Reverse discrimination is required by the Constitution.
   - **d.** Affirmative action programs died out.

8. The "don't ask, don't tell" policy applies to people in the United States
   - **a.** who have disabilities
   - **b.** who are gay
   - **c.** who are past retirement age
   - **d.** who are illegal aliens

9. In _____, the Supreme Court held that a promotion of a woman to remedy past discrimination was constitutional.
   - **a.** *Johnson v. Transportation Agency of Santa Clara County*
   - **b.** *Adarand Constructors v. Pena*
   - **c.** *Fullilove v. Klutznick*
   - **d.** *United Steelworkers v. Weber*

10. Any government-created quota system will be
    - **a.** phased out immediately
    - **b.** ruled constitutional
    - **c.** ruled unconstitutional
    - **d.** subjected to "strict scrutiny"

	a	b	c	d
1	a	b	c	d
2	a	b	c	d
3	a	b	c	d
4	a	b	c	d
5	a	b	c	d
6	a	b	c	d
7	a	b	c	d
8	a	b	c	d
9	a	b	c	d
10	a	b	c	d

Essay Question

Explain when affirmative action policies began, what their purpose is, and why they are given that name.

Public Policy and Comparative Government

Topics

Accompanying Activities in the *Activity Book*

Objectives

- Identify and define steps in the government's policy-making process.
- Explain how the government manages the economy through monetary and fiscal policy.
- Analyze government policies regarding raising and spending money.

Vocabulary

free enterprise	deficit	national debt
monetary policy	fiscal policy	entitlement

BACKGROUND

In an era of great prosperity, it seems strange to talk of recession and depression. Yet much of what concerns us today revolves around fear of depression and recession. Government economic policies seem to work better today, but many economists often appear at odds about what we should do next.

Economic solutions for economic policy have gone from theories about the demand-side to the supply-side, from Keynesian "pump-priming" to trickle-down. Is it computers and high-tech solutions that have helped things work better, or are we just in a cycle of prosperity that will change no matter what we do? Many scholars believe that the increased production of goods during World War II saved us from the Great Depression, even though New Deal policies helped. Would we need another war to save us from such a debacle again? Given the weapons of mass destruction we have today, such a war has the potential to end civilization as we know it.

Generally governments espouse policies that try to ensure citizen acceptance of the legitimacy of that government. In their book

Comparative Politics Today: A World View, Gabriel Almond and G. Bingham Powell, Jr., state that public policy can be evaluated using four major questions:

1. How does the political system develop and implement policies to extract resources from the environment, whether human, natural, or capital?

2. How does the political system develop and implement policies to allocate resources to individuals and groups in terms of goods and services?

3. What policies does the political system develop and implement to regulate the behaviors of the people who produce and consume resources?

4. What appeals does the political system make to the patriotism, history, ideology, and values of its citizens to spur them to participate in the system and to comply with the policies it sets forth?

Applying Almond's and Powell's questions to the policy-making processes of the United States should serve to make the government's economic policy more understandable.

Further Resources

Federal Reserve Bank of Minneapolis. "United States Monetary Policy."
     http://woodrow.mpls.frb.fed.us/info/policy/
Heilbroner, Robert L., and Lester C. Thurow. *The Economic Problem.*
     7th ed. Englewood Cliffs, NJ: Prentice-Hall, 1984.

For Discussion

Review

1. *What are the steps generally followed in the government's policy-making process?* (They are establishing the problem, formulating a policy, adopting the policy, implementing the policy, and evaluating the policy.)

2. *What do the terms* deficit *and* national debt *mean?* (They refer to conditions arising when the government owes money and spends more than it receives.)

3. *What action does the Federal Reserve Board take to control monetary policy?* (It can set discount rates, set margin requirements, set reserve requirements, and create more money.)

4. *What is the difference between regressive taxes and progressive taxes?* (Regressive taxes tend to hit the poor harder than do progressive taxes.)

Critical Thinking

1. *Why do you think that some U.S. citizens, such as presidential contender Steve Forbes, have proposed a flat tax rate on incomes?* (Have students calculate how a flat tax rate works compared to a progressive rate.)

2. *Who has the most power in determining the federal budget?* (Have students refer to the chart on page 355 as they explain their views.)

3. *Why do you think that the federal government spends such a large percentage of its budget for* *military defense?* (Encourage students to consider the American military obligation today and historical significance of the cold war before they answer.)

4. *Should the Constitution contain an amendment requiring the federal government to balance its annual budget? Why or why not?* (Encourage students to think about the power of the Constitution and national emergencies such as wars.)

Skills Development Activities

1. **WRITING:** Policy Making

   Have students write a short expository essay about a policy of their school. If possible, have them analyze the five stages of the policy-making process, concentrating on how the policy is being (or was) evaluated. Policies might be about dress codes, eligibility for athletics, absences, and so forth.

2. **CURRENT EVENTS:** Federal Reserve Board

   Have students locate a news report about recent actions of the Federal Reserve Board. Ask them to summarize the information orally.

3. **INTERNET:** The National Debt

   Have students determine approximately how much the national debt increases in a day, a month, or a year.

4. **SPECIAL SOURCES:** Budget Review

   Have students locate and skim part of the Government Accounting Office's annual audit of the budget. Talk with them about who uses the information and for what purposes.

Study Guide

Name: _____

Complete each item as you read Chapter 17 (pages 342–356).

1. List and explain the five stages of policy making.

   a. _____

   b. _____

   c. _____

   d. _____

   e. _____

2. America's economic system is based on _____.

3. The _____ is responsible for _____,
   or the control of the money supply.

4. The two main theories of U.S. fiscal policy are _____ economics and
   _____ economics.

5. The largest source of federal revenue is the federal _____

6. _____ taxes hit the poor harder; _____ taxes vary
   with a person's ability to pay.

7. The three largest expenditures of the federal government are for _____, national
   _____, and the national _____.

8. About 70 percent of items in the budget are _____.

Vocabulary

Read each description, and write the letter of the correct term on the line.

1. _____ Economic system in which private businesses compete for profit

2. _____ Government spending exceeding government revenue

3. _____ Total money borrowed by the federal government but not yet repaid

4. _____ Policy that controls the money supply

5. _____ Policy that controls government revenue and spending

6. _____ Payment required by law

a	deficit
b	fiscal policy
c	free enterprise
d	monetary policy
e	national debt
f	entitlement

Multiple-Choice Test

Name: _____

Find the best answer for each item. Then completely fill in the circle for that answer.

1. Which stage in policy making occurs FIRST?
   - **a.** adopting a policy
   - **b.** evaluating a policy
   - **c.** implementing a policy
   - **d.** recognizing the problem

2. The _____ is the sum of money the federal government has borrowed but not yet repaid.
   - **a.** budget deficit
   - **b.** national debt
   - **c.** regressive tax
   - **d.** budget resolution

3. Who manages monetary policy?
   - **a.** the President
   - **b.** Congress
   - **c.** the Federal Reserve Board
   - **d.** the Office of Management and Budget

4. Fiscal policy is concerned with
   - **a.** taxing
   - **b.** spending
   - **c.** borrowing
   - **d.** all of the above

5. According to _____ economics, the government should help manage consumer demand.
   - **a.** free enterprise
   - **b.** capitalist
   - **c.** Keynesian
   - **d.** supply-side

6. Which is the single largest source of federal revenue?
   - **a.** social insurance taxes
   - **b.** income taxes
   - **c.** estate taxes
   - **d.** excise taxes

7. On what does the federal government spend the most?
   - **a.** defense
   - **b.** the debt
   - **c.** grants to states and localities
   - **d.** entitlements

8. Who pays discount rates when they borrow money?
   - **a.** the bureaucracy
   - **b.** other nation-states
   - **c.** banks
   - **d.** all of the above

9. According to the Constitution, who has the right to borrow money for the federal government?
   - **a.** Congress
   - **b.** the Federal Reserve Board
   - **c.** the Office of Management and Budget
   - **d.** the President

10. The federal budget process begins about how long before the budget goes into effect?
    - **a.** 3 years
    - **b.** 5 years
    - **c.** 6 months
    - **d.** 18 months

	a	b	c	d
1	a	b	c	d
2	a	b	c	d
3	a	b	c	d
4	a	b	c	d
5	a	b	c	d
6	a	b	c	d
7	a	b	c	d
8	a	b	c	d
9	a	b	c	d
10	a	b	c	d

Essay Question

Explain how fair you think the U.S. tax system is. Should rich people pay more than poor people?

For use with:	**Chapter 17**	**Public Policy**
For use with:	**Activity 43**	**Our Energy in 2025**

Objectives

- List several reasons why the government uses regulations to implement its policies.
- Identify several laws governing business, labor, the environment, and energy.
- Analyze the reasons why citizens support or object to various regulatory policies.

Vocabulary

domestic policy   foreign policy   monopoly

BACKGROUND

Regulatory policies occur when the government wishes to control the behaviors of individuals and/or groups in the society. Policy implementation is always accompanied by some sort of regulatory policy. Most citizens encounter such policies only when paying taxes or following traffic regulations. Some regulations will come as trade-offs or alternative costs to participating in the society. For example, to save some endangered species, we have to limit public access to certain areas. To protect people from each other, we need to have laws governing certain kinds of behaviors in public places, such as no-smoking regulations.

According to Almond and Powell, we need to pose several questions as we implement public regulatory policy:

What behaviors does the political system wish to and need to regulate?

What sanctions need to be imposed to make citizens comply with the regulations?

Who (what groups and individuals) will be regulated, what protections for rights will exist, and what appeals from sanctions will exist? Will there be equality of application of the regulations?

One of the major problems confronted by governments in democratic societies is that people wish to see others regulated but not necessarily themselves. Many people wish to see the environment preserved or zoning regulations enforced but not at their own expense. In other words, in democratic societies, whether regulations exist for business, for labor, for the environment, or for energy, someone is going to be inconvenienced by some regulations, and many individuals and groups who will often benefit from long-term trade-offs believe that their personal goals are thwarted by such regulations.

Finally, due process rights and civil liberties often confront regulations designed to help protect the majority of citizens. When such situations occur, the courts often have to intervene to decide whether or not the regulations can be enforced in the way the government would wish. Of course, in authoritarian societies, such problems seldom occur because citizen complaints carry sanctions that usually restrict all rights to relief from the regulations.

Further Resources

Niveta, Peitro. *The Politics of Energy Conservation.* Washington, DC: Brookings Institute, 1986.

Reich, Robert B. *The Work of Nations: Preparing Ourselves for Twenty-first Century Capitalism.* New York: Knopf, 1991.

Wilson, James G., ed. *The Politics of Regulation in the United States.* New York: Basic Books, 1980.

For Discussion

Review

1. *What are the meanings of the terms* **domestic policy** *and* **foreign policy**? (*Domestic policy* refers to policies relating to issues in the United States, while *foreign policy* is a body of policies the United States pursues with other countries.)

2. *Why did the Federal Trade Commission investigate the computer software company, Microsoft Corporation?* (It has been accused of trying to monopolize the software industry.)

3. *What is a conglomerate?* (It is a corporation that controls a variety of businesses.)

Critical Thinking

1. *Why do you think that some consumers and some industries might object to the Clean Air Act of 1990?* (Students might say it had the effect of raising the prices of products such as automobiles.)

2. *Do you think that the United States should refuse to trade with nations that fail to develop proper environmental policies? Why or why not?* (Encourage students to consider the environmental policies of the United States as well as our trade policies.)

3. *What do you think is a fair minimum wage for all workers?* (Urge students to imagine themselves as employers and employees as they think about their answers.)

4. *Do you think no-smoking regulations in restaurants, offices, and other public places are fair?* (Answers will vary.)

Skills Development Activities

1. **WRITING:** Air and Water Quality

   Have students write a letter to the editor of a local newspaper about pollution problems in their community. Encourage them to offer a potential solution or "next step" to take.

2. **CURRENT EVENTS:** Microsoft

   Using the *Readers' Guide* or the Internet, have students locate articles about the Justice Department's lawsuit against Microsoft. Ask students to present a brief oral report to the class about their findings.

3. **INTERNET:** Business and Labor

   Have the students locate one or more Web sites regarding aircraft unions and airline labor difficulties. Have them state the facts in each case and report their findings to the class.

4. **SPECIAL SOURCES:** Pollution

   Refer students to the Major Anti-Pollution Policies chart on page 361. Then have them conduct research about how one policy listed in the chart has affected their local communities. Suggest the value of conducting interviews with local officials.

Study Guide

Name: _____

Complete each item as you read Chapter 17 (pages 357–361).

1. _____ policy focuses on concerns within the United States, while

    _____ policy is concerned with U.S. interactions with other countries.

2. Three key laws that targeted eliminating monopolies were the _____ Act, the

    _____ Act, and the _____ Act.

3. Four key laws that sought to regulate labor were the _____ Act, the

    _____ Act, the _____ Act, and the

    _____ Act.

4. To enforce the Clayton Act, Congress established the _____ in 1914.

5. Although monopolies have largely disappeared, two newer threats to competition are the

    _____ and the _____.

6. The government agency that plays a key role in regulating the environment is the EPA, or

    _____

7. The _____

    Act has two goals: to make U.S. waters clean enough for swimming and wildlife and to end pollution of the

    nation's waterways.

Vocabulary

Read each description, and write the letter of the correct term on the line.

1. _____ Concerned with events within the United States

2. _____ Concerned with events outside the United States

3. _____ Business that lacks competition

a	domestic policy
b	foreign policy
c	monopoly

Multiple-Choice Test

Name: _____

Find the best answer for each item. Then completely fill in the circle for that answer.

1. _____ policy is concerned with the United States' relationships with other countries.
   - **a.** Regulatory
   - **b.** Foreign
   - **c.** Social
   - **d.** Domestic

2. Which was NOT passed to combat monopolies?
   - **a.** the Interstate Commerce Act
   - **b.** the Sherman Antitrust Act
   - **c.** the Wagner Act
   - **d.** the Clayton Act

3. The Federal Trade Commission was established to enforce the _____ Act.
   - **a.** Interstate Commerce
   - **b.** Taft-Hartley
   - **c.** Wagner
   - **d.** Clayton

4. The Fair Labor Standards Act
   - **a.** prohibited child labor
   - **b.** set the work week at 40 hours
   - **c.** set a minimum wage
   - **d.** all of the above

5. Which act established the National Labor Relations Board and guaranteed the rights of workers to use collective bargaining?
   - **a.** the Wagner Act
   - **b.** the Fair Labor Standards Act
   - **c.** the Sherman Antitrust Act
   - **d.** the Clayton Act

6. Which helps regulate the environment?
   - **a.** the NLRB
   - **b.** the FTC
   - **c.** the EPA
   - **d.** the BLS

7. What was originally created to manage Yellowstone?
   - **a.** the National Park Service
   - **b.** the Environmental Protection Agency
   - **c.** the Federal Trade Commission
   - **d.** the U.S. Forest Service

8. The first federal act concerned with air pollution passed in
   - **a.** 1939
   - **b.** 1979
   - **c.** 1986
   - **d.** none of the above

9. Long-term U.S. energy policy planning began after the energy crisis of
   - **a.** 1946–48
   - **b.** 1966–68
   - **c.** 1973–74
   - **d.** 1990–91

10. Regulatory policies affect
    - **a.** businesses
    - **b.** workers
    - **c.** the environment
    - **d.** all of the above

	a	b	c	d
1	a	b	c	d
2	a	b	c	d
3	a	b	c	d
4	a	b	c	d
5	a	b	c	d
6	a	b	c	d
7	a	b	c	d
8	a	b	c	d
9	a	b	c	d
10	a	b	c	d

Essay Question

Trace the development of U.S. labor policy. Discuss at least three acts passed by Congress.

For use with: **Chapter 17** | **Public Policy**

For use with: **Activity 44** | **Saving the Social Security System**

Objectives

- List and explain some of the historical reasons for the development of social welfare policies in the United States.
- Analyze the controversies surrounding the development and implementation of health care and education policies in the United States.

Vocabulary

public assistance   social insurance programs   welfare

BACKGROUND

During the Great Depression in the United States, it became clear to many inside and outside the government that traditional ways of dealing with social problems created by the extreme economic difficulties associated with the Depression were not working. At the Depression's peak, approximately one-fourth of the working population was unemployed and millions of others were underemployed. The New Deal answered many of the problems with radical solutions for the time, thwarting even social and economic policies associated with Marxism and fascism.

While the entry of the United States into World War II helped to bring about prosperity, many of the social welfare policies developed during the Depression remained in force. Such programs as Social Security and other entitlements have become a part of the social fabric in the United States. However, several entitlement programs have been, and continue to be, controversial. Many citizens see such programs as beneficial only as they apply to members of their own families and portions of their own communities.

People often see programs as wasteful when applied to others in the community or in other communities. Many see programs such as food stamps or Aid for Families with Dependent Children (AFDC) or even Medicaid as wasteful and extravagant because they are convinced that most people who use them abuse the programs—at least until they need such programs themselves.

And when the federal government got involved in education programs in the late 1950s, many citizens saw such programs as interfering with their own community's right to decide an education policy. When Title IX policies threatened to withhold federal funds from schools not providing equal opportunities for women in sports and other school activities, many schools had to undergo major changes, and their patrons were angry. Controversies continue to rage over school accountability, school vouchers, and charter schools as the federal government continues its involvement in education.

The controversy over the government's role in social policy making is also evident in the issue of health care and the fate of President Clinton's 1993 proposal.

Further Resources

Bane, Mary Jo, and David T. Elwood. *Welfare Realities: From Rhetoric to Reform.* Cambridge, MA: Harvard University Press, 1994.

Katz, Michael B. *Improving Poor People: the Welfare State, the "Underclass," and Urban Schools as History.* Princeton, NJ: Princeton University Press, 1995.

For Discussion

Review

1. *What does the term* social insurance *mean? Provide two examples of such insurance.* (It provides a safety net for people such as the elderly and the poor in terms of Social Security and Medicaid.)

2. *When we refer to entitlements, what are we talking about?* (These are payments provided for people who meet certain eligibility programs, such as Social Security.)

3. *What does the term* vouchers *mean when applied to education policy?* (They are special "credits" that allow students to attend schools of their choice.)

Critical Thinking

1. *Do you believe that it is necessary, or even appropriate, for the federal government to provide safety net policies for the poor and the elderly? Why or why not?* (Encourage students to consider how people would support themselves without such programs.)

2. *Why do you think that some people believe that the federal government is too involved in education policy?* (Ask students to think about traditional attitudes toward education as they develop their answers.)

3. *Do you believe, as some do, that the federal government should provide basic health care for all citizens? Why or why not?* (Have students review health care policies in their own community before they develop their answers.)

Skills Development Activities

1. **WRITING:** Education Policy

   Ask students to research the educational policy of the current President. Have students write a four- or five-paragraph analytical essay describing and evaluating it.

2. **CURRENT EVENTS:** Food and Drug Administration

   Have students research periodicals to find information about new drugs being tested and approved by the Food and Drug Administration. See how many different drugs the class can list.

3. **INTERNET:** Insurance

   Have students locate Web sites for the American Medical Association and/or the American Pharmaceutical Association and report their findings about positions on health insurance taken by these associations. Have them report their findings to the class.

4. **SPECIAL SOURCES:** Health Care

   After students analyze the cartoon on page 363, have them write a one-paragraph explanation of it. Discuss how its message relates to current health care issues.

Study Guide

Name: _____

Complete each item as you read Chapter 17 (pages 362–366).

1. The government has three main concerns in the American health care system:

   _____ and supervision, _____, and

   _____.

2. President Bill Clinton proposed a _____ program to Congress in 1993.

   Three interest groups who helped defeat it were the _____, the

   _____, and the _____.

3. Aid given to needy people is known generally as _____.

4. Public assistance is available to those who meet _____.

5. _____ programs help the elderly, ill, and unemployed.

6. Five important social insurance programs are _____,

   _____, _____,

   _____, and _____,

7. Most education policy is set by _____ and _____

   governments.

8. _____ have been proposed to give poor school districts a chance to improve and

   give underprivileged students a chance to choose their schools.

Vocabulary

Read each description, and write the letter of the correct term on the line.

1. _____ Public or private programs that help the needy or people with disabilities

2. _____ Aid programs funded by state and federal tax money

3. _____ Government programs created to help elderly, ill, and unemployed citizens

a	public assistance
b	social insurance programs
c	welfare

Multiple-Choice Test

Name: _____

Find the best answer for each item. Then completely fill in the circle for that answer.

1. Who carries out government health research?
   a. the Food and Drug Administration
   b. the Department of Agriculture
   c. the National Institutes of Health
   d. Medicare

2. What is Medicare?
   a. a health industry interest group
   b. a government insurance program for the needy
   c. a government health research program
   d. a public health insurance program for the elderly

3. What is Medicaid?
   a. a health industry interest group
   b. a government insurance program for the needy
   c. a government health research program
   d. a public health insurance program for the elderly

4. What is the AMA?
   a. a health industry interest group
   b. a government insurance program for the needy
   c. a government health research program
   d. a public health insurance program for the elderly

5. Who proposed a national health insurance program?
   a. President Roosevelt
   b. President Reagan
   c. President Bush
   d. President Clinton

6. Which is an example of welfare?
   a. food stamps
   b. Medicare
   c. Medicaid
   d. all of the above

7. Who is largely responsible for starting federal welfare programs?
   a. President Roosevelt
   b. President Reagan
   c. President Bush
   d. President Clinton

8. The Morill Land Grant Act provided money
   a. for school vouchers
   b. to poor people
   c. to Social Security
   d. to state colleges

9. Who is most responsible for setting education policy?
   a. the federal government
   b. the Department of Education
   c. state governments
   d. the AMA

10. A 1997 program proposed by President Clinton was
   a. Centers for Disease Control
   b. the Great Society
   c. Welfare to Work
   d. none of the above

	a	b	c	d
1	a	b	c	d
2	a	b	c	d
3	a	b	c	d
4	a	b	c	d
5	a	b	c	d
6	a	b	c	d
7	a	b	c	d
8	a	b	c	d
9	a	b	c	d
10	a	b	c	d

Essay Question

What is the difference between welfare and social insurance? Cite examples of each.

| For use with: | **Chapter 17** | **Public Policy** |
| For use with: | **Activity 45** | **Foreign Aid Policy** |

Objectives

- Identify and define major American foreign policy goals.
- Distinguish types of American foreign policy strategies, such as sanctions, coercion, and covert operations.
- Explain the role of key foreign and defense policy makers.

Vocabulary

Foreign Service   foreign aid   sanction

BACKGROUND

When the late cartoonist Walt Kelly had his cartoon character Pogo say, "We have met the enemy and he is us," he was referring to U.S. citizens' belief in their nation as the finest, most superior nation on Earth. However, the Vietnam War served notice to many in the United States that others may not see, or even wish to see, the world as we view it.

U.S. policy has sometimes been self-defeating and disastrous. Most of the time, at least during the twentieth century, our policies have served us, and sometimes the rest of the world, well. In his farewell address, George Washington admonished Americans to beware of foreign entanglements. Then, we were a young and fairly weak power. Today, we are arguably the most powerful nation on Earth, with worldwide obligations.

Depending on one's point of view, the United States is either the "Great Satan" or the world's last best hope. Our foreign and defense policies and how they are applied often determine how we are viewed. We are at once viewed as too powerful and, sometimes, too sanctimonious. Our motives are sometimes questioned. Do we encourage sanctions because we genuinely disagree with the way a nation treats its people, or do we encourage them to further our own interests?

And yet, many Americans seldom allow foreign and defense policy to influence their daily lives. When crises are imminent, when the Hitlers, the Milosevics, and the Saddam Husseins confront us with foreign policy and defense decisions, most Americans have opinions and wish to be, at some level, involved at least in the debate over policy. Most of the time, however, we wish to leave the day-to-day concern over policy to those responsible for its oversight.

Finally, most Americans living in our representative democracy wish to know how policies our elected leaders choose to follow affect our national interest. Do these policies support democratic values, do they promote foreign trade, do they affect domestic employment, and is our individual and collective interest threatened? The answers to these questions often determine how much support the policies themselves receive from the citizenry and, ultimately, the implementation of the policies themselves.

Further Resources

Keen, Sam. *Faces of the Enemy: Reflections of the Hostile Imagination.* New York: Harper and Row, 1986.

Kennedy, Paul. *The Rise and Fall of the Great Powers.* New York: Random House, 1987.

von Clausewitz, Carl. *On War.* New York: Penguin Books, 1968.

For Discussion

Review

1. *What are some U.S. foreign policy goals, according to the U.S. Department of State?* (They are preserving national security, promoting world peace, promoting democratic values, and furthering foreign trade.)

2. *What do people mean when they refer to the cold war?* (They mean a period of mostly non-military, hostile confrontation between the United States and the former Soviet Union.)

3. *What are three of the major foreign and defense policy-making agencies for the United States?* (They include the State Department, the Defense Department, the National Security Council, the Central Intelligence Agency, and the Joint Chiefs of Staff.)

4. *What do government officials mean by the term covert operations?* (They usually mean secret operations designed to avoid military involvement.)

Critical Thinking

1. *Do you think that a nation such as the United States should engage in political coercion? Why or why not?* (Encourage students to consider the alternatives to such operations when they develop their answers.)

2. *What actions do you think the United States should take before engaging in military interventions?* (Have students consider the Constitution as well as national interest and our national and foreign policy goals.)

3. *Do you think that Congress should have more of the responsibility for formulating U.S. foreign and defense policies than it does now?* (Encourage students to consider the obligations Congress already possesses as well as what the Constitution says about the executive's role.)

Skills Development Activities

1. **WRITING:** NATO

Have students research the history and goals of the North Atlantic Treaty Organization. Ask them to create a two-page brochure that would explain NATO to U.S. elementary school students.

2. **CURRENT EVENTS:** Military Intervention

Have students summarize in one paragraph a recent news article or television news report on U.S. military operation somewhere in the world. Use the summaries as a basis for a class discussion on defense policy.

3. **INTERNET:** United Nations

Have students use a Web site to identify two or three issues currently being considered by the United Nations. Ask them to report on them to the class.

4. **SPECIAL SOURCES:** Nuclear Proliferation

Have students use an almanac, search the Internet, or use the *Reader's Guide* to find information about nations that possess nuclear weapons and/or nuclear weapons' capability. Then have them construct a table, map, or graph showing a comparison of the relative nuclear capabilities of these nations.

Study Guide

Name: _____

Complete each item as you read Chapter 17 (pages 367–375).

1. What year did the cold war begin? _____ When did it end?

   _____

2. What are the four goals of American foreign policy?

   _____

   _____

   _____

   _____

3. The President takes the lead in foreign policy. What are four agencies that assist the President?

   1) _____, 2) _____,

   3) _____, and 4) _____.

4. The Foreign Service is part of the _____.

5. Three types of diplomatic policy are _____, _____,

   and _____.

6. Alliances can be an effective means of _____ to countries considering military

   action.

7. Three common defense strategies are _____,

   _____, and _____.

Vocabulary

Read each description, and write the letter of the correct term on the line.

1. _____ Diplomatic corps of the State Department

2. _____ Financial and other assistance to other countries

3. _____ A penalty against a nation

a	foreign aid
b	Foreign Service
c	sanction

Multiple-Choice Test

Name: _____

Find the best answer for each item. Then completely fill in the circle for that answer.

1. The cold war lasted from about _____
   to _____.
   a. 1950, 1972   c. 1955, 1983
   b. 1945, 1991   d. 1960, 1998

2. Which is NOT a foreign policy goal of the United States?
   a. to preserve national security   c. to promote human rights
   b. to promote world peace   d. raising U.S. educational standards

3. According to the Constitution, the President shares foreign policy-making powers with
   a. the Supreme Court   c. the Senate
   b. Congress   d. the House

4. Who administers the State Department?
   a. the Foreign Service   c. the Secretary of State
   b. the President   d. the National Security Council

5. American diplomats are part of
   a. the Foreign Service   c. the Department of Defense
   b. the National Security Council d. the Joint Chiefs of Staff

6. Whose headquarters are in the Pentagon?
   a. the Central Intelligence Agency c. the Joint Chiefs of Staff
   b. the Department of Defense   d. the National Security Council

7. An economic penalty directed against another country is called
   a. foreign aid   c. an alliance
   b. a sanction   d. deterrence

8. _____ is an alliance of the United States and western European nations.
   a. DOD   c. JSC
   b. CIA   d. NATO

9. Which is generally the last resort in American foreign policy?
   a. covert operations   c. military intervention
   b. political coercion d. economic sanctions

10. The United States sends weapons to an ally. This is an example of what?
    a. military intervention c. covert operations
    b. sanctions   d. foreign aid

1	ⓐ	ⓑ	ⓒ	ⓓ
2	ⓐ	ⓑ	ⓒ	ⓓ
3	ⓐ	ⓑ	ⓒ	ⓓ
4	ⓐ	ⓑ	ⓒ	ⓓ
5	ⓐ	ⓑ	ⓒ	ⓓ
6	ⓐ	ⓑ	ⓒ	ⓓ
7	ⓐ	ⓑ	ⓒ	ⓓ
8	ⓐ	ⓑ	ⓒ	ⓓ
9	ⓐ	ⓑ	ⓒ	ⓓ
10	ⓐ	ⓑ	ⓒ	ⓓ

Essay Question

The Framers gave Congress the power to declare war. Why do you think they wanted Congress (instead of the President) to have this power?

Objectives

- Identify and define the differences between capitalist, communist, socialist, and mixed economies.
- Describe the differences between democratic and authoritarian political systems.
- Analyze the reasons why communist political systems seem to be on the decline in the late twentieth century.

Vocabulary

capitalism   communism   Marxism   socialism

BACKGROUND

As the twentieth century turns into the twenty-first century, it appears that one of the most dynamic forces governing the lives of millions of people is failing. While communism is alive as a professed ideology in places such as China, the forces of the market are taking hold even there. Market capitalism as a dynamic driving force for delivering, producing, and using resources works, and works well, in many parts of the world.

At the beginning of the twentieth century, colonialism and neocolonialism appeared to be causing nations and peoples in many parts of the world to feel exploited by the capitalist nations of Europe and by the United States. Communism, which promised a utopia on Earth, appealed to many peoples in different places because it seemed to promise an end to exploitative capitalism and a way to gain a measure of equality and security. There are probably many reasons why Marxist communism failed. Clearly, one was the lack of incentives that capitalism provides for those who make it work.

However, capitalism too has its problems. In its provisions for competition, not all can gain security, and some fall by the wayside. Many of the most advanced capitalist nations have provided safety nets to care for those who, for one reason or another, cannot compete as successfully as others. Also, class cleavages appear under capitalism, something that Marxist communism promised to eradicate.

Some authoritarian nations such as China try to mix capitalist market systems with an authoritarian government. It would seem that in the short run they have been successful, given the fact that the gross domestic product of China has risen rapidly over the past few years. However, many predict that given the freedom necessary to operate a successful market economy, it seems likely that such efforts will either destroy the authoritarian regime or that the market economy will be abandoned. Clearly, capitalist market economies need to improve if they are going to serve all of the citizens in capitalist nations as well as they need to. However, it seems relatively certain that communism will not replace these economies soon.

Further Resources

Brzezinski, Zbigniew. *The Grand Failure: The Birth and Death of Communism in the Twentieth Century.* New York: Charles Scribner's Sons, 1989.

Theen, Rolf W., and Frank L. Wilson. *Comparative Politics: An Introduction to Seven Countries.* 3rd ed. Upper Saddle River, NJ: Prentice-Hall, 1996.

For Discussion

Review

1. *What are three of the major factors required to maintain a capitalist economy?* (They include private ownership, freedom of choice, free competition, and the laws of supply and demand.)

2. *What is the major goal of Marxism?* (It is to become a classless society, needing no government.)

3. *What are the major factors necessary for maintaining a democratic political system?* (They are freedom of communication, citizen political efficacy, competitive popular elections, and rule of law.)

4. *What is the difference between a market and a command economy?* (In a command economy, the government has greater control of the economy.)

Critical Thinking

1. *Why do you think that a true socialist (command) economy has never developed in the United States?* (A possible reason is that the United States has tried to curb the worst excesses of capitalism.)

2. *Do you believe that an authoritarian political system will survive in China if Chinese leaders continue to allow, and even encourage, a form of capitalism to exist?* (Encourage students to think about the conditions necessary for the maintenance of capitalism.)

3. *Do you think that the United States would work more effectively if a vote of no confidence could trigger an election? Why or why not?* (Encourage students to think about various possibilities.)

4. *Why do you think that Marxism has ultimately been unsuccessful in many parts of the world?* (Ask students to think about how a Marxist economy is supposed to work and about citizens as subjects.)

Skills Development Activities

1. **WRITING:** Socialism in the United States

   Ask students to research the platforms and candidates of the Socialist party in one of the last two or three presidential elections. Have them write a two-page essay explaining their findings.

2. **CURRENT EVENTS:** Democratic Political Systems

   Ask students to select a country that they believe has a democratic political system. Have them do research so they can assess how well their countries meet the six measures of democracy listed on pages 387–388.

3. **INTERNET:** Communist Leaders

   Have students explore one or more Web sites containing descriptions of the lives and works of several communist leaders, such as Mikhail Gorbachev, Jaing Zemin, and Fidel Castro.

4. **SPECIAL SOURCES:** Communism and Capitalism

   Have students locate summaries or abstracts of Adam Smith's *Wealth of Nations* and Karl Marx's *Das Kapital*. Then have them compare the basic ideas contained in these documents and report their findings to the class.

Study Guide

Name: _____

Complete each item as you read Chapter 18.

1. _____ is an economic system characterized by free-market competition and private ownership.

2. The five characteristics of capitalism are 1) _____,
   2) _____, 3) _____,
   4) _____, and 5) _____.

3. Marx explained these six principles in *Das Kapital:* 1) _____,
   2) _____, 3) _____,
   4) _____, 5) _____, and
   6) _____.

4. _____ is a system of government in which the state owns the means of production.

5. _____ is an economic system that advocates government.
   ownership of the means of production.

6. Four basic elements of socialism are 1) _____,
   2) _____, 3) _____, and
   4) _____.

7. What are six characteristics of democratic political systems? 1) _____,
   2) _____, 3) _____,
   4) _____, 5) _____ and
   6) _____.

8. Authoritarianism is a _____, while communism is an
   _____.

Vocabulary

Read each description, and write the letter of the correct term on the line.

1. _____ Economic system marked by competition in a free market

2. _____ Economic system in which the state controls the means of production

3. _____ Political and economic ideas that emphasize class struggle

4. _____ Economic system in which basic industry is owned by the government

a	capitalism
b	communism
c	Marxism
d	socialism

Multiple-Choice Test   Name: _____

Find the best answer for each item. Then completely fill in the circle for that answer.

1. Which system is most likely to encourage entrepreneurs?

   a. capitalism   **c.** socialism

   b. Marxism   **d.** communism

2. Which is NOT generally a characteristic of capitalism?

   a. private ownership   **c.** a command economy

   b. free competition   **d.** prices determined by supply and demand

3. The labor theory of value states that

   a. the value of goods comes from the workers' labor   **c.** capitalists steal from the workers

   b. in capitalism, workers are paid as little as possible   **d.** workers should own the means of production

4. Which term refers to the working class?

   a. *perestroika*   **c.** proletariat

   b. bourgeoisie   **d.** *laissez-faire*

5. Which statement is true?

   a. Socialism is the same as Marxism.   **c.** Communism is the same as socialism.

   b. Marxism is the same as communism.   **d.** none of the above

6. Under _____, many private industries are often nationalized.

   a. *laissez-faire*   **c.** socialism

   b. capitalism   **d.** a market economy

7. The term for an economy with elements of socialism and capitalism is

   a. mixed economy   **c.** super economy

   b. combined economy   **d.** market economy

8. Which is a feature of an authoritarian political system?

   a. freedom of speech   **c.** competitive popular elections

   b. rule of individuals, not law   **d.** wide recruitment of political leaders

9. Great Britain

   a. is a democracy   **c.** has a unitary system of government

   b. has a monarchy   **d.** all of the above

10. For centuries, China was ruled by

   a. presidents   **c.** emperors

   b. prime ministers   **d.** Socialist parties

1	a	b	c	d
2	a	b	c	d
3	a	b	c	d
4	a	b	c	d
5	a	b	c	d
6	a	b	c	d
7	a	b	c	d
8	a	b	c	d
9	a	b	c	d
10	a	b	c	d

Essay Question

Why is "rule of law," and not the rule of individuals, essential to a democratic political system?

State and Local Government

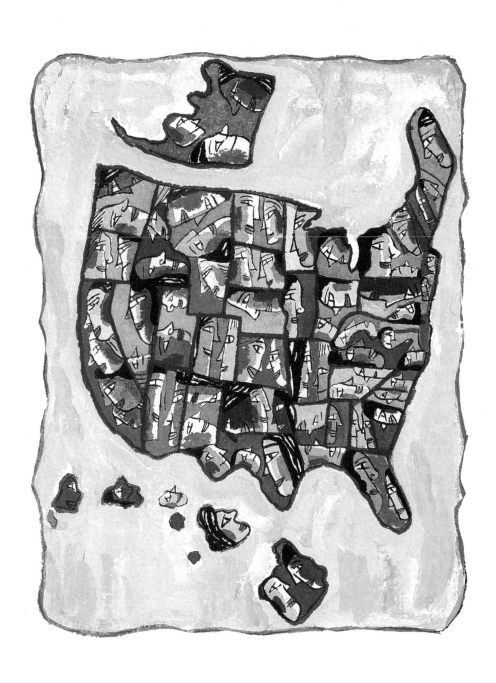

**Accompanying Activities
in the *Activity Book***

For use with: | **Chapter 19** | **Structure of State and Local Government**

For use with: | **Activity 47** | **Editing Your State Constitution**

Objectives

- Explain dispersed versus concentrated power.
- Analyze the roles of state constitutions, legislatures, courts, and governors.
- Explain the basic types of local and city governments.

Vocabulary

initiative   referendum   recall

BACKGROUND

Students spend most of their time studying and learning about the national government, but the government they most often come in contact with is the local government. Many people assume if you have seen one government, you have seen them all, but that certainly is not true. While the chapter mentions seven similarities (democratic in some way, popular elections, some appointed officials, divided branches, bicameral state and federal legislative branches, they tax, and they have court systems), there are four key differences. First, locally, people vote not only for officials but on policy choices as well. Second, at state and local levels, more than just the top executives are elected. Third, party leaders have much more influence over who gets committee chairmanships at state and local levels than nationally. Finally, federal judges are appointed while many state and local judges are elected. Some of these differences are designed to disperse power so no one part of government becomes too powerful. State constitutions vary—some have strong leadership, and some weak.

Almost all state constitutions have been designed to match the national system. All are bicameral (except Nebraska), with an executive (governor) and a court system. The legislatures vary in size, the governors vary in power, and the courts are more active than the federal courts. Many state constitutions also include provisions for initiative, referendum, and recall, all progressive reforms introduced in the early 1900s.

In addition to state governments, there are other levels of government with which people regularly come in contact—county, township, special district (such as school districts), and municipality. It's not terribly surprising that these governments come in different sizes and formats. The level having the most diversity is the municipal level, where governments tend to fall into one of three basic types: mayor-council, commission, and council-manager plan. Mayor-council is the most traditional, the commission form is least used, and the council-manager plan has become the most common form for cities between 10,000 and 200,000 people.

Further Resources

Bonfield, Edward C. *The Unheavenly City.* Boston: Little, Brown, 1970.

Donahue, John D. *Disunited States: What's at Stake as Washington Fades and States Take the Lead.* Glenview, IL: Basic Books, 1997.

Ohio Public Radio/Public Television. "Statehouse News Bureau." http://www.statenews.org

For Discussion

Review

1. *What are the four main differences between national and state or local governments?* (On local levels people vote for more than officials, many more executives are elected rather than appointed, party leaders are more influential, and judges are elected.)

2. *What is the difference between governments with dispersed powers versus those with concentrated powers?* (Governments with dispersed powers feature more positions with varied powers while concentrated governments have fewer individuals with significant power.)

3. *What is a referendum?* (A referendum is a process in which the voters of a state are asked their opinion on a piece of legislation.)

4. *What are the three basic forms of municipal governments?* (The three municipal government structures are mayor-council, council-manager plan, and commission plans. Note that there are strong- and weak-mayor council forms).

Critical Thinking

1. *Federal judges are appointed, and many state and local judges are elected. What impact do you think the different methods of choosing judges might have?* (Since they are elected, state and local judges are more likely subject to political influence and popular pressure in court decisions.)

2. *Why do you think most state constitutions are much longer than the U.S. Constitution?* (State constitution writers often wanted to limit the power of the decision makers, so they spelled out in detail where power could be used.)

3. *In the council-manager plan, the manager is a hired professional. How do you think this reform decreased the power of political machines?* (City managers have no political favors to return and, as hired employees, they are supposed to be removed from political corruption.)

4. *Do you think it's best for local government to concentrate or to disperse political power?* (Students should give reasons as they answer.)

Skills Development Activities

1. **WRITING:** Local Issues

   Have students, as a class, identify areas or issues of concern to the local community. Have each student select an issue with which he or she can identify in some way and have each write a letter to the appropriate local official, expressing his or her point of view and asking if there are any plans to address the issue.

2. **CURRENT EVENTS:** Jesse Ventura

   Have students research the issues and election surrounding Minnesota's choice of Jesse ("The Body") Ventura as governor in 1998. Have students write a one-page summary of the issues and the way Ventura, as a third-party candidate, was able to win. Have them evaluate his potential as a presidential candidate in the future.

3. **INTERNET:** State Government

   Ask students to look up either their state's constitution or their state government organization. Have students make a chart that identifies
   1) elected executive positions and occupants,
   2) the structure of the legislative branch along with the number of seats in each house, and
   3) the state supreme court justices and their terms in office.

4. **SPECIAL SOURCES:** Local History

   Have students go to their local library and research the history of their city, town, or village. Have students write a one-page summary of the history of their community. Encourage them to find and then bring in an early map of their city, town, or village.

Study Guide

Name: _____

Complete each item as you read Chapter 19.

1. The United States has almost _____ local governments.

2. In general, are state governments marked by dispersed or concentrated power?

    _____

3. _____, _____, and

    _____ are three ways voters have a direct say in government in many states.

4. In every state, the governor is chosen by _____ election.

5. Most governors have seven powers: 1) _____,

    2) _____, 3) _____,

    4) _____, 5) _____,

    6) _____, and 7) _____.

6. Most state legislatures are similar to _____ in organization.

7. There are two main kinds of state courts: _____ courts and

    _____ courts. All states have a court of appeals similar to the

    _____.

8. To select state judges, many states use the _____, a method that combines election

    and appointment.

9. There are four basic types of local government: the _____, the

    _____, the _____, and the

    _____.

10. There are three basic types of city government: 1) the _____ plan;

    2) the _____ plan; and 3) the _____ plan.

Vocabulary

Read each description, and write the letter of the correct term on the line.

1. _____ Process by which citizens propose a law

2. _____ Process by which a proposed law is voted upon

3. _____ Process by which voters can remove an elected official from office

a	initiative
b	recall
c	referendum

Multiple-Choice Test

Name: _____

Find the best answer for each item. Then completely fill in the circle for that answer.

1. Which is NOT an important difference between government on the national level and government on the state and local levels?

   a. On the state and local level, people vote for policies as well as officials.

   c. Many more executive branch officials are elected on the national level.

   b. Party leaders at the state level have a greater influence on committee chairmanships than do leaders on the national level.

   d. National judges are appointed; many state judges are elected.

2. Which word best describes power at the state level?

   a. concentrated

   c. unified

   b. centralized

   d. dispersed

3. A group of voters proposes a new state law and gets the proposal on the ballot. What is this an example of?

   a. initiative

   c. referendum

   b. recall

   d. all of the above

4. A statewide election is held to determine whether a new environmental law should be passed. What is this an example of?

   a. initiative

   c. referendum

   b. recall

   d. none of the above

5. Upset voters work to hold an election to remove a corrupt state official from office. What is this an example of?

   a. initiative

   c. Missouri Plan

   b. recall

   d. neither a nor b

6. Which is NOT a power shared by most governors?

   a. to prepare the state budget

   c. to hear cases on appeal

   b. to veto legislation

   d. to issue executive orders

7. A typical state court system includes

   a. trial courts and a supreme court

   c. appeals courts and a supreme court

   b. trial courts and appeals courts

   d. appeals courts, trial courts, and a supreme court

8. Which is NOT a basic unit of local government?

   a. county

   c. commission

   b. township

   d. municipality

9. Typically, schools and water supplies are governed through

   a. counties

   c. townships

   b. special districts

   d. municipalities

10. Which is the most common type of city government?

    a. mayor-council

    c. council-manager

    b. commission

    d. special district

1	a b c d
2	a b c d
3	a b c d
4	a b c d
5	a b c d
6	a b c d
7	a b c d
8	a b c d
9	a b c d
10	a b c d

Essay Question

Explain what a special district is and how it works.

For use with:	**Chapter 20**	**Policies and Finances of State and Local Government**
For use with:	**Activity 48**	**Identifying Local Issues**

Objectives

- Analyze key issues in education, welfare and public health, and law enforcement and public safety policy.
- Define and explain the three types of state and local taxes.
- Identify an example of a tax revolt.

Vocabulary

sales tax   income tax   property tax

BACKGROUND

In the earlier discussion of federalism, there was mention of what are called *reserved powers,* which are powers for the states only. This chapter covers three of the areas most commonly mentioned as state and local responsibilities—education, welfare and public health, and law enforcement and public safety.

All three of these issues create considerable controversy, and not everyone is satisfied with the status quo. The issue that gets the most attention in education is funding. Most agree on standards and curriculum requirements, but the disagreement revolves around leveling the spending between wealthy districts and poor districts. Many states fund schools with a combination of state tax money and local property taxes. It is this local component that gives some districts huge advantages. There have been a number of attempted solutions (such as Act 60 in Vermont) that redistribute the wealth to poorer districts, but obviously the wealthier districts are resisting.

A second area of state responsibility is welfare and public health. Most people agree that basic medical needs should be available for all, but access to welfare is another matter. The most common reforms have been a time limit on benefits and a tying of benefits to some employment, usually called *workfare.*

The final local responsibility discussed is law enforcement and public safety. People want to feel safe wherever they go, but few are willing to pay the cost. More police equal more taxes just like more jails equal more taxes. Most want the benefits but are not willing to put their money behind their wishes.

Given what all states have to do, they must generate revenue somehow. The most common methods used by states are sales taxes, income taxes, property taxes, and other assorted taxes, such as gas or inheritance taxes. Not everyone, however, thinks increasing taxes is the solution, as a number of tax revolts have occurred, forcing taxing bodies to live with less money rather than more.

Further Resources

National Governors' Association and NGA Center for Best Practices.
"NGA Online." www.nga.org
Norris, Donald F., and Lyke Thompson, eds. *The Politics of Welfare Reform.*
Thousand Oaks, CA: Sage Publications, 1995.
The Urban Institute Project. "Assessing the New Federalism."
http://newfederalism.urban.org/html/reports.html

For Discussion

Review

1. *What is a workfare program?* (It is a social program designed to help welfare recipients find and keep jobs.)

2. *What is a sales tax?* (A sales tax is a tax, or additional charge, on purchased items.)

3. *How does a property tax work?* (A property tax is a tax paid based on a percentage of the value of land and buildings.)

4. *What is an example of a tax revolt?* (The chapter mentions two: Act 60 in Vermont, which is being resisted, and Proposition 13 in California.)

Critical Thinking

1. *Some states have toyed with the idea of using vouchers for education. What impact do you think this would have on the education system within states?* (A voucher would be a credit given to the school the children attended. It would force bad schools to improve or go out of business. It might also let more students go to private schools, depending on the guidelines established.)

2. *Is setting a limit on the amount of time a person can receive welfare benefits a good idea? Explain.* (Answers will vary.)

3. *Do you support or oppose state-run lotteries?* (Review page 431 together before students respond.)

Skills Development Activities

1. **WRITING:** Tax Revolt

   Have students reread the feature on the "Revolt of the Gentry" on page 423. The goal of Act 60 is admirable—to increase funding for poorer districts—but is there a better way? Have students write a one- to two-page proposal on what they might suggest for increasing the funding for the poorer districts in the state. Students should be as detailed as possible. They may work in pairs or threes.

2. **CURRENT EVENTS:** Workfare

   Have students find magazine or newspaper articles on workfare or some other welfare alternative, either the proposals or the implementation. They should each write a one-paragraph summary of the article and present a summary to the class. Follow up with a discussion of the merits of workfare or other alternatives to welfare.

3. **INTERNET:** State Spending

   Have students find recent data on their state government expenditures. Discuss how well their information correlates to the data in the pie chart on page 427.

4. **SPECIAL SOURCES:** School District Data

   Help students locate financial information about their school or school district—the tax rate, a budget, construction costs, and so forth. Encourage them to find or create a table, graph, or chart about some of the data and share it with the class.

Study Guide

Name: _____

Complete each item as you read Chapter 20.

1. Three critical areas for which state and local government bear responsibility are

    _____, _____, and

    _____.

2. The greatest single cost for state and local governments is _____.

3. Many states are turning to _____, which requires welfare recipients to work in

    order to receive benefits.

4. In 1998 President Clinton asked _____ for a _____

    for patients.

5. Police and fire protection are primarily the responsibility of _____ governments.

6. In most states, the budget is prepared under direct supervision of the _____.

7. State and local governments rely for funding on the _____ tax, the

    _____ tax, the _____ tax, and miscellaneous

    other taxes.

8. The chief source of income for local governments is the _____ tax.

9. California voters adopted Proposition 13 in _____.

Vocabulary

Read each description, and write the letter of the correct term on the line.

1. _____ A regressive tax on purchased items

2. _____ A progressive tax on annual income

3. _____ Tax on land and buildings

a	income tax
b	property tax
c	sales tax

Multiple-Choice Test

Name: _____

Find the best answer for each item. Then completely fill in the circle for that answer.

1. Which is NOT a major responsibility of state and local governments?

    a. education   **c.** law enforcement

    b. defense   **d.** public health

2. State and local governments spend most money on

    a. police protection   **c.** education

    b. fire protection   **d.** welfare

3. Who runs most schools?

    a. counties   **c.** townships

    b. state governments   **d.** none of the above

4. The requirement that welfare recipients take and keep jobs is called

    a. unemployment compensation   **c.** welfare

    b. social security   **d.** workfare

5. To promote public health, states

    a. license health workers   **c.** set and enforce cleanliness standards

    b. inspect food   **d.** all of the above

6. Police and fire protection are

    a. primarily the responsibilities of local governments   **c.** primarily the responsibilities of the national government

    b. primarily the responsibilities of state governments   **d.** responsibilities shared equally by the local, state, and national governments

7. The role of the federal government in law enforcement has

    a. increased in recent years   **c.** remained about the same in recent years

    b. decreased dramatically in recent years   **d.** decreased slightly in recent years

8. Local governments receive most of their revenue from

    a. sales taxes   **c.** income taxes

    b. property taxes   **d.** business taxes

9. A consumer pays $2.00 in taxes on things he bought at the grocery store. He has just paid a _____ tax.

    a. property   **c.** business

    b. progressive   **d.** sales

10. Proposition _____ limited _____ taxes in _____.

    a. 11, sales, Vermont   **c.** 13, property, California

    b. 12, income, California   **d.** 15, estate, Massachusetts

	a	b	c	d
1	ⓐ	ⓑ	ⓒ	ⓓ
2	ⓐ	ⓑ	ⓒ	ⓓ
3	ⓐ	ⓑ	ⓒ	ⓓ
4	ⓐ	ⓑ	ⓒ	ⓓ
5	ⓐ	ⓑ	ⓒ	ⓓ
6	ⓐ	ⓑ	ⓒ	ⓓ
7	ⓐ	ⓑ	ⓒ	ⓓ
8	ⓐ	ⓑ	ⓒ	ⓓ
9	ⓐ	ⓑ	ⓒ	ⓓ
10	ⓐ	ⓑ	ⓒ	ⓓ

Essay Question

Do you think state or local governments should have a greater say in how schools are run? Why?

Skills Handbook

How to Use the Skills Handbook

The Skills Handbook was designed to allow you, the teacher, maximum flexibility. You can skip around or move in order through a section, cover entire sections or select particular topics within a section, work on skills development in class or assign as homework, and concentrate on a particular skill with the whole class or individualize curriculum by focusing on different skills for different students.

To help students get the most out of the Skills Handbook, the pages that follow provide three kinds of resources for each of the five skills topics.

1.   Introducing the Skills

This page provides advice about how to introduce students to specific skills.

2.   Practicing the Skills

This page offers ideas about what to say and do after students have read the Skills Handbook pages. Brief in-class activities are suggested.

3.   Skills Activity Worksheets

Worksheet 1
Worksheet 2

Two reproducible worksheets, each focusing on one or more of the skills discussed, are included for you to distribute to students. Most are designed to be completed or discussed within a single class period.

INTRODUCING THE SKILLS

Please consider the following comments before introducing these topics to your students.

Taking Notes

For students, taking notes does not come naturally. Working on homework, day-dreaming, or chatting with neighbors is much more fun, but far less helpful at test time. It is crucial to give students a chance to see that taking notes is to their benefit. The challenge, of course, is how to do that. Students have to see the connection between what is in their notes and what they will see on the test. More often than not, students will do the work if they get results. It is important, then, to be very detailed and forthcoming with information early in the year so the connection between what is given as notes and what is on the test is well established. As time goes on, students will be able to operate on less detailed and specific information, but establishing the benefit of note taking early is the key. It really doesn't matter which style students use, so long as they use something!

Annotating a Selection

Annotating a selection is something most people do in their heads as they read, without even thinking about it. If students are told to highlight what they are reading, they can do that. If they are told to annotate their reading, they won't know what you're talking about. The only real difference between highlighting and annotating is making the written notations in the margins. This is an extra step, but it can be very valuable, especially to those students who read but do not understand. The key notations are the questions or the points that are unclear. It is a good practice to ask at the start of class if there are any questions from last night's reading. If this becomes a habit, students will annotate without even realizing what they are doing.

Taking Tests

Tests are the number one assessment tool used by most teachers. It is important to stress that tests are not the only assessment, but given that, they are important. Taking tests can lead to anxiety, stress, and late nights. Test performance can also lead to good grades and growing confidence. The obvious key is not so much format, but preparation for students. If we all had dimes for every time a student said, "it's easy when you study," we would all be rich, but that really is the key. Getting students to review over a period of time versus cramming the night before is probably what makes the biggest difference.

The Writing Process

Writing for some comes very easily. For others, writing is a struggle. It is key to recognize and acknowledge that fact to students. The goal for students should not be to write novels, or even to enjoy writing, but simply to write better. As the section title implies, writing is a process. Better writers take advantage of the process, while poor writers usually shortchange it. As with most study skills, the more time students put into writing something, generally the better it will be. The process described on pages 444–447 is a good one if all the steps are followed. That's a big *if.*

PRACTICING THE SKILLS

Use the following activities to help students develop and practice their skills.

Taking Notes Practice

1. **OPEN-NOTE TEST** Give an open-note test on material from assigned reading or class lectures. Announce the test in advance so that students are motivated to take careful notes.

2. **NEW STRATEGIES** Ask students to outline, use a graphic organizer, or make a K-W-L chart to organize their notes. Suggest that they try a technique they have not used before. Discuss together which methods seemed to work best and why.

Annotating Practice

1. **SAMPLE ANNOTATION** Assign students a newspaper editorial or handout to annotate. Annotate a copy yourself. Then make a transparency so that you can show students how you have marked up the same selection.

2. **CLINTON'S RADIO ADDRESS** Have students complete Worksheet A, in which they annotate a speech by President Clinton. Use their annotations and outlines to start a discussion of how to identify the important parts of a reading.

Test-Taking Practice

ESSAY QUESTIONS As students review for a test, have them each write one essay question that covers some of the material. Put them in pairs and have each student write sample answers for his or her partner's question. After collecting the responses, choose several to discuss anonymously. Help students to identify very specifically what makes some answers better than others.

Writing Process Practice

1. **PROOFREADING AND REVISING** Have students complete Worksheet B. Encourage them to make at least ten proofreading corrections. Review the errors they have found together. Then discuss organizational and content weaknesses of the passage. For instance, the first and last paragraphs suggest the author will discuss three problems with presidential elections, but only two—cost and length—are developed.

2. **TOPICS AND THESES** Discuss with students the differences between knowing your topic and having a thesis, a point to make about that topic. Have students practice developing several thesis statements about a single topic by following the formula described on page 445.

SKILLS ACTIVITY WORKSHEET A— ANNOTATING READINGS

Name: _____

Directions

Read the following excerpts from President Clinton's speech. Using the techniques discussed on page 439, annotate the passage. Then make a brief outline of the major points. Use the back if necessary.

Radio Address to the Nation by President Clinton—May 15, 1999

Good morning. In the past few weeks, ever since that terrible day in Littleton, people all across America have searched their souls and searched for solutions to prevent this kind of tragedy from happening again, and to reduce the level of violence to which our children are exposed.

Last Monday, at our White House strategy session on children and violence, representatives of every sector of society agreed on one fundamental fact: making progress requires taking responsibility by all of us. . . .

I've always said the entertainment industry must do its part, too. In 1993, shortly after I became President, I traveled to Hollywood and spoke there, to members of the community about their responsibility. . . . After six years of work the entertainment industry is helping parents to limit children's exposure to violence, working with the administration on a voluntary rating system for television and the V-chip to enforce it; and on parental screening for the Internet and ratings for all Internet game sites. But there is still too much violence on our nation's screens, large and small. Too many creators and purveyors of violence say there is nothing they can do about it. And there are still too many vulnerable children who are steeped in this culture of violence, becoming increasingly desensitized to it and to its consequences and, therefore, as studies show, hundreds of them more liable to commit violence themselves . . .

Members of the entertainment community can make a big difference. Today, I want to issue three specific challenges to them. First, the whole industry should stop showing guns in any ads or previews children might see. Second, I challenge theater and video store owners all across our country to enforce more strictly the rating systems on the movies they show, rent, and sell. You should check IDs, not turn the other way as a child walks unchaperoned into an R-rated movie. Third, I challenge the movie industry to reevaluate its entire ratings systems, especially the PG rating, to determine whether it is allowing too much gratuitous violence in movies approved for viewing by children.

Our administration is fighting to do all we can to protect children. The entertainment industry should do everything it can, too. . . . We can do it together.

Outline:

SKILLS ACTIVITY WORKSHEET B—
PROOFREADING AND REVISING

Name: _____

Directions

Read the following selection carefully. Your task is to proofread the passage that follows and make all necessary corrections. Then on the back make suggestions to the writer as to how to improve the organization of the essay. Begin by identifying the main point and evaluating how well the paragraphs support it.

Problems with Presidential Elections Today

In the United States we hold elections every for years because the constitution directs that we have to do that. Since the time of Washington their have been many distinguished men who have filled the position of chief executive. But recently presidential elections have become more like beauty contests. The public doesn't know where candidates stand on all the issues all the time, campaigns are too long, and they're too costly.

Over the years most of the presidents came from one of the two major parties. The major partys have changed over the years. Federalists and the Democratic-Republicans were the first ones, and they were followed by the whigs and then the modern Republican party of today. The Republicans were the party of Lincon, Theodore Roosevelt, and Eisenhower, they were all well respected by the people that elected them. These presidents would not like what has happened to presidential election today.

Campaigns today are so expensive that only people with lots of money or lots of connections really have a chance of getting elected. The last election was the most expensive time ever to run. The candidates in 1996 each spent about 66 million dollars. That is to much.

Finally, campaigns today are also much longer then in the old days. Today candidates begin thanking about running for President 2 years before the actual election. In that time that is extra, the candidates will engage in that type of activity that is most to get that candidate noticed so that people will vote for that candidate. That certainly takes up a lot of time and energy. Also having extremely large campaign staffs. It is not unusual for candidates to have as many as 20 people working for them.

As I have discussed, there are three major problems with presidential elections today. They are to expensive, and they cost way too much especially for advertising and commercials. Presidents should be given money to make it possible for even poor candidates to be able to run, not just rich people. Campaigns also drag out too long. We need to fix the problems in modern presidential elections.

INTRODUCING THE SKILLS

Please consider the following comments before introducing these topics to your students.

Reading Effectively

Effective reading is not as difficult as it sounds. Students often ask how long it should take them to read something, and the answer is usually about half of what they expected. The first thing they should be told is to not just read, but to "read smart." Anyone can become a more efficient and effective reader by trying a few of the techniques mentioned in the checklist on page 448, but like most things it takes a little discipline.

Thinking Clearly

Help students recognize that every time something is learned, people make judgments and evaluations, and they compare that new information to what they already knew. By doing this mental processing, individuals are able to understand the new information and think clearly about it within a frame of reference.

Avoiding Fallacies

Fallacies are part of everyday life, and students will probably enjoy trying to recognize these logical flaws. Most advertising contains some information that may not be 100 percent factual. Political commercials are famous for presenting half-truths or slanting the story. Most often fallacies are found when statements are challenged or questioned, so the message for students is: Don't be afraid to ask!

Distinguishing Facts from Opinions

Students will probably be confident they can distinguish between fact and opinion. Fact is verifiable as true. Opinions usually reflect an emotional interpretation of attitudes or beliefs. What gets tricky is when these two are combined in something like "interest rates are down, which is great for our economic future." The key here seems to be separating head from heart, what we know versus what we feel.

Recognizing Assumptions

Students may not have had much experience identifying the unstated assumptions in what they read or hear. Help students to see that most any book is written from a certain point of view. (For instance, was George Washington really one of our greatest Presidents, or was he lucky enough to be first?) Assumptions are rarely stated but tend to appear more as attitude.

Making Generalizations and Drawing Conclusions

Generalizations are interesting creatures. There is usually some kernel of truth to them which is then applied to everyone—kind of like stereotypes. Often in generalizations the "buzz" words, such as "every," "all," or "no," appear. Introduce students to these topics by looking carefully at the chart on page 455 about women in the House.

PRACTICING THE SKILLS

Use the following activities to help students develop and practice their skills.

Effective Reading Practice

ASKING QUESTIONS Select a short passage for the class to read together. Then ask each student to write down at least three questions that occur to them as they read. Have them share their questions and use them to generate a discussion about the content and about what it means to be an active reader.

Thinking Clearly Practice

1. **VENN DIAGRAMS** Work together as a class on comparing and contrasting skills by creating a Venn diagram on the board. Choose an appropriate subject from the textbook or have students brainstorm ideas in class. Encourage students to see similarities and differences that might not be obvious at first glance.

2. **CAUSE-AND-EFFECT RELATIONSHIPS** Give students several events that have been in the news recently in your school or community—political issues, changes in rules or laws, recent elections, and so forth. Ask them to work in pairs to create cause-and-effect charts such as the one on page 450.

Fallacies Practice

1. **COMMERCIALS** Have students use Worksheet C to help them identify fallacies that may exist in TV commercials. After they share their responses, have them discuss their opinions of whether or not the fallacies make the commercials effective.

2. **FINDING FALLACIES** Bring in several editorials and letters to the editor from magazines and newspapers. Ask students to choose one or two to read carefully. Have them review the fallacies listed on pages 451–452 and then try to identify whether any of those techniques have been used.

Facts and Opinions Practice

1. **EDITORIALS** Have students work in pairs to complete Worksheet D about reasons for the American Revolution. Use class time for them to report on their findings in brief oral presentations.

2. **HIDDEN OPINIONS** Review with students the paragraph about Francis Bellamy on page 453, stressing that sometimes an opinion can be hidden in a paragraph that is filled with facts. Have them write a paragraph of their own—using the Bellamy passage as a model—about a topic of their choice. Ask them to include and label five facts and one opinion in their paragraphs.

Recognizing Assumptions Practice

1. **ADVERTISING** Assign students to complete Worksheet C about a commercial of their choosing. Encourage them to think about the sorts of assumptions that the creators of the commercials were making about the potential buyers.

2. **POLL QUESTIONS** Spend a few minutes talking about the campaign financing poll question on page 454. Then ask students to create new versions of the question that don't assume that interest group money is harmful.

Generalizations and Conclusions Practice

EVALUATING GENERALIZATIONS Have students work in pairs or threes and make a list of generalizations about things or groups of people at school (for example, government teachers are hard graders) that they believe are true. As you discuss their lists, ask them to provide specific support for each generalization.

SKILLS ACTIVITY WORKSHEET C— COMMERCIALS AND CRITICAL THINKING

Name: _____

Directions

Watch TV commercials for spots that try to sell something using one of the fallacies mentioned on pages 451–452. Describe the commercial in as much detail as possible. Then note the part of the commercial that you identified as being a fallacy and explain how it works.

A. Commercial Product _____

B. Description of commercial:

C. What fallacy was used to try and sell the product?

D. Was the commercial convincing? Explain.

SKILLS ACTIVITY WORKSHEET D— READING AND THINKING CRITICALLY

Name: _____

Directions

The teacher will put you into pairs. Within your group one person has to write an editorial as an American and the other as an English person. Each person should answer the question, "What are the causes for the American Revolution?" Be sure to support your opinions. The next day you will swap with your partner and you will try to find opinions, assumptions, and generalizations. Be prepared to briefly present your findings to the class. Write your editorial below (and on the back if needed).

INTRODUCING THE SKILLS

Please consider the following comments before introducing these topics to your students.

Interviews and Questionnaires

Interviews can be great sources of information, but teachers rarely assign them. Ask students to describe any interviews they've conducted or questionnaires they've responded to or created. Students need to realize that almost all questionnaires have bias.

Using the Library

Some students may view libraries today as old-fashioned. One of your jobs as the teacher is to highlight the differences between what one finds on the Internet and what one finds in libraries. It will be useful to find out what sort of library research students have previously done.

Using the Internet

Students need to realize that the Internet is not the ultimate solution for all of their research needs. For students it's quick, easy and relatively painless, until their search inquiry gets 894,632 responses. The challenge is to make the students focus their search.

Organizing Sources

Part of many research projects is keeping track of a large number of sources. Most students have not been dealing with projects requiring a multitude of sources, so a sheet of paper may have sufficed. Help them realize the importance of organizing their sources by assigning them to hand in their notes or photocopies.

Evaluating Sources

Finding information is easy. When research is done, especially on the Internet, students have to be very concerned with the reliability of that information. Is the source legitimate? Is the information biased in some way? Introduce the process of evaluating sources by discussing why these questions are important.

Using Sources Responsibly

Explain to students that the difference between research and plagiarism is citation. It is important to stress to students that citations are for more than just words, they're for ideas as well.

Documentation

Although many English classes go over this skill, students can always use more practice. Remind them that there are different kinds of formats. They may also need specific examples of what is considered common knowledge.

PRACTICING THE SKILLS

Use the following activities to help students develop and practice their skills.

Interviews and Questionnaires Practice

PARENTS AND POLITICS Ask students to interview one of their parents about their views on a political issue. Request that they make up a list of five written questions in advance. Have them bring in a tape recording or a written summary of the interview.

Using the Library Practice

1. **REVIEWING PERIODICALS** Assign each student one of the periodicals listed on page 459. Ask students to locate and skim a recent issue and then prepare a one-minute review of the sorts of articles and features they found.

2. **LOCATING SOURCES** Take students to the library and give them an assortment of specific facts to look up. They should find the information in two different reference works. Suggest that they work in pairs.

Using the Internet Practice

PARTY WEB SITES Using Worksheet E, have students search the Internet for as many Web sites of political parties as possible. Encourage students to evaluate the objectivity and reliability of any site they list.

Organizing Sources Practice

NOTE CARDS Discuss with students how to use index cards for taking notes—what information to include, what headings to use, and so forth. Have the class vote on a President as a research topic. Then distribute index cards to students and have them make a note card about the President. Suggest that they use the index of their textbook or an encyclopedia to locate possible information.

Evaluating Sources Practice

1. **WEB SITE RELIABILITY** Have students write a one-paragraph review of a Web site that they would consider authoritative and reliable. Suggest that they address and answer some of the questions about sources, authors, and information on page 463 as they explain their judgments.

2. **RANKING SOURCES** Bring in a wide range of different sources for a particular topic—general encyclopedias, popular magazines, academic journals, Web site data, newspaper articles, and so on. Let students look them over and then rank them according to reliability. Ask them to explain their reasoning.

Using Sources Practice

PLAGIARISM Use an old research paper (ideally one from another class, without a name), and block out the citations. Have students read the paper, identify the ways sources have been used, and discuss where they think a source citation is necessary.

Documentation Practice

BIBLIOGRAPHICAL ENTRIES Have students complete Worksheet F. Remind them that attention to detail—what needs to be capitalized, where periods should go, how lines are indented—is crucial. Have volunteers put their entries on the board so all can review answers and correct their sheets.

SKILLS ACTIVITY WORKSHEET E— USING THE INTERNET

Name: _____

Directions

The Internet is full of information, some useful, some not. Your task to practice using the Internet is to find as many political party Web sites (from the United States or other countries) as possible. In the first column below, list the party name; in the middle column, list the Web sites; and in the third column, list whether the site (after looking at it) seemed to be good, just ok, or not good at all.

Party Name   **Web Address**   **Rating ***

SKILLS ACTIVITY WORKSHEET F— DOCUMENTATION

Name: _____

Directions

You have just finished writing your research paper, and it is time to go back and put in the parenthetical citations to make your Works Cited or Reference page. Using the information below, create a sample bibliography entry for each source provided. Use MLA format throughout. Refer to the information on page 467 as well as the latest edition of *The MLA Handbook* as you work. After you are done, go back and number the bibliography entries to show how you would alphabetize them if you were really using them in a paper.

A. Newt Gingrich p. 7 *Congressional Press* Washington D.C. *How to Be Speaker* 1997 (book)

B. American Civil Liberties Union "How to File a Lawsuit" http://www.clu.org (Web site)

C. Neil Armstrong, NASA astronaut, retired May 12, 1999. Wilmette, Illinois (interview)

D. *Time* "Primaries are Too Expensive" Timothy James p. 23–24 May 14, 1996 (weekly periodical)

E. P. 14 "Campaign Reform Needed" *Newsweek* April 15, 1997 (weekly periodical)

F. *PACs Are Dangerous* 1983 Quinn Press Manchester, New Hamphshire Paul Smith and Andrew Christopher (book)

G. Katherine Elly and Margaret Bedford. "Women's Rights." *Delaware Gazette,* January 7, 1986, pages 35, 39 (newspaper)

H. Ronald Reagan (topic) *New World Encyclopedia* Vol. 14 1996 edition pg. 58 (encyclopedia)

I. *Y2k Bug Causes Headaches* Department of the Treasury U.S. Government 1999 Washington D.C., Government Printing Office (government publication)

INTRODUCING THE SKILLS

Please consider the following comments before introducing these topics to your students.

Original Documents

Help students see that original documents are both treasured finds and little riddles. They are treasured finds because they reflect a particular period of time. They are riddles because if you don't know the background or the circumstances, the original document can be like a piece of a jigsaw puzzle; you get a clue as to the big picture, but more needs to be developed.

Political Cartoons

Students will probably find political cartoons both fun and challenging. Bring in samples to show that most political cartoons, unlike the Sunday comics, are not supposed to be funny, but rather convey a message. They are really editorials done with a picture rather than sentences.

Maps

For students, maps serve to illustrate points or help understanding. While they may be familiar with roadmaps that they use in a car, it may be a good idea to discuss other types of maps and their uses. Discuss the voting map on page 472 to review how to use legends.

Graphs, Charts, and Tables

All students have seen graphs, charts, and tables in their books. Graphs and charts usually have a specific purpose or one real point to prove, while tables tend to have more general information that may support a point. Charts and graphs should have an inset box with additional helpful information, while tables have headings that are usually key to figuring them out.

Public Opinion Polls

Most people have heard of public opinion polls, usually during election seasons when they can't seem to be avoided. What students don't usually realize is there are different types of polls—open-ended response or limited response—and that questions worded the right way can help any group prove any point. Discuss together how polls are done by professional organizations and how they use random sampling to try and guarantee that the people responding are diverse and represent the population as a whole.

PRACTICING THE SKILLS

Use the following activities to help students develop and practice their skills.

Original Documents Practice

1. **SUMMARIZING DOCUMENTS** Ask students to find a document from the eighteenth or nineteenth centuries—perhaps a speech, a letter, a Supreme Court decision, a bill, or a treaty. Have students write a one-paragraph summary of what the document means and why it was important at the time.

2. **PARAPHRASING THE CONSTITUTION** After discussing the modern translation of Article III, Section 3, on page 468, assign each student a difficult section of the Constitution. Work together to develop a paraphrase in modern English.

Political Cartoons Practice

1. **ANALYZING CARTOONS** Have students complete Worksheet G. Before they begin, it may be useful to analyze a number of cartoons together. Bring in several examples for the class to examine and discuss.

2. **STATE OF THE UNION** Put students into pairs and ask them to write one-sentence summaries of the meaning of the Oliphant cartoon on page 471. Read their statements aloud and discuss any differences.

Maps Practice

1. **READING MAPS** Ask students to locate a map in their textbooks. Have them analyze it carefully and then develop a list of several questions that studying the map has brought to mind.

2. **CARTOGRAMS** Have students review the description of cartograms on page 472 and then study the cartogram on the electoral vote on page 182. Brainstorm a list of other kinds of information that might best be presented in a cartogram.

Graphs, Charts, and Tables Practice

IMMIGRATION DATA Have students study the table on immigration trends on page 297. Divide them into six groups. Have two groups make a pie chart, two groups make a bar graph, and two groups make a line graph to represent the information visually. After they have finished, discuss which style graph was best for this information and why. If computers are available, encourage students to use the spreadsheet graphing function, if they know how.

Public Opinion Polls Practice

1. **STUDENT POLL** Before assigning students to devise and administer a poll of their own and complete Worksheet H, spend some class time discussing how to word poll questions. You may want to discuss together the feature on poll questions on page 115 and/or help students to practice wording poll questions so as not to shape the answers that are given.

2. **NEWS ACCURACY POLL** Discuss together the methods and results of the Gallup Poll on the accuracy of news organizations on page 478.

SKILLS ACTIVITY WORKSHEET G— POLITICAL CARTOONS

Name: _____

Directions

Find a political cartoon in a newspaper, in a magazine, or on the Internet. Cut it out, copy it, or print it if it's from the Internet, and attach it to this sheet. Answer the questions below as they apply to your cartoon.

What is the cartoon about or what is its subject?

What is the message the cartoonist is trying to convey?

What, if any, details in the cartoon are unclear?

SKILLS ACTIVITY WORKSHEET H—PUBLIC OPINION POLLS

Name: _____

Directions

Find a partner or two, and then pick an issue (gun control, prayer in schools, Internet censorship, video game ratings, or some local school issue). Write five poll questions to find out what people think about the issue. Ask 20 students (all together) your questions, and then answer the questions below and on the back.

A. Write five poll questions on (topic) _____

    1.

    2.

    3.

    4.

    5.

B. Answer the following questions:

    1. Did the poll help you find the information you wanted? Explain.

    2. Were any of the questions biased or slanted? Explain.

    3. How careful were you to get a representative sample? What impact might your sample have had on your results?

    4. What did you learn or find out? (Be prepared to tell the rest of the class.)

INTRODUCING THE SKILLS

Please consider the following comments before introducing these topics to your students.

Giving a Speech

Giving a speech can be one of the most terrifying experiences any high school student can go through. It is key to acknowledge that and to provide ways to ease students' anxiety. The Skills Handbook does a good job, especially in the planning stage. For most students (except those with stage fright) good preparation takes much of the tension away because they are more confident when it is time to actually make the speech itself. It might be helpful to explain that teachers give a "speech" every day, and while it may look easy, sometimes it's not! Many of the skills activities included for each of the 48 topics contain ideas for specific speech assignments.

Writing a Letter

Writing a letter sounds pretty easy. It is. Writing a good letter is not quite so easy, and it requires thought and organization. Bring in several sample letters from local newspapers to discuss as examples. When writing to a politician or an editor, it is key to stick to one and only one topic. Moderate, well-supported positions are most likely to get the reader's attention, and they are most likely to be considered legitimate and merit a response or get published.

Writing a Position Paper

Position papers are simply written arguments. Ask students to think of the last time there was a discussion in class in which sides were taken. If the discussion had been cut off and students were asked to write down their comments, they would have the heart of a position paper, minus the introduction and maybe a conclusion. Position papers should be assertive, clear, and brief. Stress that students should try hard to recognize the opposition's points and refute them, thus making their position sound more valid. Suggestions for position papers are included in many of the skills activities for each topic in this *Teacher's Guide.*

Writing a Research Paper

For most students, writing a research paper is drudgery. Students may enjoy sharing past experiences (success or horror stories) with one another. As with many academic activities, preparation is the key. For many students, papers of five pages or less will be done the night before they're due. Most of these last-minute papers aren't very good, so a key topic to discuss is the benefits of beginning early: having more time to do research, having plenty of time to rewrite or reorganize, and avoiding last-minute computer problems and panic. Browse through the skills activities included for each topic to find many ideas for research paper assignments.

PRACTICING THE SKILLS

Use the following activities to help students develop and practice their skills.

Speech Practice

1. **OUTLINE SPEECH** Budget time for students to give occasional impromptu or outline speeches, especially when class debate gets heated. Have them use Worksheet I to prepare and evaluate a short outline speech. Let them choose their own topics and prepare their outlines as homework.

2. **ANALYZING A SPEECH** Videotape a speech (from a news show or from C-SPAN) and have students watch it in class. Ask them to evaluate the speaker's effectiveness by commenting on some of the items in the checklist on page 480.

Letter Practice

1. **ISSUE LETTER** Have students write letters to a local government official or their federal representative. Suggest that they pick an issue about which they feel strongly. Remind students to review the tips and format on pages 482–483. Collect the letters just to look them over before they are mailed.

2. **ANALYZING LETTERS** Bring in several letters to the editor from various magazines and newspapers. Place students into groups and let each group choose one to analyze. Ask students to consider how well the letters follow the advice in the checklist on page 482 and to summarize their judgments in one paragraph. Suggest that they speculate on why the editor chose to publish this particular letter.

Position Paper Practice

1. **TIME FOR A CHANGE** Spend a little time discussing the strengths and weaknesses of the position paper draft on page 485. Have students consider the tone, the amount of supporting evidence, and the handling of opposing views. Brainstorm together a list of other possible opening and closing strategies.

2. **INTRODUCTIONS** As students are working outside of class on an assigned position paper, use several minutes of class time to brainstorm together a list of possible strategies for effective introductory paragraphs—surprising facts, anecdotes, a quotation, historical background, and so forth. Bring in sample editorials and position papers and discuss how well their introductions work.

Research Paper Practice

1. **DEVELOPING TOPICS** Have students use Worksheet J to practice developing topics before you assign a formal research project. When all have finished, it might be good to list different responses on the board so all students may contribute their ideas and see what others have thought of.

2. **USING QUOTATIONS** Many students tend to use direct quotations too frequently. To help them recognize when they should be summarizing and paraphrasing a source—instead of quoting—bring in several articles and speeches. Read several sentences aloud and ask students to explain why they would or wouldn't choose to quote those words in a research paper of their own. Remind them that summaries and paraphrases, not just quotations, need to be cited parenthetically.

SKILLS ACTIVITY WORKSHEET I—
GIVING A SPEECH

Name: _____

Directions

In the space below, construct a brief outline of the main ideas you want to cover in your speech. You will be allowed to bring this sheet up with you, or you can put the outline on note cards. After you've given the speech, answer the questions below. Use the back if you need more space.

Topic: _____

Outline:

Answer the following questions after the speech.

1. How do you think your speech went?

2. Did you find the outline helpful? Did you refer to it a lot or a little? Explain.

3. What type of experience did your speech turn out to be? Explain.

SKILLS ACTIVITY WORKSHEET J – WRITING A RESEARCH PAPER

Name: _____

Directions

Below are two broad topics, Congress and Elections. Your job is to refine and narrow each topic as you work down the page so you can do this on your own when you have to choose your own topic.

Congress	Elections

A. List several major categories below each general topic.

Example: Leadership

Example: Campaigns

B. Pick one major category from A and list possible subcategories.

Example: Speaker of the House

Example: Advertising

C. List possible theses (main points) that your paper could develop and support.

Example: Speakers of the House have too much power.

Example: The use of television advertising in presidential campaigns has changed significantly in the last 12 years.

Answer Key

1 | The Basics of Government

Study Guide

1. the institution through which a country or society makes and enforces policy
2. nation-states
3. territory, population, sovereignty, government
4. public order, social conflicts, stable economy, public service
5. Evolution, Force, Divine Right, Social Contract

Vocabulary

1. a	**3.** c		
2. d	**4.** b		

Multiple-Choice Test

1. d	**5.** a	**9.** a
2. d	**6.** b	**10.** a
3. b	**7.** c	
4. a	**8.** d	

Essay Question

Students should provide specific support for their varying choices.

2 | Power and Forms of Government

Study Guide

1. those who control the economy; the "power elite"; bureaucrats; a wide variety of people (pluralist theory)
2. geographic, legislative, executive, the number
3. unitary
4. legislative, executive
5. rule by one, rule by a few, rule by many
6. representative democracy

Vocabulary

1. f	**3.** d	**5.** a
2. c	**4.** e	**6.** b

Multiple-Choice Test

1. d	**5.** a	**9.** b
2. c	**6.** b	**10.** c
3. b	**7.** d	
4. b	**8.** b	

Essay Question

Essays should identify the four theories of elitism—Marxist theory, Mills's Power Elite, bureaucrats, and the pluralist view—and explain why one of them best describes the elites in the United States.

3 | Beginnings of Revolt

Study Guide

1. limited government, representative government
2. Magna Carta, Petition of Rights, English Bill of Rights
3. charter
4. royal, proprietary, charter
5. Thomas Jefferson
6. natural rights, consent of the governed

Vocabulary

1. b	**3.** a	
2. c	**4.** d	

Multiple-Choice Test

1. b	**5.** b	**9.** d
2. c	**6.** c	**10.** d
3. a	**7.** d	
4. c	**8.** d	

Essay Question

Essays should focus on Locke's ideas of natural rights and consent of the governed, both of which were denied to colonists by the English government.

4 | Creating the Constitution

Study Guide

1. the Articles of Confederation
2. trade, taxes, states
3. Samuel Adams, Patrick Henry
4. Thomas Jefferson, James Madison, John Adams, George Washington
5. the agreement to create a bicameral legislature that included equal representation of the states and representation based on population
6. the agreement to include three-fifths of a state's slaves in its population to determine representation
7. Federalists, Anti-Federalists
8. James Madison, Alexander Hamilton, John Jay

Vocabulary

1. c	**3.** f	**5.** d
2. b	**4.** e	**6.** a

Multiple-Choice Test

1. c	**5.** d	**9.** d
2. a	**6.** d	**10.** c
3. c	**7.** b	
4. d	**8.** b	

Essay Question

Students' answers will vary, but they should focus on what Madison means when he writes that men aren't angels. Make sure students explain whether or not they agree with the quotation.

5 | Constitution and Amendments

Study Guide

1. popular sovereignty, limited government, separation of powers, checks and balances, federalism
2. popular sovereignty
3. Limited government
4. legislative, executive, judicial
5. the legislative branch, the executive branch, the judicial branch
6. federalism
7. Preamble, articles, amendments
8. 27, Bill of Rights
9. two, two

Vocabulary

1. e	**3.** c	**5.** a
2. f	**4.** d	**6.** b

Multiple-Choice Test

1. d	**5.** c	**9.** c
2. b	**6.** a	**10.** b
3. d	**7.** c	
4. c	**8.** d	

Answer Key

Essay Question

The six goals of the government are "to form a more perfect union, establish justice, insure domestic tranquillity, provide for the common defense, promote the general welfare, and secure the blessings of liberty." Students should explain why they think one is the most important.

6 | National Government and the States

Study Guide

1. delegated, implied, inherent
2. Elastic Clause
3. 10th
4. reserved powers
5. concurrent powers
6. republican, domestic insurrection, admit
7. state militia, elections

Vocabulary

1. b	4. e	7. f
2. d	5. g	
3. c	6. a	

Multiple-Choice Test

1. c	5. c	9. c
2. b	6. b	10. d
3. d	7. d	
4. c	8. b	

Essay Question

Students should explain that the Elastic Clause is used to "stretch" the power of the national government.

7 | The Changing Nature of Federalism

Study Guide

1. Thomas Jefferson
2. *McCulloch v. Maryland*
3. null, void
4. *Gibbons v. Ogden*
5. incorporation
6. 14th
7. grants-in-aid
8. categorical, block, revenue sharing
9. mandate

Vocabulary

1. c	3. a	5. d
2. b	4. e	

Multiple-Choice Test

1. b	5. a	9. b
2. c	6. d	10. d
3. d	7. a	
4. a	8. d	

Essay Question

Students who support unfunded mandates might cite national supremacy; students who oppose them might cite states' rights.

8 | Party Systems and Party Roles

Study Guide

1. one-party, two-party, multiparty
2. two
3. label
4. watchdogs
5. information
6. political parties
7. independents
8. grassroots

Vocabulary

1. d	3. b	5. c
2. e	4. a	

Multiple-Choice Test

1. b	5. d	9. c
2. a	6. d	10. a
3. c	7. a	
4. b	8. b	

Essay Question

Advantages of multiparty systems might include representation of more points of view and the promotion of coalitions.

9 | U.S. Political Parties

Study Guide

1. historical tradition, broad ideological consensus, winner-take-all system, single-member districts
2. system in which the person receiving the largest number of votes wins
3. Federalist
4. Democratic–Republicans
5. Andrew Jackson
6. Whig
7. Republican
8. Second Democratic Era
9. Democratic, Republican
10. economic protest, splinter, ideological, single-issue

Vocabulary

1. c	2. a	3. b

Multiple-Choice Test

1. a	5. d	9. d
2. d	6. d	10. d
3. a	7. c	
4. a	8. c	

Essay Question

Student answers should include specific references to several minor parties in previous elections.

10 | Elections and Campaigns

Study Guide

1. state, Congress
2. primary, caucus, general
3. closed primary, open primary
4. cross-over vote
5. the campaign before the party nomination, the effort between the nomination and the general election
6. New Hampshire
7. dark horse candidate

Vocabulary

1. e	3. d	5. f
2. c	4. b	6. a

Multiple-Choice Test

1. b	5. d	9. d
2. d	6. d	10. b
3. a	7. c	
4. a	8. a	

Essay Question

Students who think that processes should be uniform might cite simplicity and consistency. Students who support the status quo might cite tradition, workability, and state control.

Answer Key

11 | Campaign Financing

Study Guide
1. Federal Election Commission
2. radio, television
3. private sources, public sources
4. individual donors
5. political action committees
6. 1970s
7. Soft money

Vocabulary
1. a   **2.** b   **3.** c

Multiple-Choice Test
1. b   **5.** d   **9.** c
2. d   **6.** d   **10.** a
3. a   **7.** a
4. d   **8.** b

Essay Question
Students who support the laws might cite equality and the avoidance of greater influence for the wealthy. Students who oppose the laws might cite freedom of choice, spending, and speech.

12 | Political Participation

Study Guide
1. voting   5. Education
2. 48.8   6. higher
3. Civics   7. white
4. activists   8. education

Vocabulary
1. b   **2.** a   **3.** c

Multiple-Choice Test
1. d   **5.** d   **9.** d
2. b   **6.** b   **10.** c
3. c   **7.** b
4. b   **8.** a

Essay Question
Answers should focus on education, age, and racial and ethnic background.

13 | Voting Rights and Behavior

Study Guide
1. citizen
2. suffrage
3. property
4. 15th
5. tax, grandfather clause, literacy
6. 19th
7. 26th
8. citizen, registered
9. efficacy
10. driver's license
11. weekday voting, weak party efforts, voter satisfaction
12. candidate appeal, party identification, issues

Vocabulary
1. b   **3.** c
2. d   **4.** a

Multiple-Choice Test
1. b   **5.** d   **9.** a
2. d   **6.** d   **10.** c
3. b   **7.** a
4. c   **8.** a

Essay Question
Students should mention the key events on the timeline on pages 98–99.

14 | Political Ideologies

Study Guide
1. liberal, conservative, moderate
2. liberal
3. conservative
4. moderate
5. liberal
6. conservative

Vocabulary
1. b   **3.** a
2. c   **4.** d

Multiple-Choice Test
1. c   **5.** c   **9.** a
2. b   **6.** c   **10.** c
3. d   **7.** a
4. b   **8.** b

Essay Question
Students might point out that, for example, an individual may hold conservative views on most issues and liberal views on others.

15 | Public Opinion

Study Guide
1. public opinion
2. family, gender, religion, education, race and ethnicity, region
3. Democratic
4. economic, social
5. liberal
6. polls
7. straw
8. sample

Vocabulary
1. a   **2.** c   **3.** b

Multiple-Choice Test
1. d   **5.** a   **9.** c
2. a   **6.** a   **10.** d
3. c   **7.** c
4. b   **8.** b

Essay Question
Students should make the connections between one factor and their attitudes very clear.

16 | Politics and Mass Media

Study Guide
1. mass media
2. print, broadcast, Internet
3. newspapers, magazines
4. radio, television
5. 1st
6. Federal Communications Commission
7. equal time doctrine
8. political
9. agenda

Vocabulary
1. b   **3.** d
2. c   **4.** a

Multiple-Choice Test
1. d   **5.** b   **9.** d
2. c   **6.** c   **10.** d
3. c   **7.** d
4. a   **8.** b

Essay Question
Students should state a clear position and explain their reasoning in detail.

Answer Key

17 | Interest Groups and PACs

Study Guide
1. interest groups
2. size, resources, intensity
3. economic, social action, equality, public interest
4. business and trade, labor, agricultural, professional
5. lobbying, electioneering, litigation, and shaping public opinion
6. PACs
7. advertisements, research, events

Vocabulary
1. b **2.** c **3.** a

Multiple-Choice Test
1. a	**5.** a	**9.** d
2. d	**6.** b	**10.** a
3. d	**7.** a	
4. c	**8.** c	

Essay Question
Students should explain their choices. Most students will likely select public-interest groups.

18 | Structure and Powers of Congress

Study Guide
1. bicameral
2. Senate, House of Representatives
3. population, states
4. 2, 6
5. delegated, implied, nonlegislative
6. delegated
7. implied

Vocabulary
1. a **2.** c **3.** b

Multiple-Choice Test
1. d	**5.** a	**9.** b
2. a	**6.** b	**10.** d
3. b	**7.** c	
4. a	**8.** a	

Essay Question
Students should note the higher qualifications for the Senate and the implication that it was to be the "upper" house.

19 | Impeachment and Oversight

Study Guide
1. nonlegislative
2. impeachment
3. treason, bribery, or other high crimes, misdemeanors
4. House of Representatives, Senate
5. Andrew Johnson, Bill Clinton
6. Richard Nixon
7. oversight function
8. appropriate
9. subpoena

Vocabulary
1. c	**3.** b
2. d	**4.** a

Multiple-Choice Test
1. d	**5.** c	**9.** a
2. b	**6.** b	**10.** c
3. b	**7.** d	
4. b	**8.** d	

Essay Question
Students should identify the threat to the country or to the system of government or something similar.

20 | Leaders and Committees

Study Guide
1. 2
2. party, committee, caucuses, support agencies
3. majority, minority
4. Speaker of the House
5. floor
6. the Vice President
7. standing, select, joint, conference
8. caucuses
9. the Library of Congress, the Congressional Budget Office, the General Accounting Office, the Government Printing Office

Vocabulary
1. g	**4.** e	**7.** c
2. b	**5.** h	**8.** a
3. d	**6.** f	

Multiple-Choice Test
1. c	**5.** d	**9.** d
2. b	**6.** a	**10.** b
3. b	**7.** a	
4. a	**8.** a	

Essay Question
Students should demonstrate a good understanding of the positions listed in the chart on page 151.

21 | Bills and Committee Consideration

Study Guide
1. bill
2. members of Congress
3. public, private
4. hopper
5. committee
6. die
7. hearings
8. mark up
9. House, Senate
10. Rules Committee

Vocabulary
1. a **2.** b **3.** c

Multiple-Choice Test
1. c	**5.** c	**9.** b
2. d	**6.** a	**10.** c
3. b	**7.** c	
4. a	**8.** b	

Essay Question
Students might indicate that the complex process discourages rash actions.

22 | Debating and Voting on a Bill

Study Guide
1. quorum
2. Committee, Whole
3. rules
4. filibuster
5. cloture
6. germane
7. riders
8. to pass it as written, to table or kill it, to send it back to committee, to amend it

Answer Key

9. Christmas tree
10. Gridlock

Vocabulary

1. e   3. a   5. f
2. b   4. c   6. d

Multiple-Choice Test

1. d   5. d   9. c
2. a   6. a   10. b
3. d   7. b
4. c   8. a

Essay Question

Students should explain that the executive branch balances the power of the legislative branch by having to sign bills and that the veto is a key check on the legislative branch's power.

---

23 | Congress and Controversial Issues

Study Guide

1. seniority system
2. incumbents
3. twentieth century
4. PACs, name recognition
5. term limits
6. Malapportionment
7. gerrymandering
8. racial gerrymandering

Vocabulary

1. c   2. b   3. a

Multiple-Choice Test

1. b   5. c   9. b
2. c   6. d   10. b
3. c   7. d
4. d   8. d

Essay Question

Students should explain that advocates of term limits might see pork barrel legislation as a method incumbents use to maintain their seats at the expense of better legislation.

---

24 | The Presidency

Study Guide

1. natural-born, 14, 35
2. 4, two
3. $200,000 (as of 1999)
4. Alexander Hamilton
5. electors
6. President, Vice President
7. 12th, electors, President, Vice President
8. electors
9. 270
10. states, popular

Vocabulary

1. a   2. b   3. c

Multiple-Choice Test

1. b   5. b   9. b
2. d   6. a   10. b
3. b   7. a
4. c   8. a

Essay Question

Students who support the direct, popular vote might point out the possibility of a discrepancy between voters' and electors' choices; other students might point out that the electoral college system has worked well for more than 100 years.

---

25 | Succession and Vice Presidents

Study Guide

1. death, disability, resignation, impeachment
2. presidential succession
3. Presidential Succession Act
4. Vice President, Speaker of the House, president *pro tempore*, secretary of state, cabinet
5. 25th Amendment
6. Speaker of the House, president *pro tempore* of the Senate
7. Senate, presidential disability

Vocabulary

1. c   2. b   3. a

Multiple-Choice Test

1. d   5. a   9. b
2. b   6. b   10. c
3. a   7. b
4. c   8. c

Essay Question

Students who support a stronger vice presidency might cite the advantages of another strong ruler. Students who support the status quo might cite the advantages of a single leader for the executive branch and the country.

---

26 | Constitutional Powers

Study Guide

1. ll
2. commander in chief
3. War Powers Act
4. diplomat
5. treaties
6. executive agreements
7. executive orders
8. reprieves, pardons
9. State of the Union
10. veto

Vocabulary

1. c   3. a
2. d   4. b

Multiple-Choice Test

1. b   5. d   9. d
2. b   6. b   10. c
3. d   7. a
4. c   8. d

Essay Question

Students who want a stronger presidency might cite effective leadership and quick action. Students who support the status quo might cite separation of powers and checks and balances.

---

27 | The Evolving Presidency

Study Guide

1. economic planning, executive privilege, impoundment, persuasion
2. Franklin Roosevelt

3. the Employment Act of 1946

4. Executive privilege

5. Richard Nixon

6. Impoundment

7. Budget Reform Act

8. news releases and briefings, press conferences, photo ops and media events, sound bites, backgrounders and leaks

9. Abraham Lincoln, George Washington, Franklin Roosevelt

Vocabulary

1. b　　**2.** c　　**3.** a

Multiple-Choice Test

1. c　　**5.** b　　**9.** c
2. b　　**6.** b　　**10.** a
3. a　　**7.** b
4. a　　**8.** b

Essay Question

Reward thoughtful responses that refer to the powers of economic planning, executive privilege, impoundment, and persuasion.

28 | The EOP and the Cabinet

Study Guide

1. Executive Office of the President, cabinet, independent

2. Executive Office of the President

3. Office of Management and Budget

4. OMB, fiscal year

5. 14

6. executive departments

7. secretary, attorney general

8. advisers, heads

9. 1933

Vocabulary

1. a　　**2.** c　　**3.** b

Multiple-Choice Test

1. d　　**5.** a　　**9.** d
2. b　　**6.** c　　**10.** a
3. d　　**7.** d
4. b　　**8.** d

Essay Question

Students should demonstrate understanding of the advisory and departmental roles and mention possible competition among members.

29 | Independent Agencies

Study Guide

1. 150

2. no

3. departments, party, watchdogs

4. independent regulatory commissions, government corporations, independent executive agencies

5. independent regulatory commissions

6. U.S. Postal Service

7. government corporations

Vocabulary

1. c　　**2.** a　　**3.** b

Multiple-Choice Test

1. c　　**5.** a　　**9.** c
2. d　　**6.** c　　**10.** d
3. a　　**7.** b
4. b　　**8.** d

Essay Question

Students who think they should be abolished will emphasize their cost. Students who think they should be maintained will emphasize the services they provide.

30 | Civil Service and the Bureaucracy

Study Guide

1. spoils

2. Pendleton Act

3. bureaucrats

4. Office of Personnel Management

5. merit, Merit Systems Protection Board

6. Hatch Act

7. Congress

8. Management, Budget

9. government agencies, interest groups, congressional committees

Vocabulary

1. a　　**2.** b　　**3.** c

Multiple-Choice Test

1. a　　**5.** b　　**9.** c
2. d　　**6.** d　　**10.** c
3. c　　**7.** a
4. a　　**8.** d

Essay Question

Students should explain that *triangle* is used because there are three parties involved. The term *iron* is added to indicate their strength and power.

31 | Foundations of the Judicial System

Study Guide

1. III, Congress, inferior courts

2. jurisdiction

3. civil, criminal, constitutional

4. exclusive jurisdiction

5. judicial review

6. *Marbury v. Madison*

Vocabulary

1. c　　**3.** a　　**5.** f
2. e　　**4.** b　　**6.** d

Multiple-Choice Test

1. c　　**5.** b　　**9.** b
2. d　　**6.** a　　**10.** b
3. b　　**7.** c
4. d　　**8.** d

Essay Question

Students should indicate that judicial review enables the judicial branch to influence both the legislative and executive branches.

32 | Federal Courts and Federal Judges

Study Guide

1. Judiciary Act, constitutional, legislative, constitutional

2. federal district, appeals, International Trade

3. grand juries

4. 13

5. Military Appeals, Claims, Columbia, Territorial, Veterans, Tax

6. President, experience and background, party, ideology, gender, senatorial courtesy
7. Senate
8. gridlock

Vocabulary

1. a   2. b   3. c

Multiple-Choice Test

1. b   5. a   9. b
2. b   6. b   10. d
3. d   7. a
4. b   8. a

Essay Question

Student answers should focus on the balance of power between the executive and legislative branches.

---

33 | Supreme Court at Work

Study Guide

1. nine
2. chief justice
3. writ, *certiorari*
4. legal question, Supreme Court, parties
5. yes, no
6. majority opinion, dissenting opinion
7. concurring opinion
8. October

Vocabulary

1. c   2. b   3. a

Multiple-Choice Test

1. b   5. a   9. c
2. d   6. c   10. c
3. b   7. b
4. c   8. a

Essay Question

Students who support explanations might cite clarification and streamlining the judicial process. Students who support the status quo might cite the Court's independence and the legal issues explanations could create.

34 | Supreme Court and Policy Making

Study Guide

1. judicial review
2. precedents
3. personal values, justice, political climate, public opinion
4. Judicial activism
5. Judicial restraint
6. activist
7. enforcement, Congress, President
8. amend

Vocabulary

1. c   2. a   3. b

Multiple-Choice Test

1. d   5. b   9. b
2. c   6. d   10. c
3. c   7. c
4. c   8. a

Essay Question

Students may mention limits on cases they can hear, limited powers of enforcement, Congress, the President, and public opinion.

---

35 | Civil Rights and Civil Liberties

Study Guide

1. Answers will vary slightly. For a description of each Amendment, see page 496 of the student text.
2. civil liberties
3. Civil rights

Vocabulary

1. c   2. a   3. b

Multiple-Choice Test

1. a   5. d   9. a
2. b   6. c   10. a
3. d   7. b
4. c   8. a

Essay Question

Students' answers should focus on civil liberties as protections against government and civil rights as positive acts of government.

36 | 1st Amendment Freedoms

Study Guide

1. "Congress shall make no law respecting an establishment of religion."
2. separation
3. false
4. *Reynolds v. United States, Cantwell v. Connecticut, Minersville School District v. Gobitis, Bunn v. North Carolina, Welsh v. United States, Wisconsin v. Yoder*
5. pure, speech plus, symbolic
6. symbolic
7. 1798
8. *Schenck v. United States, Dennis v. United States, Yates v. United States, Brandenburg v. Ohio*
9. *Near v. Minnesota, New York Times Company v. United States, Branzburg v. Hayes, Miller v. California*
10. *Adderley v. Florida, Grayned v. City of Rockford, Lloyd Corporation v. Tanner, Schenck v. Pro-Choice Network of Western New York*

Vocabulary

1. a   2. b   3. c

Multiple-Choice Test

1. b   5. d   9. c
2. b   6. d   10. b
3. a   7. a
4. b   8. c

Essay Question

Students should explain that free association is required for people to engage in many communal religious practices and group speech.

---

37 | Due Process and Citizenship

Study Guide

1. due process
2. procedural due process
3. substantive due process
4. birth, birth to citizens abroad, naturalization

5. 250,000
6. 675,000
7. resident aliens, non-resident aliens, enemy aliens, illegal aliens, refugees
8. property, attend public

Vocabulary
1. b   2. c   3. a

Multiple-Choice Test
1. d   5. b   9. b
2. b   6. b   10. a
3. d   7. b
4. c   8. c

Essay Question
Students should indicate that Congress used to set quotas but no longer does.

38 | Rights of the Accused

Study Guide
1. *habeas corpus, ex post facto, attainder*
2. 4th
3. search warrant, lawfully arrested
4. exclusionary rule
5. double jeopardy
6. indictment
7. counsel, fair trial
8. cruel and unusual
9. no
10. *Roe v. Wade*

Vocabulary
1. d   3. a
2. b   4. c

Multiple-Choice Test
1. d   6. d
2. c   7. d
3. a   8. b
4. c   9. b
5. a   10. c

Essay Question
Students should provide details. Those in favor might cite the right to privacy as fundamental. Students opposed to the amendment might argue that it's unnecessary or too vague.

39 | Civil Rights Struggles

Study Guide
1. 13th, 14th, 15th
2. Jim Crow
3. *Plessy v. Ferguson*
4. *Brown v. Board of Education of Topeka*
5. Civil Rights Act, Voting Rights Act
6. 9
7. 7.5 million
8. Native American, senator

Vocabulary
1. a   2. b   3. c

Multiple-Choice Test
1. a   5. d   9. c
2. c   6. a   10. d
3. c   7. c
4. b   8. b

Essay Question
Students should identify the 13th Amendment as abolishing slavery, the 14th Amendment as granting due process and equal protection, and the 15th Amendment as protecting suffrage. All three were ratified in the wake of the Civil War.

40 | Women's Rights

Study Guide
1. Seneca Falls
2. Lucretia Mott, Elizabeth Cady Stanton
3. 19th, 1920
4. Betty Friedan
5. Title IX
6. reasonableness, strict scrutiny
7. Equal Rights Amendment, 1972
8. 1982

Vocabulary
1. b   2. c   3. a

Multiple-Choice Test
1. b   5. c   9. b
2. d   6. b   10. c
3. d   7. d
4. b   8. a

Essay Question
Reward thoughtful responses that include specific support for students' positions.

41 | Discrimination and Affirmative Action

Study Guide
1. 70
2. American Association of Retired Persons
3. 17
4. Americans with Disabilities
5. *Hardwick v. Georgia*
6. "don't ask, don't tell"
7. affirmative action
8. Reverse discrimination
9. Bakke
10. *United Steelworkers v. Weber, Fullilove v. Klutznick, Johnson v. Transportation Agency of Santa Clara County, Adarand Constructors v. Pena*

Vocabulary
1. a   2. b   3. c

Multiple-Choice Test
1. d   5. b   9. a
2. d   6. a   10. d
3. a   7. b
4. d   8. b

Essay Question
Students should infer that the *affirmative* means positive and that *action* refers to proactive policies.

42 | Policy Making and Economic Policy

Study Guide
1. Answers will vary slightly.
   a. Recognizing the Problem
   b. Formulating the Policy
   c. Adopting the Policy
   d. Implementing the Policy
   e. Evaluating the Policy
2. free enterprise
3. Federal Reserve Board, monetary policy
4. Keynesian, supply-side
5. income tax

6. Regressive, progressive
7. entitlements, defense, debt
8. uncontrollables

Vocabulary

1. c   3. e   5. b
2. a   4. d   6. f

Multiple-Choice Test

1. d   5. c   9. a
2. b   6. b   10. d
3. c   7. d
4. d   8. c

Essay Question

Students should make sure to support either progressive or regressive taxes in their responses.

---

43 | Regulatory Policy

Study Guide

1. Domestic, foreign
2. Interstate Commerce, Sherman Antitrust, Clayton
3. Wagner, Fair Labor Standards, Taft-Hartley, Landrum-Griffin
4. Federal Trade Commission
5. oligopoly, conglomerate
6. Environmental Protection Agency
7. Federal Water Pollution Control

Vocabulary

1. a   2. b   3. c

Multiple-Choice Test

1. b   5. a   9. c
2. c   6. c   10. d
3. d   7. a
4. d   8. d

Essay Question

Students' answers should include details of the federal regulations mentioned on page 359.

---

44 | Social Policy

Study Guide

1. research, cost control, access
2. national health insurance, American Medical Association, Pharmaceutical Manufacturers Association, National Federation of Independent Businesses
3. welfare
4. eligibility requirements
5. Social insurance
6. Medicare, Medicaid, Aid to Families with Dependent Children, Supplemental Securities Income, food stamps
7. school boards, state
8. Vouchers

Vocabulary

1. c   2. a   3. b

Multiple-Choice Test

1. c   5. d   9. c
2. d   6. d   10. c
3. b   7. a
4. a   8. d

Essay Question

Welfare is a general term that includes public and private assistance; *social insurance* refers to government programs designed to assist people living below the poverty line.

---

45 | Foreign Policy and National Defense

Study Guide

1. 1945, 1991
2. preserving national security, promoting world peace and maintaining a balance of powers, promoting democratic values and human rights, furthering foreign trade and global cooperation
3. State Department, National Security Council, Central Intelligence Agency, Department of Defense
4. State Department
5. foreign aid, economic sanctions, alliances
6. deterrence
7. covert operations, political coercion, military intervention

Vocabulary

1. b   2. a   3. c

Multiple-Choice Test

1. b   5. a   9. c
2. d   6. b   10. d
3. b   7. b
4. c   8. d

Essay Question

Students might cite the fact that going to war is a serious decision that should not be given to a single person.

---

46 | Economic and Political Systems

Study Guide

1. Capitalism
2. private ownership, factors of production, free competition, laws of supply and demand, freedom of choice
3. original communal societies, the class struggle, the labor theory of value, economic control of society and government, revolution of the proletariat, dictatorship of the proletariat
4. Communism
5. Socialism
6. nationalization, public assistance, heavy taxation, a command economy
7. high level of political participation by citizens, freedom of communications and speech, broad recruitment of political leaders, high effect of citizen participation, rule of law not individuals, competitive popular elections
8. political system, economic system

Vocabulary

1. a   3. c
2. b   4. d

Multiple-Choice Test

1. a   5. d   9. d
2. c   6. c   10. c
3. a   7. a
4. c   8. b

Answer Key

Essay Question

Students should explain that allowing no person to be above the law keeps power in the hands of the people, who make the law.

---

47 | State and Local Government

Study Guide

1. 87,000
2. dispersed
3. Initiative, referendum, recall
4. popular
5. to make appointments to state offices, to veto or line-item veto legislation, to grant pardons, to prepare the state budget, to issue executive orders, to command the state National Guard, to help establish the legislature's agenda
6. Congress
7. trial, appeals, U.S. Supreme Court
8. Missouri Plan
9. county, township, special district, municipality
10. mayor-council, council-manager, commission

Vocabulary

1. a
2. c
3. b

Multiple-Choice Test

1. a
2. d
3. a
4. c
5. b
6. c
7. d
8. c
9. b
10. a

Essay Question

Students may cite a school district as an example and should mention that special districts focus on particular areas and problems not handled by other local districts.

---

48 | Policies and Finances

Study Guide

1. education, welfare and public health, law enforcement and public safety
2. education
3. workfare
4. Congress, "Bill of Rights"
5. local
6. governor
7. sales, income, property
8. property
9. 1978

Vocabulary

1. c
2. a
3. b

Multiple-Choice Test

1. b
2. c
3. d
4. d
5. d
6. a
7. a
8. b
9. d
10. c

Essay Question

Students who support more state influence might cite statewide uniformity. Students who support local influence might cite more intimate knowledge of the schools and the students.

Topic Index